MW00466987

"Chuck Thoele cleverly weaves parallels between NCAA basketball—referencing real-life moments during games of play, unstoppable teams, and coaching geniuses—and essential lessons about investing. Having worked with RGT and Chuck for the past twenty-four years, I'm confident you'll find *Bulls, Bears, & Basketball* a valuable read."

—**Troy Aikman**
NFL Hall of Fame Quarterback

"In *Bulls, Bears, & Basketball*, Indiana University alum Chuck Thoele demonstrates in a unique and creative manner how the strategies and lessons learned in basketball competition can apply to personal financial management. He succeeds in instructing the reader in a decision-making process that can be easily understood, simple to apply, and entertaining at the same time."

—**Steve Alford**
Head Coach, UCLA Bruins Men's Basketball team

"Indiana University graduate Chuck Thoele, skillfully masters the art of teaching readers must-know principles to building financial security for life. By connecting two of his greatest loves—helping people manage their money and the annual NCAA Tournament known as March Madness—*Bulls, Bears, & Basketball* puts a refreshing spin on learning valuable information."

—**Mark Cuban**
Dallas Mavericks' owner, American businessman, and investor

Success in basketball coaching comes from the teaching and mastery of fundamentals. This success is paralleled with *Bulls, Bears, & Basketball* as it teaches readers of all ages the vital principles to building financial security for life."

—Homer Drew
Legendary NCAA Coach with 640 career wins

"Whether zone or man-to-man defense, *Bulls, Bears, & Basketball* will teach you a unique approach to creating a financial game plan."

—Bernie Clark
Executive Vice President
Advisory Services
Charles Schwab & Co., Inc.

"Being a huge fan of the NCAA tournament and having played and coached in it, I appreciate how Chuck draws parallels between March Madness and financial planning and investment principles."

—Bryce Drew
Former All-American
NBA Veteran
Current Head Coach at Valparaiso University

Bulls, & Bears, Basketball

RGT
WEALTH ADVISORS
www.rgtadvisors.com
(214) 360-7000

Bulls, & Bears, Basketball

Financial Planning for College Hoops Fans

Chuck Thoele

BROWN BOOKS
PUBLISHING GROUP

Bulls, Bears, & Basketball
Financial Planning for College Hoops Fans

Brown Books Publishing Group
16250 Knoll Trail Drive, Suite 205
Dallas, Texas 75248
www.BrownBooks.com
(972) 381-0009

A New Era in Publishing™

ISBN 978-1-61254-155-6 (HC)   ISBN 978-1-61254-163-1 (PB)
LCCN 2013957796

Printed in the United States
10 9 8 7 6 5 4 3 2

For more information or to contact the author, please go to
www.BullsBearsAndBasketball.com

To all avid college basketball fans who love
the March tournament yet still need money
management the other eleven months of the year.

CONTENTS

ACKNOWLEDGMENTS

The origination and creation of *Bulls, Bears, & Basketball* has been a real blessing to me. I'm thankful to my wife Beth, daughter Brooke, son Nick, sister Leigh, and my mother, Mary Lou, and my father, Ray, who passed away nine years ago for their support and encouragement.

I also want to thank my business partners, Mark Griege, Joe Nolan, Ash Narayan, and many co-workers who have been part of my education from which this book is written. It is a privilege to share the same profession and desire to help others reach their financial goals. Thank you to my pastor Stan Copeland for inspiring in me a desire to consider writing. I thank my creative writer, Lee Brookman, who took an idea and helped make it a reality. I appreciate the help provided by Gene Thoele, Joe Neely, and Bill Steding in finalizing the book. Much appreciation to Brown Publishing for greatly improving the project and helping make it something I'm proud to be associated with but didn't realize could be so well developed.

And last but not least, thanks to the Indiana Hoosiers who ignited the love of college basketball which gave me the springboard to mix the somewhat unusual combination of basketball and financial planning.

Pregame Warm-Up

"Not only is there more to life than basketball, there's a lot more to basketball than basketball."

—**Phil Jackson**,
eleven-time NBA championship coach
with highest winning percentage in league history

March Madness Meets Money Management

This is a book about financial planning. It's filled with ideas and insights to help you take control of your financial affairs and make possible the lifestyle that you've always envisioned for you and your family.

Sometimes financial planning can be boring, and that comes straight from me, a Certified Financial Planner, Chartered Financial Analyst (CFA), and Certified Public Accountant (CPA). I'm a guy who has made his living in this profession for more than thirty years. Before you drop this book and flip on ESPN, let me explain.

Although the words "personal financial management" probably don't make you bristle with excitement, they are nonetheless critical to your well-being as well as that of your spouse and kids. Most adult professionals realize this already. They know planning is important, but they fail to do it well because, frankly, they just can't bear to spend hours poring over budget spreadsheets and stock charts and insurance contracts, or whatever they imagine when they think of money management. It's not quite as daunting as they think.

The problem is a disconnect between professional money managers and everyone else. Too often, financial professionals rely on historical charts and esoteric language to make a point. The message gets lost in translation. Even though their own money is at stake, many people just don't find financial planning interesting or exciting enough to devote the time and energy required to do it right.

There is a way to change that, however, if we in the financial world communicate in everyday terms and relate to our clients using language they not only understand but enjoy. I've worked with hundreds of clients over the years, from young professionals just starting in the world to multimillionaire executives and professional athletes. One thing I've learned is that most people like a good analogy. By using familiar examples, we can make complex topics more approachable and engaging.

As you've probably guessed, that's where basketball comes into play in this book.

WHY BASKETBALL?

Using sports terms to communicate is nothing new. Business people, politicians, and professionals of all ilks are called upon to build strong teams, bring their A game, follow through, and hit the proverbial home run.

A love of sports is ingrained in American culture to the point that even individuals who are decidedly apathetic toward sports still know what it means to drop the ball, strike out, or throw a Hail Mary. For those of us who willingly make sports a part of our lives, there's a light bulb that turns on when someone compares an otherwise obscure concept to our favorite sport.

For me, that game has always been basketball—college basketball, specifically. Growing up in Indiana, I was predestined to be a basketball nut. If you've spent much time in the Hoosier State, you know that basketball isn't just popular there. For a large percentage of the population, it's an obsession like football in Texas or hockey in Minnesota. I wasn't a star athlete, but basketball spoke to me nonetheless. It still does.

As I've built my career guiding clients toward financial security, I've spent considerable downtime in the clutches of the NCAA basketball season, infatuated with the perennial drama that culminates in March Madness. I've often been struck by the parallels between these two worlds; they have so much in common. In basketball and in investing, there are star performers and reliable role players. There are good seasons and bad ones followed by rebuilding years. There are tried-and-true strategies, and there are desperate measures. Always, there is the clock ticking overhead.

Make no mistake: simple sports analogies are no substitute for in-depth financial knowledge backed by research and experience. But if you speak the language of basketball, this book can help you approach your financial affairs from a familiar, perhaps more inspiring perspective.

Why Now?

Go to Amazon.com or visit the library, and you'll find enough books on financial planning to fill a gymnasium. There's probably even one based on sports analogies. So why did I feel the need to add to the pile? Because, quite simply, the game has changed.

In late 2008, the US financial system teetered on the edge of collapse. The panic that besieged the global investment markets through mid-2009 took a painful toll on the net worth of investors everywhere. Even though smoke from the financial crisis has since cleared and the markets have mostly recovered, the economy still feels the pain. The collective mindset of the investing public has been scarred.

Most families today know they need to continue to save and invest, but their confidence in the financial system has been thoroughly shaken. They're looking for advice they can use, but they're not sure if the conventional wisdom of their parents' generation, or even five years ago, still applies. Although my colleagues and I

Who Should Read this Book?

Although I believe the information and advice in this book is applicable to a broad audience, I also understand that it's not for everyone.

You don't have to be a basketball fanatic to get something out of this book. If you've ever enjoyed playing or coaching basketball or even just watching the game as a casual observer, you'll find something to like. And you'll walk away with a new perspective on money management.

You also don't need to be a financial whiz to benefit from this book. Most of the information and advice is not geared for financial experts or the super-rich. A basic knowledge of financial concepts—investments, economics—will help you breeze through the content, but it's not required.

believe that the fundamentals of saving and investing still hold true, we also agree that new lessons emerged from the latest financial meltdown and resulting recession. Those lessons, such as the need to remain vigilant about inflation, should be a part of any holistic approach to financial planning.

Think of it in basketball terms. There are plenty of great books on that subject too. But many were published before game-changing developments such as the introduction of the three-point line or today's ultracompetitive college system in which teams aggressively recruit players from around the world. You could still learn a lot from those early books, but they wouldn't be entirely in tune with the realities of today's game.

WHAT TO EXPECT

This book will impart some valuable financial advice from a fresh perspective, drawing out the strategic Xs and Os that you must have in your financial playbook.

Like a college basketball game, the book is broken into two halves. The first half addresses the building blocks of a successful financial plan from a philosophical and a practical approach. These lessons could apply to anyone but are especially important from young adulthood through middle age. The second half covers strategies to continue building and preserving your financial well-being in life's later stages, including the transition to an empty nest, retirement, and legacy planning.

At the start of each chapter, you'll find a short account of how a memorable college basketball team in a particular year or era found victory by making precise strategic adjustments in its game plan. These stories aren't just analogies linking basketball to financial planning. They are metaphors for life in general.

Phil Jackson spoke wisely when he said, "There's a lot more to basketball than basketball." Focus, discipline, self-awareness, humility, resilience, and other qualities combine to make winners on and off the court. In this book, I believe you'll find at least a few nuggets of coaching wisdom that will serve you well on your personal path to glory.

THE FIRST HALF

CHAPTER ONE

EVALUATING YOUR TEAM

Financial Planning Begins with a Look in the Mirror

PEACH BASKET PARABLES: UCLA AND THE WIZARD OF WESTWOOD

No book that includes a college basketball premise would be complete without mentioning John Wooden. Most longtime basketball followers know Wooden's story well. Start with the fact he is generally regarded as the greatest coach in college basketball history. He coached the UCLA Bruins to seven consecutive NCAA championships (1967–1973) during a stretch in which they won ten titles in twelve years. At one point, his teams won eighty-eight consecutive games, a men's basketball record that, as of 2013, still stood. Despite his incredible .813 winning percentage over twenty-seven seasons at UCLA and the truckload of trophies, Wooden's basketball success is not his only claim to fame.

Wooden is universally respected for his philosophical approach to coaching, most notably his Pyramid of Success, through which he instilled invaluable life lessons in his players, lessons he eventually shared with the world. "What you are as a person is far more important than what you are as a basketball player," he said, and that was saying a lot because Wooden was a terrific player in his own right.

Born in 1910 and raised on an Indiana farm, Wooden starred in basketball at Martinsville High School. The arena had more seats than there were people in town—and it was still full for most games. In college, he played for Purdue and led the Boilermakers to a national championship. He also played professionally for several years, once leading the (pre-NBA) National Basketball League in scoring.

Professional athletes back then also had day jobs, and Wooden found his passion teaching English during the day and coaching sports on the side. At one point he passed up a high-paying opportunity with a traveling exhibition team to stay in his classroom job. Eventually he left high school teaching and began his career as a college coach in 1946.

KNOWING YOUR STRENGTHS AND WEAKNESSES

Wooden would later earn the nickname "the Wizard of Westwood" (referring to UCLA's Los Angeles neighborhood) although he was not particularly known as a master in-game strategist. Later in his life, he even acknowledged that making calculated changes during the flow of the game was not his strong point.

Most would say Wooden's greatest talent was his ability to maximize the potential of the players by creating a near-unbeatable system of play. It involved impeccably organized practices and a knack for challenging players to challenge themselves, knowing how to get through to each one. He encouraged players to look inward and to understand and improve themselves before they presumed to contribute to the team. The first line of his widely followed Seven-Point Creed was "Be true to yourself."

Wooden also demanded discipline, routine, and uniformity. He was not a tyrant; he wanted only to instill in his team the realization they could not control everything and therefore should take care to master what *was* within their power. He began each season with a lesson on how to put on your socks (allow no wrinkles) and shoes (lace 'em up tight). They were not going to lose games because of blisters on their feet. Long hair and beards were not permitted on his team. He believed they caused excessive perspiration that could be a distraction at a critical moment.

As Wooden's players grew into the mold he had constructed for them, he would come to know his team members as well as they knew themselves. He was then able to parlay their personal commitments into extraordinary results on the court. To this day, his pupils, including greats such as Bill Walton and Lew Alcindor (later to be known as Kareem Abdul-Jabbar), credit Wooden for their success as players and as men.

STICK WITH THE GAME PLAN

The Bruins' long-term dominance on Wooden's watch was not the result of high-tech training facilities or a brilliantly devised offense. He long insisted that the UCLA basketball dynasty was the result of sound fundamentals and a straightforward system—simple on paper yet difficult to execute without 100 percent effort from the entire team.

One of the best examples of Wooden's winning formula actually came in one of his most notable losses, a 71–69 defeat in January 1968 to Houston that ended a forty-seven-game Bruins winning streak. UCLA had not lost in two-and-a-half seasons and went into the game ranked number one. The second-ranked Cougars had not lost since UCLA defeated them the season before.

The matchup of the first- and second-ranked teams featuring the two greatest college players at the time—Alcindor and Houston's Elvin Hayes— was billed the "Game of the Century." It was the first regular season NCAA basketball game televised nationwide during prime time, and it was being played in what was then considered the ultramodern Astrodome, the world's first domed stadium. More than fifty-two thousand spectators in attendance made up the largest paid audience ever to witness a basketball game.

The marquee stars of the evening were Hayes, a six-foot-eight forward, and the seven-foot-two Alcindor, UCLA's imposing center. Though Alcindor was the best player in the country and had been (and would be) nearly unstoppable all season, he played that night with a scratched cornea that had kept him out of the previous two games.

Nevertheless, Wooden knew his team. He knew its success was built around Alcindor. He was going to stick with his system in place of any newfangled tactics designed to protect any ineffectiveness of Alcindor's.

Alcindor, however, had one of the worst games of his college career while Hayes excelled, scoring thirty-nine points. UCLA lost by two points, and there was "pandemonium in the Astrodome." Even though it was a regular season game, the next day's headlines effectively crowned a new college basketball king, and TV stations around the country replayed the game every day for a week. UCLA players, most of whom had never lost a game, described feeling shocked and dismayed by the public dethroning.

Wooden knew, though, it was only a temporary setback. He knew his players, and they believed in the system. Rather than fall into a tailspin, the Bruins went undefeated the rest of the season and went on to win the NCAA championship. Along the way, they took their revenge, trouncing the Cougars 101–69 in an NCAA semifinal. On his website, Alcindor, now known as Abdul-Jabbar, calls it the most significant victory of his college career.

Color Commentary

- John Wooden was the first person to be inducted into the Naismith Hall of Fame both as a player (1961) and as a coach (1973). He has many awards named after him, but the best-known honor might be the Wooden Award, given to the nation's most outstanding college basketball players (one male and one female) each year.
- Wooden retired in 1975 immediately after winning his tenth NCAA championship (and the Bruins would not win another national title for twenty years). He remained a visible icon in the UCLA community and nationwide until his death in 2010, just shy of his one-hundredth birthday.

Wisdom beyond Basketball

Wooden and his methods of success can teach us about financial planning. We learn from him that solid fundamentals are requisites for success and that a well-designed game plan can see you through tough times. Yet no one is invincible. Wooden's most important teaching involved self-reflection.

Wooden recruited players from disparate backgrounds and convinced them to look in the mirror and find their inner champions. That might

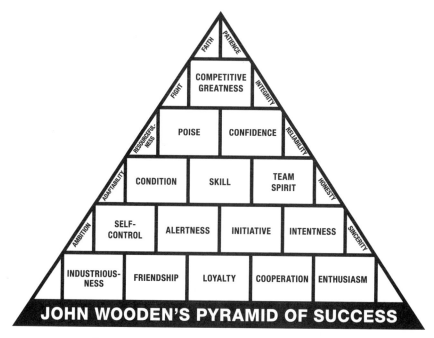

JOHN WOODEN'S PYRAMID OF SUCCESS

mean putting huge egos aside, coping with racial discrimination, or balancing basketball with political activism (remember, this was California in the 1960s). His widely adopted Pyramid of Success doesn't mention rebounding or passing or shooting percentages; it contains words such as industriousness, condition, self-control, and poise. The coach's ability to assess his players, neutralize their weaknesses, and amplify their strengths allowed him to build high-performing teams year after year.

As you create or reassess your financial plan, there is much to be learned from Wooden's legacy. Like a basketball team, the makeup of your home team matters every bit as much as external factors beyond your control. You and your family members bring personal baggage to bear on your financial style. Your upbringing, your life experiences, your marriage, your career, and especially your history of saving and investing—they all combine to shape your attitudes and behaviors concerning money.

Like any successful ball club, it is important to get a grip on those personal dynamics before you and your family can make smart financial decisions as a cohesive unit. When you understand yourselves, both as individuals and within the context of your team, you can approach the game with confidence and resolve.

In this chapter, we take a closer look at some of the factors that might affect your money mindset. This is not a questionnaire. Certainly there have been various psychological surveys designed to classify and categorize personal finance behaviors. I have never found them very useful in working with clients. A person could answer the questions very differently from one day to the next, depending on mood.

The next few pages provide an overview of typical catalysts that likely have shaped your views about money. Some definitely will apply to you. Others might not. Either way, you should finish the chapter knowing a little more about yourself than you did before. Ask yourself if and how these aspects of your life have impacted the financial decisions you have made and whether they will affect how you manage your money in the future.

INTERNAL FACTORS AFFECTING YOUR MONEY MINDSET

Your Childhood

Some of our tendencies were passed on to us by the people who raised us. Maybe it's a matter of mimicking their behaviors and preferences, or maybe some of it was embedded in our genetic code.

Countless basketball greats were coached, directly or indirectly, by their parents growing up. Others inherited the natural athleticism of their relatives. It's the same with money management.

Financial habits are often passed down through generations. You probably have at least some recollection of how your parents watched over the family finances. Perhaps they sat you down as a child and lectured you about the importance of spending wisely and setting something aside for a rainy day. They may have told you money can't buy true happiness, but it can buy comfort and opportunities.

You likely learned those lessons by watching your parents in action as they shopped for bargains, bought sensible cars, and saved enough to help put you through college. Maybe you saw how your dad's frugality throughout the years paid off in the form of unforgettable family vacations or how your single mother clipped coupons for weeks just to give you a nice Christmas. You did not realize it at the time, but you were soaking up and processing your parents' values and behaviors, which you replicated when the checkbook fell into your hands.

The lessons parents convey are not always positive. We have seen people who play fast and loose with their money, whether they have a little or a lot to squander. They might call it "living for the moment," but they give little thought to planning for the future. They assign high priority to status symbols such as brand-name clothes or expensive cars. If these behaviors were present in your household, you might have absorbed these lessons too.

For families at every income level, money can be the source of extreme stress in the home, sparking heated arguments and lingering resentment. Other families make money a taboo subject, and the kids are oblivious to their parents' financial situation however affluent or dire it might be. Perhaps your childhood was impacted by a divorce, illness, disability, or a death in the family. You might have watched as your loved ones struggled to deal with the financial ramifications through a cloud of intense emotions.

All of these experiences, positive and negative, left impressions on you. They might be impossible to erase, but they do not always manifest themselves in the way you might think or behave. Just because your parents were penny-pinchers does not mean you will follow the same path. As a teenager, you might have been frustrated by your parents' miserly ways to the point that you vowed to make your adult life more fun. Maybe your parents' ugly battles about money led you to be more understanding of your spouse's spending habits.

We are not predestined to relive the successes and failures of our families. For every basketball star who had supportive mentors for parents, there's a player who lifted himself from an abusive or drug-addled home to achieve greatness. Although past experiences do not make our lives a foregone conclusion, they are nonetheless a part of who we are.

Your Career

Your financial tendencies could have been evident early in life, such as, say, when you saved your allowance to buy a coveted toy. When you left the shelter of home and began to make your own way in the world, your preconceived notions about money management really began to materialize.

You would be in the minority if money did not play some role in your choice of career. That role is bigger for some people than for others. Did you pick your career path purely because it offered some sense of self-fulfillment or served a lofty humanitarian purpose? Or did you see an opportunity to make a nice salary with good benefits? I venture to say that for most of us, the answer lies somewhere in the middle. I, for instance, chose to become a financial planner because I saw it as a way to help people while offering a professional challenge and an avenue to afford a comfortable lifestyle for my family.

Just as money might influence your decision to pursue a certain job, your career influences your financial choices. The dominant factor is your paycheck. The more money you make, the more choices you face about when, where, and why you will spend it. For example, if you earn a minimum wage, you have few choices. You must focus on the necessities of shelter, food, and clothing. If you earn a high income, you might desire a higher standard of living—a big house, dinners at fancy restaurants, or a condo in the mountains. Or perhaps you are more focused on providing the best education for your children or donating to your favorite charity.

> **How Important Is Money to You?**
> When you chose your career field, how did the following factors influence your decision? Which was most important? Least important? Have your rankings changed over the years?
>
> • Salary and benefits
> • Interesting/challenging work
> • Image/prestige
> • Helping others
> • Work/life balance
> • Job security

The amount of money you make today and what you expect to earn in the future can have a big impact on the way you think about money in general. Money, or lack of it, might not define you as a person, but it can define the life you lead and the choices you make.

Your career is more than just your income; it is what you do and how you do it. If you are one of the lucky ones, it reflects your interests and aptitudes as a person. Are you a creative type or more analytical? Are you an innovative leader or a rule follower? Are you a micromanager or content to supervise at arm's length? Do not be surprised if your on-the-job style spills over into the way you manage your money.

Assuming you work full-time, your job also represents the biggest commitment of your time. The more demanding your schedule, the less time you have for personal pursuits, financial planning included. Even a busy financial professional, despite extensive education and a knack for working with numbers, might not have the time or the energy to come home at the end of the day and dissect the household budget.

A basketball coach spends the preseason evaluating his players' skills, preferences, and limitations. What he learns affects his decisions at game time. Sometimes that evaluation of players that leads to success can involve a start and finish that are several years in the making, as was the case when Dean Smith "finally" won his first national title at North Carolina in 1982.

"Really our first title was shaped years earlier before the moment finally came," Smith said in his book *A Coach's Life*. "The confluence of events began with the arrival in Chapel Hill of some wonderful prospects. I remember when a gangly eighth grader from Gastonia, North Carolina, showed up at our summer camp."

Smith was referring to James Worthy, who eventually joined Sam Perkins and Michael Jordan to become a three-man cornerstone of what arguably was Smith's best team in his thirty-six years as the Tar Heels' coach. Smith scouted plenty of great talent in his years recruiting players to North Carolina, and he said Worthy was one of the very few high schoolers he ever saw whom he knew on the spot would be a college star and professional player.

Acknowledging your personal attributes that influence your thinking can help you take a more successful approach to your financial plan.

Your Marriage

If you've never been married, your financial management might be easier. I am not knocking the sacred institution of matrimony. It is just a fact that marriage complicates our financial lives. Why? Because walking down the aisle represents more than the union of two souls. It usually signifies the merger of two incomes, two checking accounts, two sets of assets and liabilities, two investment portfolios . . . the list goes on. Almost always, each spouse brings into the marriage his or her own ideas of what financial security means and how it should be achieved.

Some married couples choose to keep their finances completely separate from each other, but those situations are rare. Most couples manage their money jointly, thus relinquishing the autonomy they once had with their financial fortunes. Their sole proprietorship suddenly becomes a partnership, and the partners do not always agree.

As my wife and I settled into our first year of marriage, one of our first disagreements was over who would pay the bills and balance the checkbook. That had been her mother's job in her family, so my wife naturally assumed she would fill that role in our household. I was not so sure this was a great idea. After all, I was the finance guy at work. Didn't it make sense for me to manage the coffers at home as well? There was some give-and-take, but eventually we agreed to divide the financial chores in a way that worked for both of us.

Over time, the list of money-related tasks couples must handle continues to grow: budgeting, saving to buy a home, choosing insurance limits, investing for retirement, and managing credit. These are the practical matters, the day-to-day responsibilities that go alongside mowing the grass and folding laundry. How you and your spouse divvy up and keep up with these duties certainly will shed some light on how your approaches to money management might differ.

There are also larger, more powerful influences at work—tidal forces that most couples do not discuss every day but have major implications for the marriage. These are the big-picture questions: How do you envision your lives together? Do you believe that your dream scenario is actually attainable? How, and how much, will you provide for your children? Is it more important to live for today or prepare for an uncertain future? Do you hope to retire someday, and when? What role does money play in it all?

Your answers might be based on deep-seated desires and feelings of profound responsibility formed over many years. I am no marriage counselor, but I can tell you what I have seen in decades of helping clients sort out their financial issues. That is, if your money mindset is in harmony with your spouse's, it can strengthen the bond between you. If it is in direct conflict, it can threaten to tear your marriage, and your finances, apart, but two spouses with conflicting ideas are doomed to failure. These financial convictions undoubtedly have a hand in how each thinks the household finances should be managed.

For example, your wife has been spending a lot of money eating out during her work week. You might make a sarcastic remark that could end with your wife rolling her eyes, or it could escalate into an hour-long bickering session. What you might not, but should, do is explain the deeper motivation behind your disapproval: "I would like us to control our spending so that one day we can send our kids to college and buy that beach house we have always dreamed about." Having an open and honest discussion about these expectations once in a while can prevent many arguments and help you and your partner work as a team.

Comparing marriage to basketball might be a hard sell, but let's give it a try. The players on a basketball team might have different individual approaches to the game, yet they must find ways to achieve a common goal. During some games, the group fails to jell, and the result is a discombobulated mess. Other days, they complement each other beautifully, combining their strengths to make winning look effortless. For long-term success, there must be communication and compromise.

Some conflicts are too great to overcome. As complicated as it can be for a couple to manage money, things tend to get really messy when a marriage ends. Divorce means more than just moving apart. It could mean paying or receiving alimony or child support payments and rethinking your career, your home, living expenses, insurance needs, retirement options, your estate plan, and more.

I have never been divorced, but from advising others who have, I know it can change your outlook on life. Divorce might lead to financial hardship and fear of not knowing how to handle new responsibilities, or it could provide freedoms you never experienced during your marriage. Either way, it changes your thinking about money. Coming to grips with these new realities can make a positive difference in the next segment of your life.

Your Children

Having a child is a bit like welcoming the next young phenom to your ball club. You have been waiting for his arrival with great anticipation. You celebrate when he arrives. You provide for him and nurture his development. You work hard to indoctrinate him into your system, but the young star, with his extraordinary talents, turns your whole program on its head. Your team is now built around him.

Out of necessity and out of love, we reshape our existence for our kids. The days of living only for ourselves are over. An often overwhelming sense of responsibility washes over us and remains forever.

Likewise, our financial lives can never be the same once we become parents. Face it, children are outrageously expensive. Raising kids involves a long chain of major expenses stretched across time, from diapers to doctor visits, cheerleading to cars, college to weddings, and thousands

> **Beware: Budget-Eating Babies**
> The USDA report, "Expenditures on Children by Families" estimates that the average middle-income family can expect to spend a total of $234,900 to raise a child born in 2011. That is just for the basics of food, shelter, childcare, healthcare and other necessities for seventeen years. It does not begin to account for the fun stuff you will do with your kids, nor does it include savings for college.

of pricey pursuits in between. Whether you choose to pay for all of it is up to you, but the mere fact that you are considering it affects how you manage your money.

In addition to being a provider, you are also a teacher. Just as your parents' actions made an impression on you, the financial choices you make as a caregiver can impart lessons to your kids. Your children learn by watching you, whether or not the lesson is what you intended.

> **What All Parents Should Teach Their Kids about Money (when the time is right)**
> - Distinguishing between *wants* and *needs*
> - The rewards of saving for short-term goals
> - How to balance a checking account
> - The proper use of credit
> - The value of investing at a young age

I once had an affluent client who spared no expense for his kids. "This is a hard world," he reasoned, "so I want to use my wealth to make my children happy, give them every advantage, and remove all stress from their lives."

My client's heart was in the right place, but I wondered how such a privileged upbringing would come to bear on the children once they became adults. Would they use their status as a springboard to greater things? Or would they choke on the silver spoon, growing up with a skewed sense of entitlement that, ironically, would destine them for mediocrity and unhappiness?

I have also seen parents who err to the opposite extreme. "I had to work for everything I have," the logic goes. "So my kids will, too, because that is what builds character." This tough love approach might be rooted in good intentions, but such deprivation can backfire if it means their kids become social outcasts in middle school or are unable to complete college.

These are weighty issues with no black-and-white answers. One thing is clear: The kind of parent you choose to be influences your decisions on spending, saving, investing, and insurance.

Even later in life, when your children are grown and hopefully self-sufficient, your financial choices continue to impact them. Your plans for retirement and old age can create powerful effects that stretch across generations. Will your children have to bear the expense of caring for you as you age? When you die, what will become of your home and possessions, and how much money will you leave behind for your family?

Recognizing and planning for your own mortality might not be a pleasant experience, but it is yet another way parenthood shapes your financial plan.

Your Financial History

Although your family background and current relationships exert emotional forces on your money psyche, your interactions with the financial marketplace push buttons in another corner of your mind. Your prior experiences with money management—both positive and negative— largely determine your faith in the system and your trust of people within it.

"The system" refers to the vast web of associations, corporations, government entities, and other institutions that essentially have a hand in your piggy bank. Included in this web are the stock market, investment houses, banks, the IRS, the Federal Reserve, and insurance companies, to name a few. How confident are you they will do what is best for your financial well-being?

Your answer could be influenced by major economic events during your lifetime. If your parents or grandparents lived through the Great Depression, for example, they could be forgiven for harboring some long-lasting skepticism toward the financial establishment. Perhaps you were affected in a similar way by the savings and loan crisis of the late 1980s, the dot-com boom and bust of 2000, or the financial system meltdown of 2008. You might have lost a small fortune in the plummeting stock market or read about others who did. As a result, maybe you look at banking, technology, or real estate sectors with suspicion.

Being burned can make you more cautious, maybe even resentful, but your positive experiences can be equally influential. If, despite the occasional bear market, you have watched your long-term portfolio increase over decades, you might feel more secure about your prospects for the future. Then again, a quick win with a hot stock could give you a dangerous case of overconfidence. Do any of these apply to you?

Events outside of the stock market count too. If you have ever had to replace a $5,000 air conditioner in the heat of summer, you might feel compelled to set aside an emergency fund for surprise expenses. If you have ever fallen victim to a house fire or been sued after a car accident, you probably place a higher priority on having enough insurance.

Last but not least, the people you have dealt with over the years have helped define your attitudes. A piece of ill-timed advice from your investment advisor might have left you distrustful of the financial planning profession in general, or maybe you feel that handing your tax return over to a CPA was the best thing you ever did.

> ### How Involved Will You Be?
>
> Your earlier financial experiences and your money intelligence—how much you know about investing and financial management—influence your desire to control your own financial destiny. Most clients I have worked with fall into one of three categories:
>
> - **Do-it-yourselfers:** want to be in total control at all times and might be skeptical of outside input.
> - **Executive types:** want to be involved in important decisions but rely on specialized experts to advise them.
> - **Pure delegators:** put their financial matters wholly in the hands of someone who is professionally trained and whom they trust to do the right thing.
>
> None of these types are wrong or right, but it is important to act in a way that suits your interests, financial means, and expertise.

Like all players and coaches, we have our record of wins and losses. We remember the nail-biters and the blowouts, the heartbreakers and the last-second miracles. We take something away from each of them, and these memories motivate our decisions in the next game.

Your Money Intelligence

Your past financial experiences determine your level of confidence in other people and institutions. On the other hand, your own depth of knowledge and comfort level in dealing with financial matters will affect how much faith you place in yourself. This concerns your money "intelligence"—

your command of the tools, rules, and strategies of the financial world. This could be compared to what sports fans call "basketball IQ." Great coaches and many great players (especially point guards) possess it. They have the foresight and quick-thinking skills to make the right decision when the game is on the line.

A lapse in judgment, however, can have disastrous results. One example was the 1993 NCAA championship game, in which the Fab Five of Michigan challenged North Carolina. In the closing seconds of the game, Michigan was down by two points when its explosive big man, Chris Webber, secured a defensive rebound. Webber dribbled up the floor and called a timeout with eleven seconds left. It would have been a sensible decision, allowing Michigan to design a play to tie or win the game at the buzzer. There was only one problem—Michigan was out of timeouts. Webber's mental error resulted in a technical foul, and North Carolina sank both free throws to dash Michigan's title hopes.

A lack of information or the absence of poise under fire can lead to bad financial decisions as well. A high money IQ can prevent them. It does not matter if your money intelligence was attained through formal education or informally by reading books and articles about financial planning. Sometimes effort and good intentions are not enough—what matters is that you understand money, how it works, and how you can make it work for you when the time is right.

Even more important is knowing what you do not know. Do you know what advantages a Roth IRA holds over a 401(k)? Can you explain how rising interest rates affect your investment portfolio? Do you understand the purpose of hedge funds? And are you prepared to make investment transactions that limit your tax liability?

The intent here is not to scare you into hiring a financial planner. It is to get you thinking about where you fall on the scale of financial aptitude: Are you an expert, a novice, or somewhere in-between? Can you trust yourself to call the right play when your financial championship is at stake?

If you can look at yourself objectively and answer these kinds of questions honestly, you will have taken a step toward building a sound, rational financial plan for the future.

ADDING IT UP:
HOW THESE INFLUENCES COMBINE TO
IMPACT YOUR FINANCIAL SUCCESS

Experienced basketball coaches know you can stand in front of your players and lecture them for only so long. After a few minutes, they'll tire of your carefully prepared speech on "the intangible qualities of a winner," and they'll be itching to get back on the court. So in a minute, we'll head out of the locker room and onto our court and get into the more practical matters of financial planning. But before we do, let's recap.

Financial planning should be a unique process for every individual and family. There is no one-size-fits-all solution. Before you can develop a plan to fit your life and goals, you have to know yourself—not just how much money you make or how much you want to have but the real *you*, the deep impulses that define your money mindset and drive your everyday financial decisions.

I'm not suggesting that a good financial plan requires a complete psychological evaluation or a journey of spiritual enlightenment. I am simply proposing that the influencing factors we discussed in this chapter can have real-life implications in your planning process. They can help you determine why you feel inclined to make the choices you do and whether your gut feelings are really the right ones for your family's financial security.

I'll give you a hypothetical example of how your money mindset might manifest itself in your financial planning process. Let's use the fictitious Mike as our subject. When Mike was growing up, his parents were not exactly long-term thinkers. They put away little for his education or their own retirement. Nevertheless, when Mike finished college and got a job, he attended a

Traits of a Successful Investor

- *Education*—on investing concepts and trends.
- *Organization*—of important records and financial affairs.
- *Patience*—to know that real, lasting success takes time.
- *Objectivity*—to base decisions on facts, not emotions.
- *Discipline*—to set aside money to invest regularly.
- *Perseverance*—to ride out down markets.
- *Skepticism*—to question the masses.

financial seminar that convinced him to start saving. He did, but a few years later, his 401(k) balance burst along with the dot-com bubble.

Maybe his parents had it right after all, he figured. Fearing another huge loss, he pulled back his 401(k) contributions to a trickle. Now in his mid-thirties, Mike has a new baby at home, and the mounting expenses lead him to keep every penny of discretionary income in his checking account. He believes he can't afford to "throw money away" in the stock market.

Obviously, Mike's path through life has shaped his thinking about money. He has a low risk tolerance despite the common and correct rule of thumb that a person his age should invest mostly in equities for long-term growth prospects. He is also distrustful of professional financial advisors—after all, he lost his shirt the last time he listened to them.

Confusion and doubt have clouded Mike's judgment, and he has difficulty seeing the big picture beyond his limited interactions with the financial universe. Sadly, his opportunities to attain wealth slip away with every passing year.

You don't have to be like Mike. By honing your ability to assess yourself objectively, you can recognize when your instincts are the right ones and when flawed logic or emotions are blocking your path to financial success. You might even conclude that you are incapable of separating your deep-rooted money mindset from your actions. In that case, there are honest, skilled financial professionals to help you achieve that objective perspective.

Know yourself. Know your strengths and how to use them. Know your weaknesses and how to overcome them.

As Wooden used to tell his players, "Success comes from knowing that you did your best to become the best that you are capable of becoming." It all starts with a good look in the mirror.

CHAPTER-ENDING THREE-POINTER

1. List the important lessons you learned about money while growing up.
2. Note the differences in perspectives between you and your spouse regarding spending, saving, and investing.
3. Be aware of investment strategies you favor or dislike based on your past experiences.

CHAPTER TWO

SCOUTING THE OPPONENTS

Sizing up the Forces that Stand between You and Your Financial Goals

PEACH BASKET PARABLES: NORTH CAROLINA VS. KANSAS, 1957 NCAA CHAMPIONSHIP GAME

If Indiana has a rival for the right to claim itself as "most basketball-crazy state," North Carolina would have to be in the mix. Three NCAA championship-caliber programs are located within thirty miles of each other in North Carolina: North Carolina State in Raleigh, with two titles; Duke University in Durham, with four trophies; and, of course, the University of North Carolina at Chapel Hill, boasting five championships (all as of 2013). Since the NCAA Tournament started in 1939, these three schools have won about 15 percent, approximately one out of every seven, of the championships played. Students and local residents still bathe themselves in blue or red and camp overnight to score tickets to games.

It has not always been that way. UNC was voted national champion in 1924 before there was an actual NCAA Tournament, and it made one Final Four appearance in 1946. Basketball fever did not really grip the area completely until March 23, 1957, when the Tar Heels made their debut NCAA Championship Game appearance.

Led by Coach Frank McGuire, the Tar Heels finished the regular season undefeated and were ranked number one in the nation, but the odds were stacked against them in the title game. Only a day earlier, UNC survived a grueling, three-overtime semifinal game against Michigan State. In those days, there was no day of rest between the semifinals and the title game, so the Tar Heels had to be fatigued going into the final. Their opponent, a 24–2 Kansas team, had easily defeated San Francisco the day before, allowing them to rest their star players in the second half.

On top of all that, the location for the tournament final was Kansas City, a thousand miles from Chapel Hill but merely forty miles from the Kansas Jayhawks' campus in Lawrence. By a cruel twist of fate, the NCAA Championship, which is always supposed to be played on a neutral court, had become a virtual home game for Kansas, with screaming Jayhawks fans flooding the arena and nary a speck of UNC's powder blue.

Kansas also boasted a not-so-secret weapon in its ranks—a seven-foot-one sophomore center who had taken the game by storm during an era when seven-footers were extremely rare in pro basketball. He averaged thirty points and eighteen rebounds per game, blocked shots almost at will, and was deemed by the media as the most unstoppable player in the country. The goliath's name was Wilt Chamberlain.

The cards might have been stacked in favor of Kansas, but McGuire had seen them play. He had taken notes, and he had a plan for his Tar Heels.

MIND GAMES

The coach's strategy started with the opening tip. Spectators were befuddled when UNC's Tommy Kearns, just five-foot-eleven, made his way to the center circle for the jump ball against Chamberlain. The rest of the considerably taller Tar Heels readied themselves in a zone defense.

From the first possession, the UNC zone suffocated Chamberlain. They triple-teamed him near the basket, doing all they could to deny him the ball and collapsing on him when he did get his hands on it. With one defender in front of him, one behind, and a third swooping in from the side, the frustrated Chamberlain was consistently forced to pass it outside or put up a difficult shot.

Of course, UNC's Chamberlain-centric strategy left the other Kansas shooters wide open much of the time. But McGuire was willing to take that risk. All tournament long he had watched the Jayhawks struggle from outside. Unquestionably, Wilt the Stilt was Kansas's bread and butter, and McGuire was going to make someone other than Chamberlain beat the Tar Heels. By halftime, his plan was paying off—Kansas shot only 27 percent from the field in the first half, and UNC led 29–22 at the buzzer.

Kansas recovered in the second half, however. As UNC tried stalling to hold onto the lead , the Jayhawks forced turnovers and clawed their way back. The Tar Heels' star Lennie Rosenbluth fouled out, and at the end of regulation, the game was tied at 46–46.

OUTLASTED, OUTSMARTED

In overtime, the Tar Heels continued to hound Chamberlain relentlessly, just as they had done for the forty minutes of regulation, but the game moved at a snail's pace. Each team scored only one basket and then tried to run out the clock or hold the ball for the game-winning shot. The strategy didn't work for either team, and the first overtime ended at 48–48. The pace slowed even more in the second overtime with neither team scoring, and for the second time in two nights, the Tar Heels headed into triple overtime.

This time, UNC went on the attack, scoring two consecutive baskets, although the Jayhawks rallied back to take a one-point lead. With six seconds left in the third overtime, UNC's Joe Quigg was fouled and went to the line for two free throws. He made both to put the Tar Heels back in front by one.

The final play of the game was typical of what had gone on all night. Kansas, still trusting in Chamberlain to save them, attempted a lob pass to the big man in the low post. The Tar Heels were ready for it. Quigg deflected the pass. Little Tommy Kearns (the guard who had gone up against Chamberlain for the opening jump ball) came up with the stolen ball and threw it high in the air to run out the clock. UNC had slain the giant to take home its first tournament championship.

It was the first and still only time the NCAA title game went into triple overtime. And it is hailed by many as one of the greatest games in college basketball history.

COLOR COMMENTARY

One especially noteworthy Kansas alumnus watching the game that night was a diehard fan of Jayhawks basketball, having played on the 1952 championship squad before becoming an assistant coach after graduation. The young man was reportedly devastated by Kansas's heartbreaking loss to UNC, which is understandable if you know the competitive fire of Dean Smith, who was that Kansas alum. In an interesting twist of fate, Smith would later be hired by McGuire to be an assistant coach at UNC and go on to serve as head coach of the Tar Heels for thirty-six seasons. In that time, he won two NCAA championships and eventually ended his career as college basketball's winningest Division I coach with 879 victories. He went down in history as one of the greatest basketball coaches of all time.

THE VALUE OF SCOUTING

Clearly, UNC's McGuire had done his research before that incredible game. It was not hard to identify Chamberlain as the focal point for his defense, but McGuire had also studied the rest of the Kansas team. The Jayhawks had other good players, but he was confident that Kansas could not win when forced to shoot long-range jumpers, and he was right.

Chamberlain scored twenty-three points in the game and was chosen Most Outstanding Player of the Final Four, but UNC's swarming tactics held him well below his season average. That was just enough for the Tar Heels to secure the victory.

Scouting upcoming foes, as McGuire did so well, has become commonplace in sports. Coaches and their teams spend many hours collecting data and reviewing video of upcoming opponents, hoping to learn their strategic tendencies on offense and defense to devise a counterapproach or expose an Achilles' heel. Perhaps they design a play to exploit a weak defender, draw a shot blocker away from the basket, or even intentionally foul a horrible free-throw shooter.

This strategic approach for getting to know your competition, attacking their strengths, and exploiting their weaknesses is another reason basketball is comparable to financial planning. Success never occurs in a vacuum. There are always opponents—forces working against you that must be overcome. It is a two-sided proposition.

Basketball is different from a sport such as golf or figure skating in which the contestants are focused on themselves and their performances. They have no direct influence over how their rivals perform unless you can envision golfer Phil Mickelson dashing across the green to block a Tiger Woods putt.

In basketball, as in financial planning, you can do more than what a Mickelson or a Woods can do. You can study your competition and find ways to shut them down while devising ways to earn the victory.

So, you ask, if financial planning is like a basketball game, who are my opponents? Any number of obstacles could stand between you and your financial goals. Your adversaries usually will not include real people aside from a boss who denies you a raise. The financial opponents most people face are more intangible, a dynamic lineup of powerful forces that threaten to delay, diminish, or altogether destroy your chances of success in the financial marketplace.

In this chapter, we divide the competition into two main categories—factors you can control and those that are external. Factors within your personal control could include failing to budget your money or making poor investment decisions. Although these are more internal opponents, they can be viewed as your competition because they must be defeated along your path to financial happiness.

Among the external factors over which you have little or no control are interest rates, inflation, market performance, and world events, all of which are intertwined and wield great power in your investment portfolio. While you might not dictate their actions as you do your own, you can often "scout" them effectively and devise a plan to minimize their impact—just as UNC did to the "unstoppable" Chamberlain.

THE ENEMIES WITHIN:
BAD HABITS AND OTHER PITFALLS TO AVOID

There are unfriendly foes hiding inside your head, most of which can be overcome if you are willing to make the effort and believe you can win.

For the UNC Tar Heels of 1957, their mental obstacles included coming off a triple-overtime game the night before and having no fans to support them in the final game. They would have had good excuses had they lost, but they defied the odds and had no need for excuses when it was all over.

Likewise, in financial planning, defeating your inner enemies comes first. What follows is a short list of self-defeating behaviors that can result in sabotaging your own financial success. In basketball terms, you could also think of these blunders as unforced turnovers. As coaches like to say, you have to "take care of the ball" when it is in your possession. Your strategy to bring down the other team will not matter if you can't keep from beating yourself. Believe it or not, preparing a team not to lose instead of preparing them to win has been identified as a more important success philosophy by some of the game's greatest coaches.

Start with former Army, Indiana, and Texas Tech coach Bob Knight, who happens to be the first coach to break Dean Smith's record for career Division I victories.

Knight, known as "The General," is a strong proponent of the school of coaching that says more games are lost than won, a sort of glass-half-empty perspective. In his 2013 book, *The Power of Negative Thinking*, Knight builds a case that your team's won-lost success is built more on identifying your team's weaknesses and training to avoid mistakes than it is on focusing on what you do well and exploiting your strengths to the max.

A quick footnote: the legendary coach John Wooden, whose game-time demeanor was much lower wattage than Knight's, echoes Knight's more cynical view in his own books, saying that more games are lost than won.

In his most recent book, Knight uses the illustration of a sculptor to explain his negative approach to coaching, saying that the sculptor carves what he does not want out of a slab of marble to end up with the proper contours of the figure he or she is creating. "Negative material is eliminated to create a harmonious work of art," Knight writes.

He continues: "As I looked to every game and every season, my first thought was always: 'What vulnerabilities do we have and what can we do to minimize them, to get around them, to survive them—and give ourselves a better chance to win?'"

Case in point was Knight's underdog Indiana team pulling off a 72–68 upset of the Michael Jordan-led North Carolina Tar Heels in an NCAA Tournament game. Knight knew that one of his team's potential downfalls in the game would be its ball handling against North Carolina's trap and double-team defenses that Dean Smith crafted so well.

Knight explained that in preparing for that game, he changed tactics with his players. He told them to abandon their usual cutting and screening offense and switch to an offense that would instead utilize more quick passes to open teammates. This would reduce the chances of too much ball handling leading to too many costly turnovers. In other words, it was a way to protect the ball without holding onto it as long, an act of negative thinking that produced positive results.

OVERSPENDING AND SAVING TOO LITTLE

Early in my financial career, I learned an important lesson: Winning at the saving and investing game is less about how much you make and more about how much you keep.

It sounds simple, yet millions of Americans continue to act as if the opposite is true. They spend their adult lives in a never-ending pursuit of more money, not so they can attain financial independence but so they can spend more. They use whatever discretionary income they have in a vain attempt to satisfy materialistic urges or to fill the lifestyle mold that society expects from them. It is never quite enough, though, and the habitual acquisition of stuff only stokes the desire for more.

These sorts of folks chase after their idea of a wealthy lifestyle like a greyhound pursues the fake rabbit. In the end, they are left with little real wealth or at least much less than they could have had if they had spent less and saved more.

You have probably heard of "keeping up with the Joneses"—always trying to win the approval of or outdo your friends and neighbors with snazzier shoes, the newest iPad, or season tickets closer to the court. That behavior is a symptom of the larger problem of consumerism. To the detriment of American families, consumerism is ingrained in our culture. It is an addiction of sorts, fueled by the commercialization of almost every aspect of our lives. Ubiquitous advertising, corporate sponsorships, and product placements assault our desire to save money as they convince us to buy, buy, buy. Every purchase, no matter how small, is another lost opportunity to save for the future.

If it sounds as if I am preaching from my high horse, I really don't have a right to. I, too, am guilty of having a fondness for the consumer lifestyle. I am just like everyone else. If I wasn't, I would never buy a brand new shirt, eat out, go to the movies, or pay five dollars for a soda at a ball game, but life would not be very much fun if we saved every penny.

Things would go terribly wrong if everyone suddenly stopped spending. Our economy is built on consumerism. With no one willing to buy the goods and services American companies are selling, these businesses would go belly up, the stock market would nose-dive, and everyone's nest eggs would implode. That is an oversimplification, but such a bleak scenario is close to what our country experienced in the Great Depression and to a lesser degree in the more recent Great Recession.

No one is saying you have to live a Spartan existence to attain financial security. Enjoy your life today, but devote enough of your income to saving and investing so you will be able to enjoy life in the future as well. Resist the temptation to one-up the Joneses of the world, and take pride in the fact that you are building something that might be less conspicuous yet far more important and fulfilling.

Like the heated battles between rivals that occur every season, would-be savers wake up every day to fight a never-ending battle against the forces of consumerism. The idea of "spend less, save more" is rudimentary, but for most people it is a mental challenge that never goes away.

STARTING TOO LATE

No coach worth his salt has ever told his players, "Let's take it easy in the first half, and then we'll turn up the heat late in the game." No, the standard coaching rhetoric is give it all you've got from the opening tip to the final horn. Jumping out to an early lead is always preferable to playing from behind.

In financial planning, starting early is even more important. Why? Because for most of us, a retirement nest egg or college fund represents a mountain of money that can't be scraped together on short notice. Meeting these goals takes years—often a lifetime—of planning and commitment. The good news is that the sooner you start saving, the easier it will be thanks to the power of compounding.

If you have read much about investing, you already know about compounding. If not, here is a primer. In the investing sense, compounding refers to the way your money builds on itself. As your investments earn returns and you reinvest the profits, your returns earn more returns. As the returns pile up, your account balance grows exponentially, and you are rewarded with a total that is much more than just the contributions you put away.

Let us look at a very simple example in numbers. You start with $10,000. Whether through bank interest or increasing stock values, that $10,000 earns a 10 percent return in one year, and you now have $11,000 in your account, a gain of $1,000. In the next year, the $11,000 earns another 10 percent return, and your balance has grown to $12,100, a gain of $1,100. In the third year, your $12,100 earns the same 10 percent return and you now have $13,310, a gain of $1,210. See how the gains keep getting larger? In a little more than seven years, you will have doubled your money without contributing another cent.

The Rule of 72

Want to know how quickly you can double your money through the magic of compounding? Use the Rule of 72. To find out how long an investment earning 8 percent takes to double, simply divide 72 by 8, and the answer would be about 9 years (not accounting for any taxes and fees). It works the other way too: to find out what rate of return you would need to double your money in five years, divide 72 by 5. The answer is 14.4 percent.

That is the power of compounding. At higher dollar amounts and with continuous contributions, the effects become much more pronounced so much so that disciplined middle-income earners can become millionaires—if they start investing early and give compounding plenty of time to do its work.

Time is your ally. Procrastination is your enemy. Waiting around for the perfect time to invest can cost you dearly. Delaying only a few years could rob you of the potential to earn thousands—perhaps tens or hundreds of thousands—of dollars through compounding.

I encourage young people to start saving for retirement in their twenties, even if it means starting with small contributions and increasing the amount as their income grows. Those who wait until their thirties, though still relatively young, will have to work much harder, contributing much more money to reach the same savings goal.

Can you expect to earn a 10 percent rate of return year after year, as in the example I provide? Probably not, especially if the financial markets continue their rollercoaster ride of recent years. Having time on your side puts you in a better position to weather the short-term ups and downs of the markets and to come out ahead in the long run.

The Cost of Waiting

In investing, time is your best friend. In the table below, Jack starts saving at age twenty-five, invests $5,000 annually for ten years, and never contributes another dime. After forty years, he still has more money than Jill, who contributed much more but started later than Jack. And of course, James, who started at age twenty-five and never stopped, has much more than both of the others.

	Jack	Jill	James
Investment contributions during ages 25–35	$5,000 annually	$0	$5,000 annually
Investment contributions during ages 35–65	$0	$5,000 annually	$5,000 annually
Total Invested	$50,000	$150,000	$200,000
Ending Balance	$850,000	$661,000	$1,511,000
*Assuming an 8 percent annual return on investments			

On a related note, starting earlier and having more years until you will need the money you invested allows you to take on more risk, such as investing primarily in stocks and other growth investments as opposed to bonds. As such, you give yourself the potential for even greater long-term gains.

The sooner in life you start to save and invest, the better your chances of creating wealth. But it does not mean that all hope is lost if you find yourself behind in the game. There are strategies to catch up, which we will discuss in Chapter 8.

SAVING INCONSISTENTLY

Great athletes "practice how they play and play how they practice." In other words, they work on the same movements (be it a jump shot or a pick-and-roll play) over and over again until the mechanics become ingrained in their muscle memory. Come game time, those fundamentally sound movements present themselves by second nature, without a moment's hesitation.

The Hidden Value of Consistency

This table shows the benefits of dollar-cost-averaging. Rick and Lisa invest the same sum of money ($1,500) in XYZ stock. Rick does it all it at once, while Lisa starts at the same time but invests $250 per month for six months. Lisa's strategy buys fewer shares when the stock price is high and more shares when the price is low. As a result, after six months Lisa owns more shares and her investments are worth more.

Month	XYZ Stock Price	Rick's Investments	Lisa's Investments
January	$10	$1,500 = 150 shares	$250 = 25 shares
February	$8	None	$250 = 31.25 shares
March	$6	None	$250 = 41.6 shares
April	$4	None	$250 = 62.5 shares
May	$6	None	$250 = 41.6 shares
June	$8	None	$250 = 31.25 shares
Ending Balance:		150 shares = $1,200	233 shares = $1,864

The same type of systematic approach can and should be applied to your financial plan. Ideally, that means making frequent, consistent contributions to your retirement accounts, college funds, and other investments. Financial success comes much easier if you make investing a habit rather than an afterthought. Put another way, it is not enough to invest early. You should also invest often.

The best and easiest way to do this is by paying yourself first. Make your savings and investment contributions every month before you make other discretionary purchases. It is as easy as setting up an auto-draft from your paycheck to your investment accounts. After a while, it becomes a routine. You naturally adjust your spending habits to make do with whatever money is left, and you no longer feel the pain of socking away regular savings.

Unfortunately, too many people take the opposite approach. They understand the need to save, and they promise themselves they will put something away just as soon as the stars align—"when I get my bonus," "once my car is paid off," "after I pay my taxes." Maybe they follow through, and maybe they don't. What usually results from this passive approach are fewer, inconsistent contributions (at best) and smaller dollar amounts. This is the reason they have failed to make investing a top priority. By comparison, the systematic investor's account balance grows steadily and compounds over time, resulting in a huge savings advantage as the years go by.

Aside from making more frequent contributions, there is another reason to invest on a consistent basis: dollar-cost-averaging. You have undoubtedly heard the old axiom "buy low, sell high." Well, systematic investing helps you do just that. By contributing the same amount of money every month or quarter, you are automatically buying more shares when prices are down and fewer shares when prices are high. Over time, this simple strategy has proven to be more successful than trying to time investment purchases based on market conditions.

Like a dedicated player who shoots a hundred free throws to start or end every practice, building systematic contributions into your "muscle memory" will make you a more effective investor.

Emotional Decision Making

How many times have you watched a ball game where a talented yet inexperienced team is pitted against a squad of battle-hardened veterans? It's a classic story. The young phenoms look athletically superior, but they make critical mental errors. They celebrate too early when they take an early lead. Then they panic as the lead dissolves. Ultimately, they crumble down the stretch. The veterans, meanwhile, have stayed the course and allowed the volatile youngsters to take themselves out of the game.

Sometimes maturity can make all the difference. Overcoming powerful emotions and maintaining an even keel is also a requisite skill for successful investors. That's easier said than done because money is an emotional topic. It is your livelihood at stake, after all. No matter. Alarmist investing decisions rarely pay off.

The financial crisis of 2008–2009 provides a perfect example of alarmist decisions causing losses. As stocks slid ever-downward and doomsday headlines popped up all over, millions of average individual investors pulled the plug on their portfolios. They simply could not bear to watch their hard-earned savings continue to evaporate, so they cashed out while they still had something left. Even as the economy began to rebound, many victims of the financial meltdown sat on the sidelines, hesitant to step back into the fray. As the markets rose again, these people missed out on the chance to recover their huge losses.

Given the calamitous events of those years, it might seem difficult to blame investors for acting out of fear and doubt. But history has shown that making major investment decisions based on current events is a strategy for failure.

Experienced investors learn to take emotion out of the equation. They know (based on reams of historical data) that circumstances will eventually turn back around and their holdings will regain—and probably surpass—their value of a few months or years earlier. Many investors see temporary declines as opportunities to buy more shares "on sale" with the expectation of making a hefty profit when the market returns to positive territory (see the Cycle of Market Emotions).

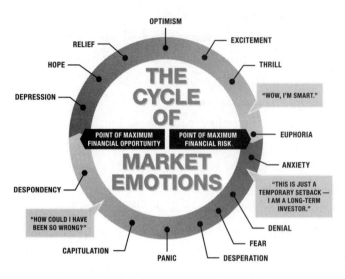

Ironically, the point of maximum financial opportunity is often when investors feel the most reluctant.

True, there is no guarantee that any single investment will recover from a crash, but in the big-picture view, the stock market overall has risen steadily over many years. If you have at least five years to invest, odds are good that a well-structured, diversified portfolio will increase in value over the long term. Your job as an investor is to think like a seasoned point guard—analyze the situation with cool objectivity, keep your nerves in check, and give your team the best chance to win.

One of the greatest point guards in women's college basketball was Connecticut's Diana Taurasi, who also played shooting guard in college. During Taurasi's four years at UConn under head coach Geno Auriemma, the Huskies won three consecutive national championships in large part because of Taurasi's great court skills as well as her inspirational leadership. She is one of the most talented and passionate players ever to play the women's game and had a sharp mind able to handle the pressure of one big game after another, but she was not perfect.

Auriemma, in his book *Pursuit of Perfection*, tells of the 2002 NCAA Championship game in which Taurasi was having one of her worst games even though her team was winning. Unabashedly in-your-face with his players, Auriemma confronted Taurasi during a timeout late in the game.

In full view of her teammates, he chastised her after she had made a flurry of mistakes, keeping Oklahoma within striking distance.

Many players, male or female, might have wilted during Auriemma's tirade against Taurasi, but she did not. She took the verbal attacks in stride, basically just shrugging her shoulders. Moments later, she made the biggest shot of the game, scoring a key basket while getting fouled by Stacey Dales, one of the Lady Sooners' best players. That was Dales's fifth foul, disqualifying her from the game. Taurasi then nailed the free throw to complete the three-point play and effectively seal the victory.

In the world of financial planning and dealing with risk, what kind of a point guard are you?

WISHFUL THINKING

While freaking out is never advisable in a basketball game or in financial affairs, neither is utter complacency.

On the court, it is not enough to sit back and assume that the hot-shooting opponents will cool off or that your teammate will save you with a game-winning shot. Winning takes hustle, aggressiveness, and determination from every player on the floor.

Financial planning is no different. I meet a surprising number of people who stake their futures on uncertain, often unreasonable, expectations. For example, you might expect that your aging parents will leave you a tidy inheritance that will put you on Easy Street. You might believe that your brilliant real estate investment of years back is going to make a big profit. Or, in an extreme case of self-delusion, you might have convinced yourself that all those years of buying lottery tickets will one day end in a jackpot.

If any of these events happen, great, but don't count on them. Things could change. Your parents could decide to leave their money to charity. Your real estate investment could decline. And—I can say this with near-100 percent certainty—you are not going to win the lottery. When these plans fall through, you will find yourself in trouble if you have been waiting around to save and invest on your own.

There is a saying in my business that makes a lot of sense: "Hope for the best, but plan for the worst." Ultimately, you are in control of your fate, and you must take an active role in your own success. Often, that means finding a trustworthy professional to manage your money for you.

THE SHORTCUT MENTALITY

Alongside the fallacy of wishful thinking comes the ill-fated shortcut mentality. We would all like to believe that there is some magic formula that can make our dreams come true overnight.

In the sports world, the most inflammatory example is the use of steroids to get bigger, faster, and stronger in short order. For investors, it is the get-rich-quick schemes you see on late-night TV, in the bookstore, and, increasingly, on the Internet. You know the ones: "I made $27,000 last month by using this simple technique." They claim to have figured out a way to beat the system or take advantage of some loophole that opens a secret door to riches. Amazingly, this "expert" you have never heard of has devised a brilliant scheme that all the Ivy League MBAs on Wall Street have somehow never discovered. Of course, you are left to wonder, if one of these deals is as good as he or she says it is, then why are they willing to share their secret with the rest of the world? Because they know a whole lot of folks will pay good money—to them—to get in on "the bonanza."

Although most of the programs you see advertised are not illegal, they are deceitful. They prey on the naiveté of inexperienced investors and their visions of financial independence. If you have ever considered buying into one of these schemes, be warned: You would probably be better off stuffing your money under a mattress.

Not just wet-behind-the-ears investors get pulled into the shortcut mentality. Even those experienced in the ways of Wall Street can be lured by temptation when the bait is more convincing. Just look at the Ponzi scheme that put the now-infamous Bernie Madoff in prison in 2009. Madoff, the head of a New York investment firm and a former nonexecutive chairman of the NASDAQ stock exchange, wore a mask of credibility that won the trust of many investors. They were promised access to an exclusive investment opportunity that yielded consistently high returns quarter after quarter, but Madoff's investors failed to ask how that could be possible when the rest of the market was in a crisis of volatility. Perhaps they just did not want to hear the answer. Ultimately, the Madoff scandal defrauded investors of billions of dollars and went down as the largest financial fraud in US history.

The more sophisticated the swindle, the more difficult it is to spot. The lesson here is a simple one you have heard a hundred times: If something seems too good to be true, it probably is.

BAD ADVICE

Most, if not all, extremely skilled basketball players had at least one great coach during their rise to stardom. It could have been the youth coach who taught the proper shooting form or the college coach who perfectly communicated the intricacies of the motion offense. What if these talented young athletes had had awful teachers? What if someone—even someone with good intentions—had taught them all the wrong things from day one? Obviously, those players would not have made it very far.

As you pursue your financial goals, you will encounter plenty of people who will give you advice. It might be foundational instruction investing or more advanced techniques like minimizing capital gains taxes. The difficult part for you will be knowing when to listen and when to tune out.

My advice: the harder someone is trying to sell you on an idea, the more suspicious you should be. This applies to the get-rich-quick schemes we discussed earlier, but it is also important with regard to everyday financial dealings.

For example, you might be approached by a seemingly professional financial advisor who seems eager to help you amass a fortune. He gives you a slick presentation and compels you to invest in some obscure product you do not understand without taking time to learn about your financial goals and risk tolerance. If that makes you uncomfortable, your instincts are correct. Advisors like this are not really advisors at all—they are salespeople. They earn a commission if you follow their advice— whether investing in a mutual fund or buying whole life insurance—and that creates a serious conflict of interest.

Bad advice can also come from people who really do want to help you but simply lack the credentials or experience to give you effective counsel.

That might be your Uncle Paul, who lets you in on a can't-lose real estate deal or even a licensed financial advisor who just has not been around the block enough times. Chapter 3 includes more detailed guidelines on how to choose a financial planner.

Much of what investors read in the financial media is bad advice. Popular publications and websites such as the *Wall Street Journal*, *Money*, and *Kiplinger's Personal Finance* feature plenty of credible material, but much of it can be easily misinterpreted. Beyond discussions of sound investing principles, they fill their pages with analyses of investing minutiae such as "When is the right time to buy precious metals exchange-traded funds?" or "How to capitalize on the downturn in Swiss francs." This can be good information if you know exactly how to use it, but most people do not.

Always remember the ultimate purpose of these publications is not to help you reach your financial goals—it is to keep their readership high so they can sell advertising space and make money. The only way to do this is by churning out enormous volumes of fresh, exciting content because nobody wants to read the same old advice every month, even if it is still true.

The information overload of today's financial media fosters the idea that to be a real investor, you have to tinker with your portfolio on a regular basis. That is bad advice.

So how is one supposed to pick the few pieces of good advice from the avalanche of misinformation? In short, be critical. Ask first about the credibility of the person who is offering guidance. Do they have the education and experience to really know what they are talking about? Then ask whether that person has your best interests in mind. If he is a glorified salesperson, the answer is most likely no. Finally, ask yourself whether the advice being given is in line with your personal financial goals. A journalist, for instance, no matter how qualified, can't possibly give advice that is tailored to your unique circumstances.

Think of yourself as an All-American athlete being recruited by top schools around the country. Unlike when you were a kid, this time you get to pick who coaches you. So choose wisely.

ON THE OTHER BENCH: FORCES BEYOND YOUR CONTROL

Identifying and dealing with these internal struggles as they relate to financial stumbling blocks, however, is only half the battle. It's time to think past the psyche and limitations of your own team and start considering the opposing powers that are psyching up in the other locker room. For the 1957 Tar Heels, those wicked forces were personified by the giant Wilt Chamberlain. UNC studied his play and formulated a plan to defeat him.

The opponents to your financial plan are more diverse. They attack from all angles and feed off each other. Here, we scout out the habits of their most dangerous starters. Although you can't always stop them completely, you can work to contain their impact on the game.

BUSINESS PERFORMANCE

If stockholders of a company had to choose one thing that influenced their investment value the most, it would logically be the performance of the business. Is the company profitable? Is it growing? Is it positioned to be a leader in its market?

This is not a lesson on how to pick stocks. It is a reminder that stocks and the companies behind them probably make up a significant portion of your investment portfolio. To some extent your financial goals are dependent on how well those companies, and the people behind them, do their jobs.

We are looking at business performance in terms of an opponent because it is something over which you have no control that can make or break your investment success. Unless you are in a position of power within that company, you have no direct bearing on whether it prospers or goes bankrupt.

The best you can do is make buy-and-sell decisions based on what you can learn about the company's management, its financial standing, and its prospects in the industry. If you invest in mutual funds, you pay a fund manager to do much of that research for you and spread your money, and your risk, across many different stocks.

The idea of business performance goes beyond individual companies. It also applies to entire industry sectors and subsectors. If you own stock in Coca-Cola, for example, you are not only concerned about whether the company is outselling Pepsi, but you also are considering how well the carbonated beverage industry is doing as a whole. You might be asking yourself if the movement toward healthier food choices in American schools is going to hurt all soft drink sales.

Taking another step backward, you are looking at the performance of the entire food and beverage sector. Will high unemployment create a slowdown in demand for nonessential snack foods, including sodas? And how will struggles in the restaurant industry, a major soda buyer, affect beverage makers?

If you own hundreds of stocks through mutual funds, you can't analyze every company in much depth. You can remain cognizant of broad industry trends that could affect where and when you choose to invest.

There are also influences at work that even the largest companies can't control, but they will have an impact on their fortunes and yours.

INFLATION AND INTEREST RATES

I mention these two forces in the same breath because they are inextricably linked. Though they are not inherently evil, when ignored they can form a dastardly duo that ransacks your investment growth.

I will spare you the long textbook explanation of inflation and assume you are familiar with the very basics: inflation means that prices for goods and services are on the rise, which means that the dollar in your pocket can buy less today than it did yesterday. If you want a more in-depth tutorial, go to Google.

Let's skip right to the part about how inflation and interest rates are related and what their implications are for your financial plan. First, it is important to understand that interest rates for most loans (mortgages, auto loans, business loans, credit card purchases) are largely influenced by the rate of inflation—more specifically, the anticipated rate of inflation in the future.

Some inflation is not a bad thing—it is a sign that business is flowing smoothly and the economy is growing. But when financial prognosticators, such as the Federal Reserve, sense that inflation is increasing too rapidly, they deal with it by raising interest rates. Higher interest rates discourage people and businesses from borrowing and then spending money, which slows down demand for goods and services and ultimately keeps prices from shooting through the roof. It also works in reverse. When the economy is in a slump, such as experiencing stagflation or deflation, the Fed lowers interest rates to encourage borrowing and spending, and that gives a shot in the arm to American companies.

So how does all this business of inflation and interest rates affect you, the investor? There is no simple answer because it depends on which types of securities we are talking about and when you buy and sell them.

With fixed-income investments such as bonds, inflation is a serious concern. If you buy a bond that pays a 4 percent annual yield and mounting inflation causes interest rates to rise to 6 percent, you have two problems. First, your bond loses value. Investors can buy newly issued bonds that pay a 6 percent yield, so they certainly will not want to pay full price for your bond, which only pays 4 percent. If you need to sell your bond while rates are still high, you will have to sell it for less than you paid for it. Second, your income loses purchasing power. Due to the effects of inflation and its rising prices, the income you receive from your bond can't buy as much as it once did. Your real return is smaller than the 4 percent printed on your account statement.

If, like most conservative investors, you have not one but hundreds or thousands of these bonds in your portfolio, it is easy to extrapolate and see how rising inflation and interest rates could run counter to your financial goals. Retirees living on a fixed income, for example, could find themselves burning through their nest eggs faster than they expected.

In general, investing in stocks provides a good hedge against the inflation and interest rate risks we just discussed. It is true that rising rates can hurt companies and their stocks in the short term because costs of doing business go up and customers tend to buy less. But, given time, these effects are usually neutralized as company earnings increase alongside other inflated prices in the marketplace—a rising tide lifts all boats. For long-term investors, stocks provide a good opportunity to earn a real return that outpaces inflation and keeps their purchasing power intact.

Entire volumes have been written about the complex interplay between inflationary forces, interest rates, and the economy as a whole, and I would encourage you to further your education. Suffice it to say that inflation and interest rates can have powerful effects on your investing success. Those effects can be negative, especially if you ignore the problem and take no measures to counteract it. Skilled money managers, however, can mitigate the risks through investment diversification. And in some cases, they can take full advantage of these economic movements and, in a manner of speaking, use the opponents' strengths against them.

OTHER MACROECONOMIC CONDITIONS

Inflation and interest rates are ever-present trade winds that blow through the investment markets, but there are other economic currents that arise to kick up dust in the financial world and cloud the decisions of investors. They could strike quickly, like the panic-inducing savings and loan crisis of the 1980s, or build slowly, like the global shift in economic power that has been occurring for decades. To varying degrees, these events impose their will upon business performance, unemployment, and consumer spending, upsetting whatever harmony existed in the financial markets at the time.

Unless you are an economist, you probably do not stay up nights analyzing these developments in great detail. But you should stay apprised of their broad potential impact on your financial plan.

We recently emerged from one such episode, which I have mentioned already—the financial crisis of 2008–2009. Succinctly, the debacle was caused by the convergence of multiple harmful economic trends that collided and exploded like the proverbial perfect storm. Among the contributing factors were loose monetary policy and easy credit conditions, inflated housing values and the eventual bursting of that bubble, subprime mortgage lending and the boom of extremely complex mortgage-related securities, and the massive overleveraging of financial company balance sheets.

The failures of the financial industry set off a domino effect through the US and global economies and eventually cut deep into the value of most investors' portfolios. Could you have predicted the plunge and made changes to protect your assets? Realistically, probably not. Most respected financial oracles say they did not see the crisis coming, but your actions in the months after the crash might have greatly impacted how much damage you sustained and how well you recovered.

Looking at this chart of the S&P 500's performance over a five-year period, consider these three scenarios. If, in early 2009, you sold all of your battered stocks and ran for cover, you are probably still in the red today. If you changed nothing and allowed your holdings to ride the roller coaster, you were able to enjoy the ride back up as stocks regained much of their value over the next few years. If, however, in 2009, you were prescient enough to start buying up good stocks that had suddenly become dirt cheap, you could have made a fortune as the market rebounded.

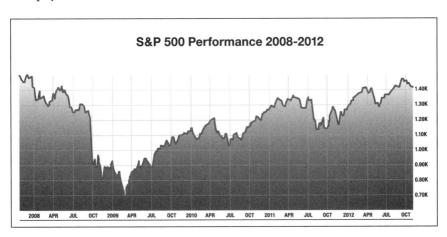

Hindsight is 20/20, of course, and I am not advocating market timing as an investment strategy. But there are lessons to be learned from these experiences that you can put to use the next time turmoil strikes—and it is never far away. In 2013, the European financial system continued to experience a crisis of its own that threatened to send big shockwaves across the pond and rock US markets again.

When bad news surfaces, the stock market reacts seemingly faster and to greater extremes than in prior decades. I would suggest that this increased sensitivity of the market is a phenomenon that investors must consider carefully. A globally connected economy, ubiquitous and near-limitless information via the Internet, easier access to do-it-yourself trading technology, and more money invested in short-term/high-activity investments such as hedge funds all add up to create a hypersensitive market, one in which the slightest tap of the mallet elicits a violent, knee-jerk reflex.

WORLD EVENTS

There are economic upheavals that are intrinsic to the financial system. They are problems that bankers and investment managers fret about daily, but the financial world is not an island that is immune to outside influence. Everything has financial ramifications—even events that, at first, seem unrelated to the stock market.

Several good examples can be found in the three-year period from 1999–2001. Remember the Y2K scare? Computer experts acknowledged that, due to a grave programming oversight, machines all over the globe might suffer catastrophic crashes when their internal clocks rolled over to the year 2000. Panic spread as people imagined the worst-case scenarios—businesses thrown back into the Dark Ages and planes falling from the sky at midnight on New Year's Day.

We look back and laugh about it today because New Year's Day came and went with hardly a hiccup. But at that point, people took the Y2K threat very seriously, even the experts at the Federal Reserve. Fearing that frightened citizens might make a run on the banks and withdraw all their funds, the Fed took preventive measures by loosening credit restrictions to make it easier for banks to borrow money if they suddenly found themselves short on cash.

Meanwhile, the stock market did not act scared. It continued rising steadily into 2000, fueled by a boom in the information technology sector as companies around the world spent billions to prepare for Y2K. Alongside the dot-com craze, the Y2K spending spree helped set the stage for the next big event: the rise and bursting of the technology bubble.

While the markets were still reeling eighteen months after the tech collapse, two jets crashed into the financial capital of the United States on September 11, 2001. This was not only a human tragedy, but it was also another economic crisis. Insurance companies experienced massive losses from the devastation. The airline and tourism industries suffered as our country put a freeze on travel plans. A general feeling of uncertainty grasped the nation and slowed down consumer spending.

As a result of 9/11, the US went to war in Afghanistan and then Iraq. Sky-high military spending over the next ten years pushed the country's national debt ever higher. Arguments could be made that it has devalued the US dollar and weakened America's stature as an economic superpower.

Remember the loose monetary policy that the Fed set in motion before Y2K? Those easy credit conditions continued after 9/11 for most of the next ten years. For

Historic Developments Affect the Economy and Investment Markets

- The mainstreaming of automobiles and airplanes
- The rise of Hitler, the bombing of Pearl Harbor, and WWII
- The start of the Baby Boom generation
- The discovery of DNA
- The Kennedy assassination
- The personal computer
- The spread of AIDS
- The collapse of the Soviet Union
- The rise of the Internet
- The Y2K scare
- September 11, 2001
- The explosion of mobile phone technologies
- Hurricane Katrina and the devastation of New Orleans
- 2008–2009 U.S. financial crisis
- The European debt crisis

businesses, easy access to credit provides an incentive to finance expansions and other major projects with borrowed money. That is exactly what many US companies did throughout the last decade, taking on enormous amounts of debt to finance rapid growth. But when a weak real estate market and flawed investing strategies caused their revenue streams to dry up, it became impossible for these companies, which included major financial giants, to pay back their massive debts. These developments led to the financial system meltdown of 2008 and sent the economy into recession.

The story goes on and on and will never end. Seemingly disparate worlds of science, technology, healthcare, culture, religion, and every imaginable aspect of society become entangled with politics, economics, and high finance. However nonfinancial they might appear, major national and world events—elections, government regulations, wars, natural disasters, diseases, scientific discoveries—reverberate through the financial markets.

The effects are not all negative. After 9/11, spending on security, both physical and technological, increased, benefiting those industries. In the midst of war, defense contractors see their stocks rise, and after natural disasters such as Hurricane Katrina, billions of insurance dollars flow into construction companies to repair and rebuild.

Every event sends ripples across the financial waters. And there, at the edge of the pond, sits your investment portfolio. So what can you do?

Your goal should not be to predict these specific events and take pinpointed actions in advance. That approach is rarely fruitful. Rather, accounting for the fact that stuff happens and understanding that financial markets will react allows you to build a financial plan that is generally stronger and fortified against any eventuality.

Watching how the market behaves under pressure, understanding its tendencies, anticipating its movements—it all comes back to the idea of scouting your competition, like a ball player studying video in a dark locker room. The better you know your opponents, the better you can prepare a complete game plan that positions you for victory.

CHAPTER-ENDING THREE-POINTER

1. Prepare a realistic savings plan for the next five years.
2. List the three biggest concerns out of your control that will keep you from reaching your goals.
3. Consider and record your reaction to the financial crisis of 2008–2009 as it affected your financial planning strategies.

Chapter Three

Devising a Game Plan

Essential Elements of Successful Financial Strategies

Peach Basket Parables: Kansas vs. Oklahoma, 1988 NCAA Championship Game

We have discussed the story of how the Kansas Jayhawks lost to North Carolina in the 1957 NCAA Championship game, so it's only fair to give Kansas its due by putting the Jayhawks on the winning side of one of these parables.

As many college basketball fans know, the annals at Kansas are full of happy endings. Like North Carolina, Kansas has been among college basketball's traditionally elite programs for much of the last century, in no small part because of the influential legacy of James Naismith, who invented the game of basketball in 1891 and was the Jayhawks' first official coach.

Following Kansas's loss to the Tar Heels in 1957, however, thirty-one years went by before the Jayhawks made another trip to the NCAA Tournament's final game. Strangely enough, that game was played in Kansas City, like Kansas's previous title-game appearance all those years earlier. Despite the fortunate proximity to their home campus for the 1988 championship game, the Jayhawks were considered the underdogs.

Kansas had not had a terrific season. It had started off a shaky 12–8 and finished the regular season with a solid but-less-than-sensational record of 21–11. Seeded sixth in its NCAA Tournament regional bracket, Kansas managed to reach the Final Four without playing any powerhouse teams.

The Jayhawks championship opponent was a different story. The Sooners from the University of Oklahoma (OU) were a number one seed, and for good reason. Their roster included three future NBA first-round draftees: Mookie Blaylock, Stacey King, and Harvey Grant. They had finished the season 35–4 while garnering national attention for their up-tempo, high-scoring style. They had scored 100 points twenty times that season, including a remarkable 151 in one game, and had crushed twelve opponents by 30 points or more. Most importantly, they had beaten their conference rivals, the Kansas Jayhawks, in both regular season meetings.

No one had expected Kansas to reach the championship game, let alone win it, which was just fine with Coach Larry Brown. He had devised a game plan that he believed could at least keep his team close—perhaps just close enough to pull off a shocking upset.

Unlike UNC's unrelenting strategy of smothering Wilt Chamberlain thirty-one years earlier, Brown's game plan was a symphony of complementary components, which the Kansas players executed—if not perfectly, at least well enough to work.

- The first priority was getting through OU's vicious full-court press, which was notorious for forcing turnovers and creating easy baskets for the lightning-quick Sooners. Brown's predesigned play broke down the press and led OU to call it off in the second half.
- Brown substituted players regularly to prevent fatigue against OU's blazing speed. He made forty-two lineup changes to OU's twelve.
- Kansas's defenders pushed OU's dominant big men out of position, forcing them to catch the ball far from the basket, out of their comfort zone.
- To take OU further out of its running game, Kansas slowed the pace in the second half, waiting until late in the shot clock to

attempt high-percentage field goals. The fact that the Sooners had been forced to retreat from their full-court press played right into Brown's hands.

Against the odds, the Jayhawks hung around. It was 50–50 at halftime. When the Sooners took a five-point lead with twelve minutes left, Kansas did not panic. Brown, who had expressed complete faith in his star, Danny Manning, put the ball in his hands and let him go to work. In a grind to the final horn, Kansas won by four points.

The box score showed that Kansas shot a sizzling 71 percent from the field. Manning scored 31 points and grabbed eighteen rebounds. The championship team would come to be known as "Danny and the Miracles," but the basketball media did not hesitate to credit Larry Brown for his masterful performance as orchestrator.

Houston Chronicle sports writer Eddie Sefko, who called Brown's game plan "flawless," summed it up: "It was like a hodge-podge of obvious ingredients that Brown mixed into a potion nobody else could conjure up."

COLOR COMMENTARY

The basketball community is a small world, especially for a frequent mover like Larry Brown. In the 1960s, Brown had been a standout point guard for the North Carolina Tar Heels, first under Frank McGuire and then Dean Smith. He had also coached two seasons at UCLA in the post-John Wooden years. The Hall of Famer has also coached ten different professional teams (he is the only coach in history to win both an NCAA title and an NBA championship). As of this writing, Brown is back in the college ranks on the high side of seventy, coaching Southern Methodist University in Dallas.

WHAT IS ON YOUR CHALKBOARD?

Kansas's well-planned strategy to beat Oklahoma in 1988 is simply one dramatic example of the process that takes place every year on every practice court before every big game. Good coaches do not lead their teams blindly into battle and hope for the best. Instead, they consider their own strengths and weaknesses, study their competitors, and make changes in their approach, however slight or drastic, to bend the shape of the game in their favor.

A truly holistic game plan is not limited to a single facet like cutting down on turnovers or making your free throws. A master strategist accounts for all the angles. He knows there are many pieces to the puzzle—offensive plays, defensive matchups, rebounding, substitutions, pacing—and that each component must align with the others and move in concert like a well-oiled machine. Equally important, the coach has a backup plan if the first one fails.

You could view your personal and family financial plan in the same way. Relying on raw talent or good luck to achieve financial success will rarely result in ultimate victory. Champions plan meticulously. And just like in basketball, there is a checklist of key components that must be addressed in your financial game plan. These include categories such as goal setting, debt reduction, budgeting, short-term savings, and investing for college and retirement.

Things might not always work out exactly as you planned—in fact, you almost certainly will encounter setbacks. That is the reason, like a veteran coach, you have contingency plans: emergency savings, insurance, and a will, for starters.

In this chapter, I will provide a brief overview of these key building blocks and their roles in your financial success, but to start, you need to address one very important question.

Do You Need a Financial Planner?

One of the key decisions you have to make as you develop or revamp your financial game plan is whether you should seek or continue receiving professional advice or rely solely on your own expertise.

For many investors, the answer has become more elusive in the wake of the US financial crisis and recession. Some have lost faith in their advisors as they have watched their portfolios languish in recent years. Others have taken the turbulent economy as a sign they need help now more than ever.

Certainly, there are arguments in favor of a do-it-yourself approach. No one is more familiar with your personal goals, risk tolerance, and financial habits than you are. So it is possible to build a highly customized financial plan on your own and execute it with dedicated personal attention. The money you save in advisory fees can be invested to capture even higher returns.

In reality, however, the majority of individual investors do not have the combination of knowledge, desire, and free time required to create and manage a comprehensive financial plan and finely tuned investment portfolio. This might be especially true if you are somewhat affluent with a busy career and more complex financial needs. In that situation, a financial planner can help.

> ## Can You Afford to Pay for Advice?
>
> As you might expect, how much you'll pay for financial advice depends on how in-depth and personalized you want to get.
>
> Some financial services companies will offer account holders some basic financial guidance for free or create a base plan for a modest fee.
>
> For a comprehensive financial plan tailored to your specific needs, expect to pay more. You might be charged a small percentage of your invested assets per year (usually in the range of 0.5-1.5%), an hourly rate (typically $100-$200 per hour), or an annual fee (which might be $1,000-$15,000 or more).
>
> Prices may vary, but one thing is for sure: gambling with your finances can cost you much more than what you pay for professional planning.

Think of a financial planner as a trusted assistant coach—not the aspiring young apprentice, but the old sage who pulls the head coach aside and whispers in his ear at those crucial moments in the game. You are always in control of the overall game plan, but the wise assistant is there either to validate your decisions or offer constructive criticism.

A good financial planner not only has in-depth knowledge of a wide range of investments but also can help you build a solid game plan for all aspects of your financial well-being, such as insurance, taxes, education savings, and retirement planning. Investors with specific needs may also seek specialized advisory services in business investments and succession planning, charitable giving and foundation management, or estate planning and wealth transfer.

Ideally, an advisor builds a plan that grows alongside your ever-changing needs, protects the assets you have accumulated, and preserves a lasting legacy for your family. Perhaps most importantly, an advisor has the ability to remain objective, helping you make the most rational decisions when the pressure is on.

Am I biased in suggesting that you work with a financial planner? Yes, there is no argument there. That's how I make my living, but based on my experience, I can tell you that most people receive tangible and intangible benefits from professional financial advice that offset the costs. In most cases, the return on investment is far greater—that is, if the advisor is a good one.

HOW TO CHOOSE A FINANCIAL PLANNER

Whether you are comparing financial planners for the first time or re-evaluating your current relationship, asking the right questions can help pair you with the best person for the job. There are many criteria by which to evaluate a planner. Here are some of the major considerations.

- **Credentials:** Top advisors will hold one or more certifications that indicate a high degree of professional education and a commitment to ethical standards. The Certified Financial Planner (CFP) designation is generally at the top of the list, requiring the advisor to maintain a fiduciary duty to his clients. Other designations to look for are Chartered Financial Analyst (CFA), Certified Public Accountant (CPA), Chartered Financial Consultant (ChFC), Certified Private Wealth Advisor (CPWA), or Chartered Retirement Planning Counselor (CRPC).

    Investors should also take care not to mistake certain securities licenses (for example, Series 6, 7, or 63) for signs of experience or academic excellence. These licenses simply allow the bearer to sell financial products legally and follow a loose guideline to make suitable recommendations to clients. They do not require a strong commitment to act in the client's best interests. Put another way, a securities license might be compared to a driver's

---

What to Bring to Your First Meeting with a Financial Planner
- Personal financial statement (lists of assets and liabilities)
- Statement of income and expenses
- Insurance policies
- Wills and trusts
- Outline of family financial goals

license: it gives people access to the roads, but it does not mean they are skilled or even considerate drivers.

- **Experience:** Credentials do not always equate to experience, so it is also wise to ask how long the advisor has been in the field and how long the firm has been in business. Breadth of experience is also important. If you are looking for more than an investment advisor, make sure to ask about his or her knowledge of insurance coverage, tax-reduction strategies, estate planning, and other areas.

- **Custody:** One of the most important questions to ask is, "Who is going to hold my money?" Some advisors double as securities brokers, so it is in their best interests, not necessarily yours, to have your assets housed at their firm. To help eliminate this potential conflict of interest, many investors prefer independent advisors who are not affiliated with brokerages.

- **Compensation:** To go along with the question of custody, you should insist on full transparency of how your advisor gets paid. In addition to fees for their advice, many advisors are paid commissions when they sell certain financial products, creating motivations that might not always serve their clients well. Fee-only advisors, by comparison, generally are paid an advisory fee and/or a percentage of the client's assets in return for independent advice that draws upon the entire universe of financial products.

- **Personalization:** In investing, there is no such thing as "one size fits all." Yet some advisors follow a single-minded strategy and invest every client's assets identically. A qualified advisor should spend time up front to learn about your goals, objectives, risk tolerance, and time horizon and then draft a unique plan tailored around those conditions.

- **Post-Recession Considerations:** While the criteria above apply in any market condition, the recent financial crisis and recession could warrant additional questions when comparing financial advisors. You might ask if and how the advisor's investment style has changed based on lessons learned from the crisis and how those changes might apply to your portfolio. The financial health of the advisory firm also becomes more important. You should walk away from the first meeting with confidence that the advisor will still be around next year and that he is not under too much pressure to bring in additional revenue at the expense of his clients. It might be tough to find definitive answers to these questions, but simply asking might reveal more than you would expect.

FOUR KEY COMPONENTS OF YOUR FINANCIAL GAME PLAN

Whether you decide to hire professional help or go it alone, there are some common factors that any complete financial game plan will address. Remember, just as basketball is not only about scoring points, financial planning is not only about investing to build wealth. It is also about preserving what you already have and minimizing what you will owe to others.

One could find a hundred different ways to break down these essentials to financial success. For now, we will keep it simple and focus on four major categories: setting attainable goals, spending and saving with discipline, investing for the future, and planning for contingencies. Making room for each of these aspects in your financial game plan will give you a strong framework upon which to build.

Attainable Goals

In the book *I Can't Accept Not Trying: Michael Jordan on the Pursuit of Excellence*, the world's greatest basketball player had this to say about setting goals: "I approach everything step by step. I had always set short-term goals. As I look back, each one of the steps or successes led to the next one. When I got cut from the varsity team as a sophomore in high school, I learned something. . . So I set a goal of becoming a starter on the varsity. . . . When it happened, I set another goal, a reasonable, manageable goal that I could realistically achieve if I worked hard enough. . . I gained a little confidence every time I came through."

Setting goals is an obligatory step in financial planning too because you will never reach your destination if you do not know where you want to go.

As Jordan suggests, pie-in-the-sky dreams should not be confused with practical milestones. He never says that his goal was to become a legendary NBA icon; he mentions a "reasonable, manageable goal that I could realistically achieve." First it was to make his high school varsity team, then become a starter, and so on. A lifetime of setting and achieving those down-to-earth goals—through college and then the NBA—culminated in the superstar known as "His Airness."

That is not to say that you should not have long-term financial goals. Thinking years, even decades, down the road is an important part of the planning process. Every goal you set, like Jordan's, should have two features: specific and realistic.

Let us talk first about specificity. When I ask new clients about their goals for retirement, a common first response is, "To retire comfortably and not have to worry about money anymore." That sounds nice, but what does it mean, exactly? That vague description of the ideal retirement scenario provides no information that we could actually use to create a financial plan. A specific goal, on the other hand, would include details about when you want to retire and how much money you want to have by then.

Assuming you do not just pluck dates and dollar figures out of the air, arriving at meaningful details will take a fair bit of introspection and calculation. You will have to think carefully about some tough questions: How do you

Take Retirement Goals Personally

You might have heard a rule of thumb that says your nest egg should be large enough for you to spend 80 percent of your pre-retirement income during retirement.

Do not believe it—at least not until you have considered all of the variables that go into retirement planning.

Your lifestyle is unique today, and it will still be unique in ten, twenty, or thirty years. Want to travel the world in style when you retire? That will cost much more than passing your golden years by a fishing hole in the country.

Thus, your retirement savings goals should be as unique as you are. It might not be possible to pinpoint the magic number you'll need, but you can get close by making some assumptions about your life in the future.

Some online retirement calculators are helpful—*if* you know which numbers to plug in. A flesh-and-blood financial planner can ask the right questions and help you arrive at realistic answers.

envision your lifestyle in retirement, and how much money will it take to live that way? How will inflation affect the purchasing power of your money? How much will you get from Social Security? And how long do you expect to live—that is, how long does your money need to last?

Right about now, you are probably muttering some variation of "How the heck should I know?" Obviously, these are hard—maybe even impossible—questions to answer with any degree of certainty, especially if you are a younger adult with a whole lifetime ahead of you. Nevertheless, making educated guesses about your future is better than wandering blindly with no target in mind. If you are not comfortable doing your own research to come up with some answers, a financial planner can help. When you have made your overall goal specific, it might look something like this: I want to retire at age thirty-five with a net worth of $10 million.

Did this get your attention? Good. Because this leads us to the next point. Not only should your goals be specific; they should also be realistic—something that does not require a miracle to achieve. Michael Jordan could have retired at thirty-five with $10 million, but those of us who can't dunk from the free-throw line need to set our sights a bit lower. This is especially true if your goals are out of touch with reality. You only set yourself up for failure. When you see no real progress toward your vision of grandeur, it is all too tempting to give up and abandon your plan altogether.

Set financial goals that are challenging yet achievable based on what you know about your own life. For example, think about your career earning potential. If you are an elementary school teacher, there is nothing that says you can't save enough to retire comfortably, but in all likelihood you will have fewer opportunities to become as wealthy as, say, a plastic surgeon. It might not be fair, but it is the truth. Unless you want to change careers, it is best to accept the limitations and work within those confines.

We have used retirement as one example, but setting specific, realistic, measurable goals can apply to any area of your financial plan.

If you have kids at home, it is not enough to say you want to pay for their college education someday. A useful goal would also answer some important questions. How many years will it take your child to graduate—

four, five, six? Public or private school? In-state or out-of-state tuition? Tuition only or also books and living expenses? And how much will all that cost?

You might conclude that you want to save enough to pay for four years of tuition and all living expenses at one in-state public university starting in the year 2023. Using some simple online tools to make assumptions about the rising costs of college, you might come up with a target savings goal of about $200,000–$225,000. From there, you can figure out how much you would need to save each month. There are no guarantees that your child will follow the path you envision or that costs will rise at the rate you predict. At least you are working toward something.

This type of goal-setting can work as you save for shorter-term purchases and as you plan how much you want to leave behind. Once you have clear and rational parameters for what you want, you can go about finding ways to make it a reality.

How Much Will College Cost?

The College Board reports that for the 2012–2013 academic year, the average **annual** cost for tuition and fees at an in-state, public, four-year college is $8,655. Tack on another $9,205 for room and board.

The price shoots up dramatically when you start looking at schools out of state or at private colleges. For 2012–2013, tuition and fees for an out-of-state public school cost $21,706, and private schools cost $29,056 on average.

Moreover, in recent years, college costs have risen at double the overall rate of inflation, meaning 2013 might seem like the good old days by the time today's toddlers graduate high school. The College Board projects that by 2025, the total bill for the average four-year public school will be in the neighborhood of $175,000 (though the increasing popularity of online coursework might help bring the costs down).

The numbers can be frightening, but by starting early and exploring options for scholarships and financial aid, paying for college does not have to be a nightmare.

On the other hand, the high costs of college are causing more parents and students to question whether a degree is even worth the money. Would that $175,000 have a more meaningful impact if it were left in an investment account to fund your child's retirement instead or used to help them start a business? It is a contrarian notion that is becoming more popular every day.

Spending and Saving Discipline

The most well-defined goals in the world don't mean much if you are not committed to reaching them. On the basketball court, commitment might manifest itself in terms of hustle—the pure passion to outwork the competition, stick to your defensive assignment like glue, and execute the offense with unshakable focus.

When it comes to meeting your financial goals, the closest comparison I can think of is your willingness to save money. It is harder than it sounds. As consumers, we are constantly bombarded by pressures to part with our hard-earned dollars. And the economic uncertainties of the day (whatever they might be) can instill fear in investors like Shaquille O'Neal staring down a green freshman.

The quest for victory demands a steely resolve. A disciplined approach to spending and saving has to be a definable part of your game plan. That means taking action to make the most of your discretionary income— the portion of your take-home pay that is not used for essentials such as food, shelter, and transportation. If you are not putting at least some of that money toward saving and investing goals, there is no point in setting goals in the first place.

Before you ever get into the realm of stocks and bonds, your financial game plan truly begins with a simple household budget, which enables you to gain more control over what you do with your income. To start, I suggest tracking your expenses for at least a month—recording every little thing you purchase—and categorizing each one (housing, groceries, eating out, car payments, gas,

---

Ditch the Debt First

Investing while carrying too much debt can be like trying to fill a leaky bucket. Here is a simple example.

You have $50,000 in an investment account that earns 8 percent in one year (making you $4,000). You also have $15,000 in credit card debt that charges a 10 percent annual percentage rate (costing you $1,500). When you take the investments and the debt together, you really only made $2,500—a 5 percent return.

Even as you keep adding to your investment bucket, the interest you are paying to carry debt drains the gains right out of the bottom.

That is the reason, in most cases, paying off high-interest debt should be a top priority ahead of saving and investing.

insurance, medical costs, clothing, entertainment, and so on). By the way, there are plenty of excellent software programs and apps for mobile devices that can make this task relatively painless.

Your analysis will provide a clear picture of fixed expenses that you can't or wouldn't skimp on versus discretionary spending that could be put to better use. If you have ever suspected that a mischievous gremlin empties your bank account each month, this process will reveal the shocking truth: the gremlins, in fact, have names like Target, Starbucks, iTunes, and HBO.

Most importantly, you can compare the numbers with the financial targets you have set. Then ask yourself the all-important question: "Will I be able to put aside enough money every month to meet my savings goals?"

A word of caution here: budgeting your finances to meet financial goals can present a chicken-and-egg scenario. Do you first tally up your expenses and then set realistic savings goals based on how much you can comfortably spare? Or do you decide first how much you need to save and then adjust your spending to meet those goals?

I would say most people do the former—they prioritize other discretionary spending above saving and investing—and it is a killer mistake.

For most of us, our financial goals are not just about money. They represent our hopes and dreams, our vision for a happy future and a fulfilling life. Do not make them an afterthought in your budget. In terms of priorities, saving and investing might come right after your basic living expenses, but they should always come before your daily latte and, alas, even your cherished season tickets.

As a reminder, commit to paying yourself first by contributing to savings and investment accounts automatically with every paycheck. That way, your financial goals are not put on the back burner.

Taking a fundamental practice, which saving and investing should be, and turning it into a habit is something that Duke Coach Mike Krzyzewski—the winningest Division I coach and three-time national champion—knows a lot about. In his book *Beyond Basketball: Coach K's Keywords for Success*, co-authored with Jamie K. Spatola, Krzyzewski devotes a chapter to fundamentals. In it, he says that turning fundamentals into habit "requires intensive, intelligent, and repetitive action." It has to be done with a purpose, which is a good thought whether you are trying to win on the basketball court or trying to win at financial planning.

"This is why, in every practice, even late in the season, I always have my team continue to work on fundamental drills," Krzyzewski says. "It is vital that the athletes actually drill these basics. I constantly remind myself of the most basic formula of teaching: you hear, you forget; you see, you remember; you do, you understand. And when you truly understand, that is when the basics become habitual."

Try explaining that to the parent of a young boy at one of Coach K's summer basketball camps, where young players eight to eighteen from all over the world gather to learn basketball fundamentals. Krzyzewski tells of one of the mothers who approached him at camp registration and told him her son would be attending two of the three sessions. She wanted to know what he would be doing differently during his second week of camp.

"I explained to her that the second week would be more of the same (from the first)," Krzyzewski writes. "There would be different coaches and different competition, but the focus would continue to be on the basics of basketball. I explained to her about fundamentals becoming habits and how the drills we do in camp are a step toward that."

Once you are in the habit, you will probably find that it is not so hard to continue living a comfortable lifestyle without that extra cash burning a hole in your pocket. But if you truly find yourself squeezed to make ends meet, you will have to make a choice: dial back your savings goals or make changes in your discretionary spending to free up more money.

I would encourage you to do the latter. Almost everyone, with some effort, can find places to save more money without really sacrificing their quality of life, whether it's taking a sack lunch to work or quitting smoking.

Use your budget analysis to outline a detailed spending and savings plan. It should include a specific limit for how much you can spend in each category each month. Make a promise to yourself to stay within the budget, and take it one month at a time until it gets easier.

It's all about commitment. Or, as your favorite cliché sports motivator would say: Put in the work. Find it in your heart. Dig deep. Gut it out! Hustle!

Like the "Cinderella stories" of small schools that make it to the Big Dance, you might be surprised how far sheer willpower can take you.

Investing Strategy

You have set clearly defined financial goals. And you have set aside a portion of your income that will be dedicated to meeting those goals. Now what? What do you do with that money?

You could stash it in a shoebox and let it pile up over time, and one day you would take out exactly what you put in. However, that is simply not enough for most people to achieve their goals of financial independence. For one thing, as we discussed in chapter 2, inflation would gradually nip away at the purchasing power of those stagnant shoebox funds so you would effectively lose money over the years. Second, unless you are already wealthy, it is next to impossible to sock away enough cash to build a nest egg large enough to retire, pay for college, and meet other big goals.

That, of course, is why we invest. Investing gives us the opportunity to turn money into more money. In exchange for taking on risk, we are rewarded (if all goes well) with a return on investment, taking out more than we put in. Investing gives us the best chance to amass the big sums necessary to meet major financial goals. It will work, though, only if it is done correctly.

Investing without a strategic plan is a bit like picking the players for your basketball team at random. Some potential recruits are big scorers; others are defensive specialists; some do a little bit of everything; and some, well, just need to figure it out. You would not let just any of them suit up for your team. You have to find the right combination of strong contributors who will complement each other and put the odds in your favor.

In the same way, different types of investments serve different roles in your investment plan. Some are designed to grow quickly. Others just work to protect the money you put in. Many do a little of both.

Naturally, choosing the right lineup of investments depends on what you are trying to accomplish and how quickly. For example, an investment plan for a twenty-five-year-old with a new baby at home would look much different than one for a fifty-five-year-old approaching retirement.

With that disclaimer out of the way, what follows is a rundown of key players that could form the core of a sound investment game plan. No credible financial advisor will allow you to overlook these key components if they apply to you, but be sure to consider them if you are working on your own.

- **Qualified Retirement Account:** A qualified account will likely be the star player in your investment plan because it is the tool you will use to fund your biggest and most important long-term savings goal—retirement. Qualified plans are so called because they "qualify" for special IRS privileges that allow you to save more and pay less in taxes over the long run, provided you do not withdraw the money until at least age fifty-nine and a half. Examples include the 401(k) or 403(b) plan you might have at work or outside accounts such as a Traditional Individual Retirement Account (IRA) or Roth IRA.

  The rules and the pros and cons of each type of account can be researched at length on most financial websites. I won't spell out the details here. Suffice it to say that one

---

Do Not Miss the Match

Do you have a 401(k) retirement plan at work? Many employers will match your contributions up to a certain amount. For example, say your company's policy is to add fifty cents to your account for every dollar you contribute, up to 6 percent of your salary. That means if your salary is $100,000, the company will put as much as $3,000 into your retirement fund each year. It is a great way to boost your savings rate. And not contributing is like turning down free money. So be sure to contribute at least enough to your 401(k) to get the full company match.

---

  of these plans, sometimes a combination of two or more, should probably take center stage in your investment strategy if you have hopes of leaving the working world behind.

- **College Savings Fund:** Most parents dream of sending their children off to college some day. The proactive ones start saving early to give their kids a realistic shot at affording a good school.

  As with retirement funds, there are several types of qualified investment accounts that are designed specifically to save for the high costs of a university education. Perhaps the most popular are state-sponsored 529 investment plans, which allow you to grow your savings free from capital gains taxes and make tax-free withdrawals for education expenses. Alternatively, in a 529 prepaid tuition plan, your investment contributions buy tuition credits at an in-state public college at today's prices, effectively locking in a lower overall cost.

You might also check out the benefits of a Coverdell Education Savings Account (CESA), which has lower contribution limits than a 529 but can be spent on any education expense—not just for college. Finally, if you have large sums of money to invest, look into the tax advantages of the Uniform Gift/Transfer to Minors Act (UGMA/UTMA) or establishing a trust.

- **Personal Investment Account:** Retirement and (if you have young kids) college might be the focal point of your investing strategy, but it does not mean you can't have other goals. Maybe you are working toward starting a business, expanding your art collection, or funding a sailing expedition around the world. Whatever your interests, your personal investment account is the catch-all term for everything outside of qualified plans for retirement and college.

  Working with an advisor or a broker, you build an assortment of assets in your personal investment account designed to meet specific goals. Your portfolio could include individual securities such as stocks and bonds, pooled accounts like mutual funds, alternative assets such as real estate or limited partnerships, or (likely) a combination of all of them.

  While these types of investments might be used to meet targets that are closer on your time horizon, it is important to recognize that they still run the risk of declining in value. Therefore, I typically don't recommend investing in anything with much risk if you are going to need the money in less than five years. For very short-term goals, consider an interest-bearing savings account or a short-term bond mutual fund.

A pretty simple way to structure an investment plan is retirement, college, and everything else. Of course, it gets more complicated as you begin to choose exactly which types of stocks, bonds, and funds you use to fill those major holding tanks. I am referring to what we in the financial business call asset allocation, and we will talk more about that in the next chapter.

Contingency Plans

In a perfect world, you would set specific goals to achieve your wildest dreams. You would spend just enough money to enjoy the sweet life but save plenty too, and you would invest your way to financial security and lifelong happiness without blinking an eye.

Unfortunately, life is not all roses and rainbows. Bad stuff happens. There are layoffs, accidents, natural disasters, lawsuits, diseases—any one of which could throw a wrench into the works of your otherwise flawless system. That is why no Plan A is complete without a Plan B.

Basketball coaches are familiar with the concept. If a star player sprains an ankle, they don't throw in the towel. They call on the eager understudy who has been waiting for his moment in the spotlight.

In basketball, it pays to have what's called a deep bench, and similarly, you will want one for your financial plan. If you have prepared well, you will have a system—a backup plan—in place that will soften the punches that life throws at you and your family. It might even protect your financial well-being from a would-be fatal blow.

Here are three essential components to your contingency plan.

- **Emergency Fund:** If you lost your job tomorrow, what would happen to your financial outlook? If you are like most people, you would stop investing, maybe take out a premature loan from your retirement account, or max out your credit cards to make ends meet. You would suffer a major setback to meeting any long-term financial goals. But it does not have to be that way—not if you have a safety net. I recommend setting aside enough cash in a savings account to cover three to six months of living expenses. Keep it as your financial cushion for life's unexpected crises—

major medical expenses, emergency home repairs, and other mishaps that might not be covered by insurance. You will sleep better at night knowing the money is there.

- **Insurance:** Most people already know that insurance, in general, exists to protect you from financial ruin when something goes horribly wrong. We are talking about things that go beyond the reach of your emergency fund—such as your house burning down or paying the medical bills of everyone involved in the four-car pileup you caused.

  What many folks are not clear about, however, is which types of insurance they need and how much. While you probably have health, homeowners, and auto insurance, a little research could reveal that you should increase your limits to be adequately protected.

  Other types of insurance are equally important, yet fewer people buy the coverage because they are not required by law or the terms can be confusing. Nevertheless, you should investigate your needs for life insurance, disability insurance, renters insurance, long-term care insurance (if you are middle-aged or beyond), and possibly an umbrella policy to make up for any coverage shortfalls in other areas. We will discuss each of these options in more detail in chapter 5.

- **Estate Plan:** If you have never done any structured financial planning, the words "estate plan" might sound like something only very wealthy families need to worry about. In reality, it is something every family should consider. The purpose of an estate plan is to predetermine what will happen to your assets when you die or become incapacitated. If you do not leave any plans behind, state law dictates who gets your money and who takes care of your minor children.

  It is worth the expense to prevent that possibility. An attorney can help you draft a will and create a trust. These legal measures provide clear instructions for how your affairs should be handled, how your assets should be distributed among your survivors, and who will take care of your kids if necessary. In some states, the trust will also keep your assets from going through probate court upon your death, which can be time-consuming and expensive for your loved ones.

Other estate planning tools you might consider include a durable power of attorney, which allows a person you choose to access your accounts and make financial decisions in your name, and an advance healthcare directive, which tells doctors exactly how you want to be treated if you can't tell them yourself. For example, you could direct doctors to save your family the prolonged emotional pain and expense of keeping you alive via machines if there is no hope for recovery.

None of these estate planning measures is much fun to think about, which is why so many people do not do them. But, if the time comes when they are necessary, your family will thank you for thinking ahead.

WHERE TO BEGIN?

By now, it should be clear there is a lot more to financial success than just filling up your piggy bank. Developing a winning game plan requires some careful thought about your long-term and short-term goals, your household budget, your investing strategy, and your plans to deal with unexpected events. Understandably, trying to tackle it all at once can be overwhelming, so much so that it leads many people to freeze up and do nothing at all.

Do not let that happen to you. Take it one step at a time, shoring up specific areas of your financial plan until you are confident that your bases are covered (if I may switch sports for a moment).

But how do you know where to start? The short answer is that it is up to you. Financial planning is rarely a perfect, linear process. Rather, it is a web of interdependent elements that need to be repeatedly examined and adjusted. Pull on one string, and others move along with it.

If a basketball team devotes every ounce of energy to aggressive defense, tired legs might prevent them from making shots down the stretch. If it focuses too intently on offensive rebounding and sends every player to the boards, it might give up a few fast breaks on the other end. As with so many things in life, achieving balance between various elements, all of which are necessary and important, is the key to success.

Speaking practically, you only have so much money to put toward your goals, so there will be times when you will have to assign priorities and choose one path over another. Sometimes, logic provides clear direction. For example, I would say that getting out of debt, saving toward an emergency fund, and buying adequate insurance should come before buying a second home as an investment. I would also tell you to ensure your retirement savings are on track before you funnel thousands of dollars into your child's college fund. While there are scholarships and financial aid available for students, there is no such thing as a retirement scholarship.

Other times, the right decision might prove elusive. Only you can decide what is best. Return to your goals, think carefully about what is most important in your life and the lives of your family, and direct your money there first.

With that said, every game plan has to start somewhere. In the next chapter, we will talk about offense—specific strategies to accumulate wealth in your investment portfolio.

CHAPTER-ENDING THREE-POINTER:

1. Specify your three most important financial planning goals/dreams.
2. Determine which types of retirement accounts are available to your family.
3. Consider the risks you need to insure and whether you currently have coverage.

CHAPTER FOUR

GOING ON OFFENSE

Accumulating Wealth in Your Investment Portfolio

PEACH BASKET PARABLES: INDIANA UNIVERSITY, BOB KNIGHT, AND THE MOTION OFFENSE

In Indiana, the love of basketball has a name: It is called Hoosier Hysteria. It is not limited to the Hoosiers of Indiana University (IU) or the annual high school state tournament that goes by that name. The euphoria surrounding the game extends to other Indiana colleges such as Notre Dame, Indiana State, Purdue, Butler, Ball State (mentioned here as a nod to noted alum David Letterman), and Valparaiso, and it is palpable throughout the state at every level, from stuffy junior high gyms to the Pacers' pro arena.

Hoosiers have reveled in basketball glory nearly as long as the game has existed. But in 1971, a man rode into town carrying a personality big enough to overshadow Hoosier Hysteria. His name was Robert Montgomery Knight, the brash former Army head coach who had come to take the helm at IU.

Skip ahead forty years or so, and Knight (now retired) has a well-deserved dual reputation as one of college basketball's most successful and sometimes most notorious coaches of all time. He is considered successful because he won 902 Division I basketball games, eleven conference titles, three NCAA championships, one NIT championship, an Olympic gold medal, and a Pan Am Games gold medal, among other achievements. And he is considered notorious because Knight is as well-known for his fiery temper as he is for his coaching and teaching genius.

A 1976 *People Magazine* article summed it up in this headline: "Bobby Knight throws tantrums, kicks chairs—and wins basketball games."

In many respects, the volatile Knight was the antithesis of the gentleman philosopher John Wooden. Knight's unofficial curriculum vitae includes verbally abusing referees, throwing chairs across the court, physically accosting his players and other coaches, and unleashing profanity-laden tirades against anyone who tested his patience.

He showed a particular disdain for members of the sports media, once calling their profession "one or two steps above prostitution." In at least one news conference, Knight told a reporter, "All of us learn to write in the second grade; most of us go on to greater things."

While you didn't want to be on Knight's bad side, his no-nonsense style and passion for basketball earned him a level of respect among his players and fans. And there's still no denying that his impact on the game was monumental.

ON THE ATTACK

Perhaps it is fitting that Knight, with his often offensive public persona, played a major role in changing the way American teams play offense in basketball games. He is widely credited with developing and popularizing the free-flowing style known as the motion offense, which has since been emulated and adapted by coaches at every level of play.

Today's basketball fans might think of the motion offense as commonplace, but it was innovative in Knight's early years.

Most teams that ran any organized offense relied on one-off plays or a continuity offense, where players execute a repeating pattern of predefined movements. Each player sets up in the same spot every time, sets the same screen, runs to the same corner, and so on, until they wind up back where they began and the play starts over. These types of offenses have their advantages, but their biggest weaknesses are predictability and a lack of flexibility. If something's not working, it's hard to change.

A motion offense is far less rigid. Players are given the freedom to read the defense and choose the action that will give them the best chance to score. Rather than stick to a defined path like a trolley car on rails, they move like fluid along the path of least resistance. Pass and screen. Drive and dish. Flash to the high post. Curl and flare to the elbow. Take what the defense gives you. Options, options, options.

To the untrained eye, the motion offense might appear completely random. But there are rules (Knight's rules) that players must follow. These dictates include an emphasis on proper spacing (always be fifteen feet from the next guy), timing (hold your spot for two seconds then move on), and constant movement (never just stand and watch).

Aside from its limitless adaptability, the beauty of the motion offense is its ability to utilize the strengths of all five players on the floor simultaneously. Unlike set plays designed to get an open shot for a particular player, in the motion offense, the ball can get to the basket in any number of ways. The whole becomes greater than the sum of its parts.

THE PERFECT SEASON

Bob Knight's three championship teams at Indiana provide a case in point. His rosters were not built around individual offensive juggernauts such as Wilt Chamberlain or Lew Alcindor. Knight recruited intelligent (if not supremely athletic) players who understood that a solid screen or a perfect pass could be just as valuable as a pretty jump shot.

As Knight perfected his system, IU improved its record every season through his first five years as head coach. In 1974–1975, the Hoosiers finished the regular season 29–0. But they entered the NCAA Tournament without their best player, Scott May, who had broken his arm just weeks earlier. They made it to the Elite Eight before falling to Kentucky.

That loss, however, was only the intermission in what Knight eventually called "a two-year quest." The next season, with May back in the lineup alongside co-captain Quinn Buckner, the Hoosiers were literally unbeatable. They started and finished the regular season as they had the previous year, waltzing past most opponents and narrowly escaping defeat a few times. Come March, they entered the NCAA Tournament at full strength, again with an undefeated record.

The dominant Hoosiers sailed through all but one of their five tournament games, winning by an average of thirteen points, and ousting Big Ten rival Michigan by eighteen in the championship game. The Hoosiers had won their third national championship (Knight's first) with a record of 32–0. It wasn't the first time a college basketball team had a perfect season (Wooden's UCLA Bruins did it four times), but as of 2013, no one has done it since the 1976 Hoosiers.

Knight's innovative motion offense does not deserve all the credit, of course. Indiana also had a lock-down defense, usually man to man. But one thing is for sure: Those Hoosiers had the offensive freedom, flexibility, and diversity to pile up the points, no matter what their opponents threw at them.

COLOR COMMENTARY
- At the 2013 Final Four in Atlanta, the seventy-fifth NCAA Tournament, more than 250,000 fans voted to name the 1976 Hoosiers the greatest tournament team of all time.
- Until recently, Bob Knight, with 902 victories, held the record for the most victories by a men's coach in NCAA Division I history. In 2011, the record was broken by another famous coach, Duke's Mike Krzyzewski (featured in chapter 9). Where did Coach K play his college ball? Army, where his coach was Bob Knight.

READ AND REACT
A successful investing strategy has a lot in common with a motion offense in basketball. First of all, investing in general could be considered the offensive component of your overall financial game plan. Just as the purpose of offense is to score enough points to put away the win, the purpose of investing is to rack up enough gains to secure a comfortable retirement, pay for college, or meet other big financial goals.

Recall the concept of the continuity offense, where players methodically repeat a pre-set path around the court. When it works, it works. When it does not work, you're stuck. Such rigidity would be ill-advised in an investing plan. Imagine continuing to invest in the same fund year after year, even as you age, economic conditions evolve, and your financial needs change. Bad idea.

You must have the flexibility to make adjustments in your plan, examine the situation that you face, and be prepared to go left when the "defense" shifts right. Moreover, your portfolio should be diverse, taking advantage of various strengths, not solely dependent on one star shooter. Your investing plan should be like Knight's motion offense (minus all the yelling).

In this chapter, we will take a closer look at your offensive (investing) options and discuss some of the key concepts required to build and manage a high-performing portfolio that is in tune with your financial goals.

FOR STARTERS, SAVE MORE

As previously discussed, your investment plan could be grouped into buckets. This could include your retirement savings, kids' college funds, and a personal investment account devoted to other goals. Choosing the right types of investments to fill those buckets is important. It is why many investors find it worthwhile to pay for professional advice.

Here is one piece of advice that might surprise you: *how much* you invest is probably more important than *where* you invest it. That's not to say that you can throw money at any investment and expect positive returns every year. What it means is that if you allocate your portfolio in a reasonably common-sense manner, choosing the perfect stock or fund in every category is *not* what will make or break your long-term success.

A Putnam Investments study tested this theory by looking at the performance of employer-sponsored retirement plans (such as 401(k) plans) over a fifteen-year period, from 1990-2004. The research concluded that someone who makes consistent contributions in a generally appropriate allocation will, on average, be nearly as successful as a person who had the exceptional skill (or luck) to pick only high-performing investments.

Here is a hypothetical example using some numbers from the actual Putnam study. Say Joe is thirty years old and his salary is $40,000 a year.

He starts contributing 2 percent of his salary to his company 401(k) plan. However, Joe does not know much about investing, so he does not put much thought into which mutual funds he chooses within the 401(k). He continues to contribute 2 percent for the next fifteen years, never changing his allocation or rebalancing his portfolio (we will discuss these concepts later). His uneducated fund choices cost him because over the next fifteen years, all of the funds he chose performed in the bottom 25 percent of their category (the Putnam study used historical rankings by the fund-tracking firm Lipper). Even with his misfortune, Joe accumulates $39,731 after fifteen years.

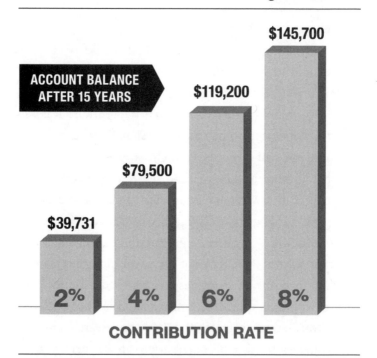

Joe's Retirement Plan Performance When Invested in Lower-Performing Funds

ACCOUNT BALANCE AFTER 15 YEARS

$145,700

$119,200

$79,500

$39,731

2% 4% 6% 8%

CONTRIBUTION RATE

Numbers adapted from 2005 study by Putnam Investments. This example uses historical fund performance to illustrate the value of increasing contributions to a retirement plan. It is no guarantee of the future performance of any investment.

What would have happened if Joe had been an expert at analyzing mutual funds and had picked only the best ones? Would he have become a millionaire? No. If, instead of picking all losers, Joe had chosen only funds that performed in the top 25 percent of their category, he would have ended the fifteen-year period with $41,869—a difference of about $2,000 after fifteen years, which isn't much to crow about.

But what would have happened if Joe had worried less about his fund choices and more about how much he was saving? If uneducated Joe (the guy who picked all so-called bad funds) had contributed 4 percent of his salary instead of 2 percent, he would have amassed about $79,500 by the end of fifteen years. Contributing 6 percent of salary would have produced $119,200. Eight percent—$145,700!

The lesson is simple: saving more is your best move in order to meet your retirement savings goals, regardless of the rate of return you are able to achieve. Again, this does not give investors a free pass to make investment choices that are way off base. But if you are tearing your hair out trying to build the perfect portfolio, you might redirect that effort toward putting more money in your account.

Xs and Os of Asset Allocation

We have established that your savings contribution rate is probably the most important factor in your investing success. That said, we can move on to discussing what you should be investing in. The key phrase here is *asset allocation*—how you distribute the money you save (your assets) across various types of investments.

As mentioned earlier, shaping your investment plan is like shaping your roster in basketball—choosing the right mix of attributes to put a well-rounded game plan into motion. Asset allocation takes that idea a step further. A coach must decide which players on his roster are going to start the game, who can provide a burst of energy off the bench, who might play a limited but strategic role for a single possession, and who will be on the floor when the final buzzer sounds. The lineup will look different depending on how much time is left and who is winning. The way you choose your asset allocation is similar. It will change depending on which stage of the game you're in.

Here's where it gets more difficult: A basketball coach might have a list of ten to twelve players from which to choose. As an investor, you have thousands of potential investment choices—stocks, bonds, mutual funds, real estate, and so on—that are all eager to get some playing time with your money.

So how do you begin to narrow down the universe of choices and identify the right investments for your needs? First, go back to your goals—the realistic and measurable targets discussed earlier. Your asset allocation will be different for each one of them. Each goal has unique requirements for how much money you need to stockpile and when you will need to start spending it.

To find investments that can satisfy these demands, you will need to consider a number of important factors. The next few pages provide an overview of the big ones.

- **Time Horizon:** Your time horizon can be defined as how many years you have to invest before you'll need to liquidate that investment. For example, if you have a goal to accumulate $100,000 to start a business in three years, your time horizon is pretty straightforward—three years. Saving for retirement, however, makes things more complicated. If you start saving in your twenties, you probably have at least thirty years before you will need to tap your retirement fund. But your time horizon does not end there because you will not cash out the whole nest egg. You will want it to last for the rest of your life. That requires you to take an educated guess at your time horizon based on how long you think you will live. These distinctions are important because the more years you have to save and stay invested, the more it makes sense to choose investments that could be volatile in the short term but pay off handsomely given enough time.

- **Required Rate of Return:** You have a goal in mind, and you know how much money you are able to put toward your goal each month (contribution rate) and how long you have to reach your goal (time horizon). There is one factor still missing from the equation: How much do your investments need to earn in order to hit that magic number? In other words, what is your required rate of return?

For the purposes of this conversation, we are assuming you actually need to earn investment returns. If you are working to reach a modest short-term goal by next year, you can probably scrounge up enough cash without the help of interest or capital gains. Your required rate of return would be zero percent. But for the big goals, you will need to invest money to make more money.

Say you want to have $1 million to retire in twenty-five years. Your annual salary is $100,000, and you decide that you can commit to putting 10 percent of your pay toward your company 401(k). That amounts to about $833 per month. If you started with nothing and set aside that $833 per month for twenty-five years, you'd have saved $249,900 in principal—far from your million-dollar goal. To get there, you would need to earn an average after-tax investment return of about 10 percent each year. So that's your required rate of return—10 percent.

Earning 10 percent annually is not beyond the realm of possibility, but given the historical performance of the stock market, it is pretty optimistic. Does that mean you should give up on the $1 million goal? No, because there are other variables we have not talked about yet.

If you have twenty-five years until retirement, chances are you'll get at least a few pay raises between now and then. So if you keep contributing 10 percent of your salary to your 401(k), you'll be putting more and more money toward your goal each time you get a pay increase. If you have the potential to get bonuses at work, 401(k) contributions are typically deducted from those checks too.

There is also the 401(k) company match to consider. If your employer kicked in fifty cents for every dollar you saved up to 6 percent of your salary (a common policy), that would be another $3,000 saved each year you made a $100,000 salary. Again, as your paycheck increased, so would the company match.

When you run the numbers with these new parameters, that $1 million goal starts to look more realistic. Because your contribution rate increases over the years, your required rate of return decreases. In fact, in this scenario, if you got average annual pay raises of 2 percent and took advantage of the full company match, an average return rate of 6 percent (a reasonable expectation) would get you to your goal.

Your personal goals and career outlook will vary, of course, but you can see how working with the numbers you have available will help you figure out how much your investments need to earn. This matters immensely in how you shape your portfolio since some types of investments have the potential to produce higher returns than others.

By the way, you can easily perform all of these calculations using simple calculators on the Internet. There is probably one on the website for your bank, broker, or retirement plan administrator.

Sound simple so far? Well, things get a little more complicated from here on. But don't fret. There are more basketball analogies on the way that will help clear it up.

- **Risk Tolerance:** There are no guarantees in investing. All investments come with a certain degree of risk—that is, the possibility that you could lose the money you put in. Essentially, your risk tolerance is your ability to accept that fact and live with it.

  That might sound bleak until you consider that there is an upside to risk. This is fundamental knowledge that all investors must understand: The more risk you are willing to take, the greater your potential for long-term rewards. It is a fact that is built into our financial system, and it is why millions of investors are willing to put their life savings into the stock market when they know there is a chance they could lose it in as little as a year. The potential to see their savings grow through higher investment returns is worth taking intelligent risks.

  On the flip side, if you risk nothing (keeping all of your money in a basic savings account, for example), you also gain next to nothing. Your account balance will never go down, but whatever low interest rate you earn will not be enough to outpace inflation let alone amass the large sums of money needed for retirement and other big goals.

Either scenario could be appropriate depending on which goal you are saving for and when you will need the money. Your time horizon, your required rate of return, and your risk tolerance are inexorably linked.

Going back to the examples from the last section, let's say you want to have $1 million to retire on in twenty-five years. At this point in your life, you can afford to accept a higher level of risk in your retirement fund. Why? Because although your account balance might fluctuate due to finicky financial markets from month to month (and even year to year), history has shown that the markets follow a general upward trend in the big picture. True, you never know what will happen in the future, but seeing how the markets have behaved over prior decades gives us confidence that the prospects for long-term investors continue to be good. So a longer time horizon should equate to a higher risk tolerance.

And what about the $100,000 you need to start your business in three years? Your risk tolerance for that savings goal should be lower. You would not want to put those funds into stocks because if the market took a temporary tumble, your savings could take a big hit and not have time to recover. In this case, investing in stocks would not be much better than walking up to a roulette table and betting everything on black. A more appropriate savings vehicle would be one with little risk, such as a money market account or short-term certificates of deposit (CDs).

Speaking of risk-reward, an interesting basketball scenario unfolded over the summer of 2013 while I was finishing this book. In a surprising move, Brad Stevens left behind a successful, secure coaching position at Butler to jump to the NBA as coach of the Boston Celtics. As much as Butler has been in the college basketball spotlight in recent years, the school is still tagged with the label of mid-major. As successful as he was there, Stevens really had little, if any, pressure on him to succeed year to year. In going to the Celtics, he was about to inherit a handful of high expectations that will really put him out on a limb.

In effect, Stevens gave up what is practically a no-lose situation at Butler to take on a pressure-packed job with the Celtics, where anything short of a deep run in the NBA playoffs is considered a failure. It will be interesting to see how this plays out over the next several years, assuming Stevens lasts that long in a league where team owners are not known for their patience or generosity. Stevens decided to take the risky plunge, giving up a job where he was adored by program supporters and pretty much able to write his ticket around Indianapolis in favor of grabbing for the bigger check in the NBA. If this works out for him, it could be a great investment with a huge payoff beyond anything he ever could have achieved at Butler, even with a national title, which his teams came close to winning a couple times.

Logically, how much risk you can accept should be defined mostly by your time horizon. Your risk tolerance might change as you get closer to meeting your goal. As you approach retirement, for example, you should consider taking less risk with the funds you have accumulated because you might need them soon.

But there is also an emotional component to risk tolerance that has little to do with logic. Some people just can't stand the idea of losing money. They get queasy every time their account balance dips even though they do not need that money for twenty years and are well aware of the market's long-term buoyancy. This mindset is probably even more common with the dreadful financial crisis of 2008–2009 still fresh in the public's memory. If you are entirely risk averse, you're certainly entitled to your point of view. But you had also better take a hard look at your financial goals and decide if you can meet them without playing the risk-reward game. In many cases, you will find the answer to be no.

Act Your Allocation

How you divide the assets in your portfolio is a personal decision that depends on your goals, time horizon, risk tolerance, and other considerations. The charts below provide examples of how the assets might be weighted in three different retirement accounts.

● **STOCKS**   ● **BONDS**   ● **ALTERNATIVE ASSETS**

Growth Allocation: An investor with a long time horizon (at least 20 years before needing the money) might invest a large percentage of her portfolio in stocks. By accepting a larger degree of interim volatility and fluctuations in account value, investors have historically been rewarded with higher long-term rates of return.

Balanced Allocation: Someone with a mid-range time horizon (10–20 years) should consider an allocation with a substantial proportion of less risky, fixed income instruments (i.e. bonds) while still allowing for enough volatility (through stocks) to continue growing his assets.

Conservative Allocation: For someone nearing or already in retirement who may have reached his savings goal, advisors typically structure the portfolio for income and capital preservation rather than growth with a bond-heavy asset allocation and fewer stocks. It's important to note, however, that even the most conservative portfolios should maintain some element of growth to offset the risk of inflation.

- **The Effects of Taxes:** It seems old Uncle Sam wants a piece of everything, and your investing success is no exception. There are taxes on investment income, capital gains, stock fund distributions, and other tax triggers that can combine to take a sizeable bite out of your savings.

  You can't get around paying taxes altogether (not legally, anyway), but you can invest in such a way that you are required to pay less. That is why every investing decision you make, including the way you allocate your assets, should include some thought about the tax ramifications. The pinnacle of tax efficiency, of course, is to achieve the highest returns possible in your portfolio while incurring the least amount of taxes.

If you contribute to a tax-advantaged retirement plan such as a 401(k) or an IRA, you are already working to lower your tax burden since these accounts give you an up-front tax deduction and tax-deferred earnings (or tax-free earnings in the case of a Roth IRA).

But your tax-saving ways do not have to end there. Achieving tax efficiency also means finding the best mix of assets between tax-advantaged accounts and taxable accounts (investments outside of retirement plans and college funds). Throwing every dime you can into your 401(k), for example, could save money now but trigger a tidal wave of taxes when you withdraw the money at retirement. Instead, saving a portion of your available funds in well-chosen taxable investments can smooth out your tax obligations over your lifetime.

The specific choices you make within your personal investment account also can make a difference in your returns. For instance, different types of mutual funds can have varying tax consequences depending on what they invest in, when they invest, and how often they make transactions within the fund.

It is about now that most average investors feel a headache coming on, their eyes getting glassier with each additional mention of the IRS. That's OK as long as you understand the main idea behind tax planning: Ensure you are progressing toward your goals as quickly as possible without giving the government a free lunch.

Depending on your comfort level, you can take broad strokes to keep taxes at bay, or you can dive into the intricacies of the tax code in an attempt to keep every penny allowable by law. In either case, but especially the latter, I would

---

Lower Interest Rates = Lower Bond Income

Since the 2008–2009 recession, the Federal Reserve has kept interest rates extremely low (at least through mid-2013). That is good news if you are borrowing money but bad news if you are seeking income from interest-bearing instruments such as bonds. Do not be surprised if your financial planner recommends other sources of income, which might include dividend-paying stocks or alternative assets such as real estate.

recommend working with a financial planner and/or a CPA to ensure your strategy is sound.

- **Current Income Needs:** When most young adults think of investing, they think of investing for growth and piling up enough gains to meet their long-term savings goals. When their investments produce income, as with bonds or stock dividends, that income is usually reinvested to achieve even more growth.

  But that perspective starts to change as you get older. For retirees, especially, there is a need for investments to generate income—income that can be turned into cash and actually spent at the supermarket or the golf course. Naturally, this shift in investment goals requires a subsequent shift in asset allocation.

  A common approach in retirement, for example, is to invest a larger percentage of the portfolio in lower-risk bonds. This not only protects your principal but also can produce a stream of income that allows you to support yourself in retirement without depleting your nest egg too quickly.

  You might have other needs to produce investment income even before retirement. Whatever those needs might be, they should be weighed accordingly with respect to your time horizon and risk tolerance.

- **Liquidity Needs:** Yet another important factor in the asset allocation mix is liquidity. Liquidity is the ease with which you can convert your investments into cash without penalty.

  The simplest example of a liquid asset would be the money in your checking account. You can use it to buy things right away even without a call to the bank. By comparison, shares of a mutual fund held in your brokerage account would still be considered liquid but somewhat less so because you would have to access your brokerage account to order a sale and maybe wait a day or two to receive the funds. On the opposite end, your IRA would be very nonliquid. You can't make withdrawals until age fifty-nine-and-a-half without incurring some steep penalties (some exceptions apply), so those funds are essentially off-limits for younger investors.

Why does liquidity matter? Because it's a good idea to have easy access to at least some of your savings so you are able to deal with emergencies, make major purchases, or seize new investing opportunities. You might want to help your sixteen-year-old daughter buy a car, or you may find yourself facing shockingly high funeral expenses when a loved one passes away. If all of your money is tied up in nonliquid assets, your options are limited. Liquidity keeps your options open.

Investment goals, time horizon, rate of return, risk tolerance, income, and liquidity needs—there is a lot to think about. If you are a novice investor, you might find yourself approaching each of these factors separately and deliberately, and that is not a bad thing. But as you gain investing experience, you will begin to view these overlapping determinants as one big, moving picture. Like a guard initiating the motion offense, you read the situation in front of you and react with the right moves. Or, like a coach, you see what your team needs in a given situation and make strategic substitutions to have the right lineup on the floor.

In the next section, we will talk about some of the options you have at your disposal—the specific investing tools you can use to get your offense rolling.

IDENTIFYING YOUR GO-TO SCORERS

On the offensive end of the floor, you will have playmakers, spot-up shooters, slashers, and brute-force players near the basket. Most will do one or two things very well but will be limited in other areas. Your big guy might be great at rim-rattling jams, for instance, but stink at free throws. Your point guard might distribute like FedEx but be unable to jump over a piece of paper.

Investments have their pros and cons too. Stocks, bonds, funds, real estate, and so on—each could contribute to your investment offense in different ways and could slow it down in others. Taking into account the factors we discussed earlier (time horizon, risk tolerance, etc.), your challenge will be to assemble a lineup of assets that is appropriate for each of your goals.

I could use this spot in the book to reel off an exhaustive list of investment types and discuss their specific attributes (the differences between growth and value stocks, for example), but you can easily find that information elsewhere. Instead, I will offer some general observations and recommendations based on my experiences with clients over many years. These can help you decide what to do with all that information.

KNOW WHAT YOU ARE BUYING AND WHY: STOCKS VS. BONDS

Whether you are working with an advisor or just reading articles about how to allocate your portfolio, you will almost always be advised to split your money—not necessarily evenly—among stocks (for growth), bonds (for safety and income), and perhaps some alternative assets to serve a specialized purpose. The percentage you put into each asset class will depend on how aggressive or conservative you want to be.

In my opinion, however, many investors follow these rules of allocation based on conventional wisdom without really understanding why they are doing it. So the following is a quick review.

When you buy a stock, you are buying a small piece of a company. Because shares of that company are traded on the open market, the stock value is subject to the forces of supply and demand. When the majority of people think the long-term prospects for the company are good, they want to buy the stock. As a result, the stock price goes up and your investment increases in value. Conversely, when more people are trying to get rid of the stock, the price goes down. There are lots of reasons why people form positive or negative opinions about certain stocks, but in the end, it's always supply and demand that causes the stock price to fluctuate.

The reason stocks are generally labeled risky is because there is no limit to how far—or how fast—the stock value can fall. Market forces exert themselves so quickly that a stock could be riding high one morning and be virtually worthless later that afternoon. That is an extreme example, but it does happen.

In practical terms, the stock market is extremely unpredictable in the short term, but it has always risen as a whole when given decades to do its work. And that, in a nutshell, is why you as an investor are encouraged to put a larger portion of your portfolio in stocks when you are young and less as you get older and closer to your goals.

Traditionally, bonds make up another major piece of the portfolio pie. Bonds are used to provide a measure of predictability, that is, security, in your portfolio and offset the volatility of stocks. The downside is they tend to produce lower investment returns compared with stocks.

When you buy a bond, you are giving a loan to the organization that issued the bond—a government or a corporation. The issuer agrees to pay you interest over the life of the loan. So if you buy a $100,000 bond with a twenty-year term and a 3.5-percent yield, the issuer pays you $3,500 for every year you hold the bond. If you hold onto the bond for the full twenty years, you will have collected $70,000 in interest, and the issuer returns your principal of $100,000, bringing your total to $170,000.

The interest payments (income) you receive from bonds, combined with the high probability that the issuer will return your principal, create a safety net of sorts. It's something you can count on, which is why bonds are generally considered less risky than stocks and why you are encouraged to move more of your money into bonds as your investment time horizon grows shorter.

Do Not Stereotype Your Investments

It makes sense to classify and form general expectations of your various assets, but painting with too broad a brush can lead to mistakes. After all, just because your seven-foot-tall center can't shoot from outside does not mean he'll fail to toss one in every now and then.

So take the aforementioned generalizations about stocks and bonds with a few grains of salt.

Stocks are not always high-risk, high-reward. The stocks of mammoth, blue-chip companies that have been around forever and are not going anywhere (think Coca-Cola or Wal-Mart) are decidedly safer bets than a promising solar technology company few people know about—

again, lower risk but lower potential return. A well-diversified portfolio might include some of each to reduce the overall volatility within the stock asset class.

Bonds are not always low-risk, low-reward. There are different classes of bonds, ranging from extremely conservative, as with US Treasury bonds, to aggressive and risky, as with low-grade corporate bonds, known as junk bonds. Bonds with lower credit ratings pay a higher interest rate because they are more likely to default on the loan and not return your principal.

Bonds face other risks as well. If you need to sell the bonds before they reach maturity, you encounter interest rate risk. For example, let's say that three years ago you bought a $100,000 bond paying 2 percent per year. Since then, interest rates have risen to 4 percent. Today, bond buyers will not pay you the full $100,000 for your bond because for that amount they can get a bond that pays 4 percent. You would have to sell your bond at a discount, effectively losing money on the investment.

Finally, bonds are subject to inflation risk. You're losing money if your investment isn't earning more than the rate of inflation.

The main takeaway here is to examine every investment for what it is, not for what you assume it should be.

INDIVIDUAL STOCKS AND BONDS—JUST SAY NO

By design, my explanations of how stocks and bonds work have been oversimplified. I mentioned earlier that there are lots of reasons the powers that be push stock prices up and down—anticipated corporate earnings, the strength of a company's balance sheet, industry trends, etc. The same goes for bonds—expected interest rate changes, credit ratings, yield curves—all can affect a bond's value on the market.

Some people really like contemplating this stuff. Most people loathe it. So here is the good news: To invest successfully, you do not have to become a financial wizard. You do not have to conduct mind-numbing research and hand-select each stock and bond in your portfolio. And you do not have to monitor their performance obsessively, making calculated trades at precisely the right times. In fact, I would go so far as to say you shouldn't even *try* these things.

Don't take that the wrong way. I'm sure you're intelligent enough to pull it off. It's just that you have your own life—a career, a family, friends, and hobbies, presumably. To think you can manage (and enjoy) all that and be a crack portfolio manager on the side is not just unrealistic, it's foolhardy.

Despite what many websites and magazines would have you believe, the average investor is not on an even playing field with the professional analysts and traders who rule Wall Street. These people spend all day, every day, scrutinizing the finest details of every stock and bond, running sophisticated algorithms using data that laypeople cannot easily access. It is like comparing an amateur pilot in a single-engine Cessna to an Air Force fighter jock in an F-16.

This matters because by attempting to identify high-performance investments one-by-one, you are presuming to know something that these highly trained professionals somehow overlooked. When, in reality, anything you can learn about a particular stock and its growth potential has already been dissected by Wall Street and is reflected in the current stock price.

So what is an average Joe to do?

MUTUAL FUNDS FOR THE MASSES—A DISCUSSION OF BENEFITS
Do not go panning for nuggets of gold in the river. Buy a gold mine.

In other words, instead of spending countless hours hunting for individual investments that might make you rich, you will probably serve yourself better by investing in broad swaths of the market at once, reaping the collective rewards of many small gains over time.

This is the idea behind mutual funds, which allow you to pool your investment dollars with other people to share in the ownership of a widespread portfolio of stocks, bonds, or other securities managed by financial professionals.

If you contribute to an employer-sponsored retirement plan or a college savings plan, you probably own shares of mutual funds under that umbrella. But funds can be put to good use in your personal investment account as well. As an advisor, I recommend them over individual securities for several reasons:

- **Professional money management:** When you invest in mutual funds, you are no longer pitting yourself against the financial experts who know the markets like their own skin. They are working for you. They put in the endless hours of research and analysis required to manage a strategic portfolio so you don't have to.

- **Convenience:** Aside from the convenience of leaving stock picking to the professionals, there is the convenience of systematic investing. Most mutual funds allow you to start small and set up automatic contributions to take advantage of dollar-cost-averaging. Moreover, there are mutual funds designed to meet every investment goal, whether you're seeking aggressive growth or capital preservation. Some funds, often called target funds, take your time horizon into account and automatically adjust the asset allocation (shifting from aggressive to conservative) as time goes by. Finally, mutual funds are marketable, meaning they are easily converted into cash or transferred to other funds as your needs change.

- **Access:** Some mutual funds invest in securities that individual investors cannot or will not buy on their own, either because the minimum investment is too high or because it requires specialized knowledge. These might include alternative assets such as energy-related limited partnerships, commercial real estate securities, international stocks, precious metals, or other commodities. Through a mutual fund, managers can use these assets (when appropriate) to maximize your portfolio's performance.

- **Good judgment:** A side benefit of investing systematically in a fund run by professionals is that it prevents you from making some of the bad decisions we discussed in earlier chapters. If you own your hand-picked collection of individual securities, for example, you might be more likely to try to time the market, buying low and selling high, which sounds good in theory but is rarely a viable strategy for average investors. A related mistake is commonly called performance chasing, in which you hear about stellar returns in a particular sector and try to get in on the action.

Trouble is, by the time you buy into that hot market, there's a good chance it will have already finished its run. With mutual funds, you choose a strategy and the manager of that fund sticks to it, usually to your benefit.

- **Diversification:** I saved the most important benefit for last. Mutual funds are typically made up of many—often hundreds—of different stocks or bonds. Even if you invested in just one fund, you would probably achieve a much greater diversity of assets than you could ever obtain by buying individual securities. Spreading your investment dollars over many different stocks and/or bonds reduces volatility and risk in your portfolio because it dampens the impact of any one security losing value. If you understand the meaning of "don't put all your eggs in one basket," you get the gist of diversification. By the same logic, of course, diversification also dilutes the effects of one stock's great performance because lower returns in other areas might balance it out. But balance is the whole idea— achieving a greater level of predictability in your portfolio with the expectation that, as a whole, it will move upward over time.

  Diversification is of such fundamental importance to your investing success that this mere mention of it is not enough. We'll explore the idea in more depth in chapter 5.

Mutual funds are not perfect, and some are better than others. But by doing some due diligence on the funds you choose and then investing consistently, you stand a better chance of reaching your goals than if you buy only individual securities.

One downside of mutual funds is that they come with fees attached. You didn't expect to get professional money management for free, did you? Most do not charge anything to buy in, but there are usually administrative expenses that take a small percentage of your earnings every year whether the fund is up or down. These fees are higher for actively managed funds that make changes to the portfolio on a regular basis. They are lower for passive funds that simply hold on to the same stocks year after year (an S&P 500 Index fund, for example).

It pays to know which is which and to compare apples to apples in terms of fees and historical performance of the fund. Do your comparison shopping at Morningstar.com, which offers fund ratings that are about as unbiased as you can get.

SEPARATELY MANAGED ACCOUNTS

Investing in a handful of carefully chosen mutual funds can be a good offensive strategy for most investors. But I'll also mention another option that can be well suited to investors with a sizeable amount of money to invest—the separately managed account.

Mutual funds offer professional money management but that manager is paid to pursue the goals of the fund itself and works on behalf of thousands of investors in the fund. By comparison, a separately managed account offers personalized attention to your goals and your portfolio. Investment experts custom build a portfolio of stocks and bonds just for you. And, on an ongoing basis, they make buy and sell decisions to maximize returns, keep your asset allocation in check, and reduce your tax liability.

Such individual attention is not free of charge, of course. So is it worth it? Often it is. Many high-net-worth investors come to find that as their portfolios grow, so do the complications of wealth management and minimizing taxes and fees becomes an even higher priority. Managed accounts can provide that personal, professional attention that mutual funds cannot. And when all is said and done, these investors might find that the service costs them no more than traditional mutual funds would.

If a managed account sounds right for you, your financial advisor should either offer the service or be able to refer you to a qualified provider.

GET BACK ON D!

Now that we've covered some of the basic elements of your offensive game plan (investing to accumulate wealth), it is time to fall back to the other end of the floor and work on defense. That means protecting the investment assets you already have and preventing misfortunes from derailing your financial security.

CHAPTER-ENDING THREE-POINTER

1. List your age, portfolio time horizon, and liquidity needs, and describe your risk tolerance in terms that make sense to you.
2. Consider whether stocks, mutual funds, separately managed accounts, or a combination of them are appropriate.
3. Spend time understanding the basics of long-term portfolio allocations and how they impact volatility.

CHAPTER FIVE

DEFENSIVE FORMATIONS

Protecting Your Financial Assets through Diversification and Insurance

PEACH BASKET PARABLES:
GEORGETOWN BECOMES 'BIG MAN U'

Georgetown University is a historic and prestigious Catholic school in Washington, DC, and it calls its athletic teams the Hoyas. Beyond the students, alumni, and administration, however, few people can tell you what a Hoya is.

The name is taken from a Latin phrase, *hoya saxa*, which has been a traditional cheer at Georgetown since the late 1800s. Loosely translated, it means "What Rocks!" It is unclear why the saying became ingrained in the school's culture and associated with its athletic program, but one common explanation links it to the strength of the stone (or rock) wall that surrounds the Georgetown campus. In other words, Hoya implies some sort of impenetrable barrier.

Throughout its own storied history, especially over the last thirty years or so, Georgetown's men's basketball program has lived up to its namesake by building a moving fortress around the basket. While the Hoyas have turned out prolific scorers such as Eric "Sleepy" Floyd and Allen Iverson, the team's legacy is firmly rooted in defense. More specifically, some of the greatest defensive centers the game has ever seen have come out of Georgetown, earning it the unofficial nickname of Big Man U. You can start with Patrick Ewing and go from there.

That big-man reputation has its genesis in Georgetown's most illustrious coach, John Thompson Jr., who ran the program for twenty-seven seasons and compiled an impressive .714 winning percentage. Thompson understood the big-man game, as well he should—he was one of them. An imposing figure at six-foot-ten and 250-plus pounds, a young Thompson played center for the Boston Celtics, backing up Hall of Famer Bill Russell, who is generally regarded as the best big-man defender in the game's history.

Thompson not only knew how to coach centers, but he also had a knack for recruiting them. Take the Hoyas' frontcourt of 1988–1991, which included the tandem of Dikembe Mutombo and Alonzo Mourning, two of the most fearsome shot blockers ever to police the paint. Mourning led the nation in blocks as a freshman, and Mutombo still holds the school record for twelve swats in a single game. The pair inspired a cheering section in the arena called Rejection Row. Mourning went on to earn the NBA's Defensive Player of the Year honor twice. Mutombo earned it four times.

Mutombo's reputation as a shot blocker has, in fact, made him sort of a pop culture phenomenon. In recent years he has starred in a playful television commercial for a major insurance company in which he runs around in all sorts of settings blocking everything in sight, even a grocery shopper trying to toss an item into the grocery cart.

Later years would see more dominant centers who carried on the tradition at Georgetown, such as Othella Harrington and Roy Hibbert.

CLASH OF THE TITANS

The list of Georgetown giants goes on, but they all followed in the footsteps (and never quite escaped the shadow) of the Hoyas' most famous big man of all: Ewing. He is Georgetown's all-time leader in blocked shots, rebounds, and games played, and he is second in points. He was also the Big East Defensive Player of the Year four consecutive seasons.

Ewing's dominance under Coach Thompson's control led the Hoyas to the NCAA Tournament title game in three of Ewing's four years. In 1982, they lost a heartbreaker to a powerful North Carolina team featuring James Worthy, Sam Perkins, and Michael Jordan. In 1985, they were stunned by eighth-seeded Villanova, which had one of the most incredible shooting nights in NCAA Tournament history, allowing them to beat the Hoyas by two points. Georgetown's only tournament championship to date came in 1984, and it was, fittingly, a battle of big men.

It was Ewing vs. Olajuwon, the latter being Hakeem Olajuwon of Houston, who was listed as seven feet tall even though he reportedly later said he was more like six-foot-ten. He certainly appeared all of seven feet to opponents because of how he played. For fans of the game, the Ewing vs. Olajuwon reference alone says a lot. But it would be unjust to ignore the all-around team efforts that brought both the Hoyas and the University of Houston Cougars to the title game.

Georgetown's stifling defense (intensified by outstanding perimeter defenders David Wingate and Reggie Williams) had been the best in the nation that season, limiting opponents to 39.5 percent shooting. They dialed up the pressure even higher during March Madness. In a tournament in which teams were typically scoring in the high sixties and into the seventies, none of the Hoyas' first four opponents scored more than fifty. A big Kentucky Wildcats team gave Georgetown problems in the national semifinal, but the Hoyas locked them up in the second half, holding the Wildcats to 3 of 33 shooting (9 percent).

In the championship game, however, Georgetown ran into a different breed of challenger in the form of the fast-paced Houston Cougars. They had a brand moniker all their own, Phi Slama Jama. Led by Coach Guy Lewis, Texas's Tallest Fraternity played a fast-paced, flamboyant running game accentuated with high-flying dunks. The Cougars had been to the NCAA final game just a year earlier (with a team that included Clyde "the Glide" Drexler) and narrowly lost to North Carolina State. Like Georgetown, they were looking for redemption in 1984.

In the middle of it all was an adversary that would demand Ewing's best: Akeem (later Hakeem) "The Dream" Olajuwon, or as his opponents came to think of him, The Nigerian Nightmare. It was the first time Ewing and Olajuwon met on the court—it would be the beginning of a celebrated rivalry that would last for more than a decade in the NBA.

DEFENSE WINS AGAIN

In the first five minutes of the game, Houston looked unstoppable. The Cougars made their first seven shots against the Hoyas' 2–3 zone. But Houston's good fortune changed when Georgetown switched to a man-to-man defense. The Hoyas showed off the smothering stopping power that had gotten them that far, and the Cougars started missing.

Still, Houston's nonstop offensive assault dictated the pace, allowing it to rack up seventy-five points by the game's end. Thompson sent in waves of fresh Hoyas to keep the pressure on, however, and the Cougars eventually succumbed, losing by nine points.

Neither Ewing (ten points) nor Olajuwon (fifteen points) had a huge game offensively, perhaps because each played such strong defense against the other. Something had to give. Nevertheless, Ewing was named the tournament's Most Outstanding Player, largely due to his ever-intimidating presence in the middle. In the two Final Four games, he had a total of fifteen blocks. The era of Big Man U had begun.

COLOR COMMENTARY

- With the 1984 championship, John Thompson Jr. became the first African-American coach to win the Division I NCAA title.
- Like father, like son: In 2004, John Thompson III took up the Georgetown coaching mantle from his dad. One of the younger Thompson's standout players was Patrick Ewing Jr. (2006–2008). While at Georgetown, the younger Ewing wore number 33. And while Georgetown does not have a tradition of retiring its famous players' jerseys, Ewing reportedly had to get permission from two guys who had previously worn 33: Patrick Ewing Sr. (his dad) and Alonzo Mourning.

BUILDING YOUR FINANCIAL BARRICADE

No winning team has ever focused exclusively on offense or defense. Players have to hustle at both ends of the floor or else earn a seat on the bench. But there are times when it is appropriate to put more emphasis on one end of the court or the other. Often, it is hard-nosed defense that ultimately separates champions from the runners-up. If Georgetown had not circled the wagons early in its game against Houston, the Cougars' frenetic offense might have run out to an insurmountable lead and cruised to a championship.

Similarly, there comes a point in every person's life when he has to shift his focus from scoring points to fending off an attack. Like in basketball, a flawed defense in planning and executing your personal finance plan can leave you vulnerable, allowing one uncontested shot after another until your spirit is broken and your hopes for victory are dashed. Bad financial habits, recessions, and inflation can slowly eat away at your financial security. Other times, the attack is swift and devastating, in which case a boxing analogy might be more appropriate. A fire, disease, or lawsuit could deliver a crushing defeat to your financial goals with a single merciless blow.

To stay in the game and give yourself a fighting chance, your financial plan must include a defensive strategy. A solid defense has perimeter guardians to make life more difficult for the opposing forces that try to penetrate your financial fortress. Ideally, your defense would also have the equivalent of a Patrick Ewing, a beast under the basket capable of turning away even the strongest threats to your well-being.

Importantly, the components of your defense must work together. Even in a man-on-man defense, it is never really one-on-one. There is switching off, double-teaming, and constant rotation to keep all entryways sealed. If one piece is out of position, the entire defense can fall apart and give up easy points to the competition.

We have already talked about playing offense, the process of pursuing investment returns to create wealth. Naturally, a discussion of defense would include ways to protect your investment portfolio from potentially harmful effects in the market.

But defense also extends to your life beyond investing. We have already touched briefly on contingency plans and the need for adequate insurance coverage. Later in this chapter, we will go into more depth about various types of insurance and why they are important to safeguard your financial security.

Communication is Key

The best defensive teams' players talk to each other all the time. They keep one another informed as to what is going on. Also, players encourage their teammates to stay focused and work hard. They clarify who is covering whom. They shout a warning when a screen is coming or when a cutter tries to slip in the backdoor. They are constantly communicating.

In most homes, communication is equally important when it comes to staying on track financially. It starts with simple budgeting and cash flow. Unless you are a single adult with no dependents, you are not the only one in control of your family's financial destiny. Your spouse, your kids, and maybe even your live-in mom wield their own share of power in determining how and when money is used; thus, they should share in the responsibility of watching over the family coffers.

Keeping your team on the same page defensively can help your family avoid some of the self-defeating money behaviors, such as overspending and making irrational decisions, and preserve enough of your income to fund other areas of your plan (insurance, investing, etc.). When everyone with a stake in your goals understands what you are trying to accomplish, they are more apt to follow your lead and carry their own weight.

A husband and wife might decide to split certain responsibilities. For example, one spouse accepts the challenge of keeping the family out of debt by paying off the credit card every month. The other tackles another important defensive assignment, setting up and contributing to an emergency fund in a savings account. The kids' responsibilities might be limited to spending their allowance wisely, though this can be an uphill battle for parents. Everyone communicates regularly to ensure the whole floor is covered.

Even if you are single, doing a periodic self-assessment of your own defensive coverage—communicating internally—is an important step to close any gaps that could leave you vulnerable financially.

DEFENDING YOUR INVESTMENTS WITH DIVERSIFICATION

Most people early in their lives do not have much to lose in financial terms. They cannot lose what they do not yet have. A fresh college grad might start her investing journey with a few thousand dollars in savings and thirty or more years to keep contributing and reap positive returns. She can afford to focus almost exclusively on offense in her portfolio.

But as the years pass and her nest egg grows, she becomes increasingly concerned about the possibility of losing what she has gained. Who wants to contribute their hard-earned dollars to an investment account month after month, year after year, only to watch those savings disappear into thin air? Nobody. That, of course, is why portfolio diversification is so important. Diversifying your investments—spreading your invested dollars over different assets—can be considered a defensive strategy because it reduces the overall risk in your portfolio while allowing for continued growth.

Diversification puts the odds of success in your favor. As your assets become more diverse, the odds of them all performing poorly at the same time decrease, and the odds of at least some of them doing well increases.

Diversification Mitigates Volatility

This table shows how, from 2007–2011 (including the extremely volatile years of the financial crisis), a typical diversified portfolio outperformed the stock market indices. Note the differences in standard deviation, which is a measure of volatility. Simply put, a diversified portfolio provided not just better overall performance, but a less-harrowing ride as well.

	Cumulative Performance	Annualized Performance	Standard Deviation
Diversified Portfolio	10.80%	2.07%	13.15%
Russell 2000	0.75%	0.15%	24.47%
S&P 500	-1.24%	-0.25%	18.88%

In this way, diversification helps to smooth out your returns from year to year and avoid the dramatic swings in value known to cause hair loss.

Speaking hypothetically, a portfolio not protected by diversification might go all over the place. It could jump 40 percent one year, lose 60 percent the next, and rise 25 percent the year after. With such erratic and extreme fluctuations in your account value, it is a risky game to bet that the money will be there when you need to withdraw it. By comparison, your diversified portfolio might earn 8 percent one year, lose 3 percent the next year, and then rise 6 percent. There will still be ups and downs, but over the course of decades, this method of investing has proven to produce more restrained yet dependable growth that, while not guaranteed, provides greater assurance of meeting your goals.

Investing in many different assets is safer than betting all your savings on a single holding. But there is more to diversification than just sprinkling your money far and wide. It is important to consider how those investments tend to perform relative to one another, which is what we discuss next.

UNDERSTANDING ASSET CORRELATIONS

You could say that all investments are part of one big family. But like the members of a family, they have their own personalities and behave in different ways. The degree to which two types of investments perform alike is called their correlation. Two assets (or asset classes) that tend to react in much the same way to certain situations would be strongly correlated. But if one investment tends to zig when the other one zags, they have a negative correlation. Finally, if one zigs and the other just stays put, that is a neutral correlation.

If this is all starting to sound like high school math class, bear with me. Asset correlations are important to the diversification process because you do not want all of your assets to always move in the same direction at the same time. In a perfect world, every investment you owned would always increase in value and never decline, but that is just not realistic. So to spare yourself the nauseating roller coaster ride over the market's peaks and valleys, it is wise to smooth out the journey by owning some assets that tend to go up when others go down.

Here is a simple illustration to show you how diversifying your portfolio among assets that are not strongly correlated can reduce your overall risk. Let's say you are brand new to investing and were given $50,000 to start a portfolio. You really like shopping at the Home Depot, so you decide you would like to own stock in that company. But if you used all of that $50,000 to buy Home Depot stock, you would have created the least-diversified portfolio imaginable. All of your savings would be riding on the fate of one stock. If that stock took a nosedive, you could kiss your small fortune good-bye. That is not investing—that is gambling.

So you decide you should spread out your risk and consider buying two different stocks: Home Depot and your second-favorite store, Lowe's. As you probably guessed, this idea is not much better because Home Depot and Lowe's have a very strong correlation. They are both home improvement stores, targeting the same customers across suburban America. When one business suffers, it is likely that the other will feel similar pains, and both of your stocks will lose value simultaneously.

With that realization, you make the wise decision to diversify your investments across many different stocks. You invest it in an S&P 500 Index Fund, which owns shares of Home Depot and 499 other companies. Because the companies in the fund represent many different industries, in any given year, it is likely that some will perform well and others might do poorly.

While your $50,000 is now spread among many stocks with lower correlations to each other, you could still be more diversified. Consider that all of the stocks in the S&P 500 are American companies. If the US economy hits an especially rough patch, like we saw in 2008–2009, virtually all of those stocks could be hit hard. To mitigate that risk, you could invest a portion of your money in an international stock fund. That might give you a source of positive returns even when US stocks are having a bad year.

Also to this point, let's say you have invested in various types of stocks, but all of your money still rests in a single asset class. You might think about moving some of that money away from stocks and into bonds. Doing so would add another degree of safety to your portfolio because, historically, the performance of most bonds is weakly correlated with stocks.

The bottom line is owning lots of different investments does not necessarily constitute a well-diversified portfolio. True diversification comes from investing in different asset classes, such as stocks and bonds, and even different categories, such as industry sectors or geographies, within each asset class.

Investing in noncorrelated assets is the groundwork for what investing professionals know as modern portfolio theory. Money managers rely on its principles to create portfolios that achieve maximum returns for the least amount of risk. In other words, they are looking for the perfect combination of offense and defense.

As shown in this graphic, an ideal portfolio falls along the efficient frontier line, where the highest expected return is reached for any given level of risk. The inefficient portfolio, on the other hand, takes on too much risk for too little return.

I am not recommending that you don a lab coat and cover a chalkboard with complex calculations of asset correlations and risk profiles. Leave that to the professionals. Building a diversified portfolio is a strategic process that, if done well, can help you reach your financial goals more efficiently.

Modern Portfolio Theory at Work

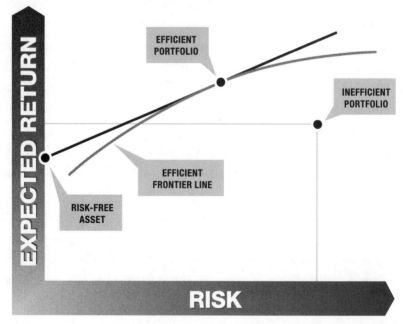

STAYING IN BALANCE

Wouldn't it be nice if maintaining a diversified investment portfolio were as easy as operating that rotisserie oven you see in the infomercials? You know the tagline: "Set it and forget it!" But the fact is that your work is not done once you have built a nice collection of noncorrelated assets. There is some upkeep involved, and it's called portfolio rebalancing. As covered earlier, the holdings in your carefully crafted portfolio are, or should be, invested in a way that matches your goals and risk tolerance. A moderately aggressive portfolio, for instance, might start out with 75 percent stocks, 20 percent bonds, and 5 percent alternative assets. But it won't stay that way for long.

Over time, your asset allocation might become off kilter as certain investments perform better than others. If stocks generate much higher returns than bonds, for example, a year later you could find that 85 percent of the value in your portfolio is in stocks, with 7 percent in alternative assets and only 8 percent in bonds. "What's wrong with that?" you're asking. "Shouldn't I be happy that my stocks did well?"

Yes, but there's just one problem. Since your stock investments outperformed the bonds, your portfolio is suddenly at a higher risk level than you intended when you selected a 75/20/5 ratio. If you change nothing, it is similar to winning at blackjack and letting it ride, leaving all your winnings in the betting circle and thereby upping the stakes dramatically. Such risky behavior might be thrilling to watch in James Bond movies, but it's not a good strategy for sensible investors.

Your portfolio needs to be rebalanced, which is the process of taking some winnings off the table and returning your asset allocation to its original levels. To get the mix back in check, you could sell off some of the stock and alternative holdings and reinvest the money in bonds or simply make new investments in bonds. Either way, in this case, your objective would be to bring the value of your holdings back to 75 percent stock, 20 percent bonds, and 5 percent alternative assets.

Protecting the lead you have built so the "bad guys" cannot come roaring right back is another way of playing defense. Keeping an eye on your portfolio and rebalancing about once a year is suitable for most average investors. You might need to do it for multiple accounts, such as your retirement fund and your personal investment account, according to the allocation goals you have set for each one. As a side note, some mutual funds and separately managed accounts will rebalance for you automatically. But it's still a good idea to stay engaged and be aware of how your asset allocation is constantly in flux.

How Portfolio Rebalancing Works

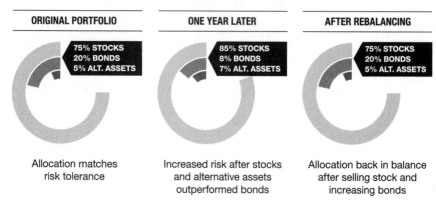

ORIGINAL PORTFOLIO	ONE YEAR LATER	AFTER REBALANCING
75% STOCKS 20% BONDS 5% ALT. ASSETS	85% STOCKS 8% BONDS 7% ALT. ASSETS	75% STOCKS 20% BONDS 5% ALT. ASSETS
Allocation matches risk tolerance	Increased risk after stocks and alternative assets outperformed bonds	Allocation back in balance after selling stock and increasing bonds

DEFENSE IN HIGH GEAR

Diversification and rebalancing are as fundamental to investing defense as sliding your feet and raising your hands in basketball. Everyone should do these things. But the craftiest defenders know how to take it to another level when the going gets tough. On the court, they dart into passing lanes or draw charges by anticipating the opponent's next move. In an investment portfolio, money managers have defensive tricks up their sleeves as well, and they are especially useful in harsh economic times.

A defensive mindset provides a blanket of protection in investing, and it's similarly indispensable in basketball, as espoused by former North Carolina Coach Dean Smith. In his book *A Coach's Life*, Smith summarizes some of his important principles of coaching, and the first one he mentions is how defense is the cornerstone of his program.

"Having a true team defense helped bring about the three goals of playing together, playing hard, and playing smart," he said. "By *team defense*, we meant having the solidarity that required each player to trust his teammates. Our defense would not work if one player was out of position."

In light of the fact that investing is usually a team concept that involves spouses as well as other members of the family, even the extended family, it is not a stretch at all to apply Smith's view of defense to the household unit when it comes to finances and investments.

Furthermore, as Smith said, "Team defense promoted team offense. When players bought into a team defense, it went a long way toward guaranteeing unselfish play on offense. We talked all the time about 'shot selection' because taking good, sound shots usually meant that a team was playing unselfishly on offense."

Few investors completely escaped the fierce bear market we experienced from 2008–2010. But while some were profoundly wounded financially, others were able to emerge with small bumps and bruises. Either they were plain lucky or they knew how to make strategic changes in their portfolios to minimize the damage when the onslaught began.

The following is an overview of some asset types that can fortify your portfolio when it comes under attack, such as when a struggling economy threatens to devour your investment value. While I would not advise pursuing these strategies on your own without more in-depth study, this section could help you understand an approach your financial planner or broker might recommend.

- **Government Bonds:** In an economic downturn, businesses have a more difficult time making money and paying off their debts. So the default risk on corporate bonds increases. The US government, on the other hand, can literally print its own money when it needs to, which is why government bonds (especially Treasuries) are generally considered safe investments. If a recession is looming, shifting a higher percentage of your portfolio to government bonds or a bond fund can provide a safe haven from the volatile stock market, and it can produce positive returns as the demand for bonds continues to rise. As always, however, it is important to remain cognizant of the other risks associated with bonds, such as the risk that inflation will outpace your returns.

- **Recession-Proof Stocks:** As I have stated earlier, I am not a big fan of individual stock-picking. But there are certain categories of stocks that tend to do better than others in a recession, and it is useful to understand why.

  Because business performance typically declines during a recession, stock prices tend to fall when analysts predict trouble on the economic horizon. At the same time, consumer confidence suffers, and people become afraid to make big, discretionary purchases. This compounds the pain for companies that sell luxury goods or nonessential services. Their stock prices fall further as fewer consumers come through the door. On the other hand, companies whose products and services are always in demand—healthcare, food and beverages, utilities, and other consumer staples—are more insulated from these effects.

  Think of it this way: When you're worried about losing your job (or you have already been laid off), do you buy a big-screen TV? Probably not. But you still have to buy groceries, turn on the lights, and take medicine when you get sick. So in a recession, Best Buy becomes a less-attractive investment than, say, Proctor & Gamble or Pfizer.

  Furthermore, when money is tight, many consumers change their routines to shop at discount stores such as Wal-Mart or Costco, which might actually boost the performance of those companies. As morbid as it might sound, people also do not stop dying just because there is a recession going on, so companies that operate funeral homes and cemeteries stay alive and kicking.

  Among these recession-resistant stocks, high-quality companies with long histories and strong balance sheets (cash reserves and not too much debt) tend to be the best bets. Again, I would not encourage you to stake your future on the success of any one company, but you might work with your broker or advisor to identify funds that invest in these general areas.

- **High-Dividend Stocks:** Some companies annually distribute a portion of their profits or cash reserves to shareholders. For every share of stock you own, you receive a tiny fraction of the payout, called a dividend. Stocks that pay relatively high dividends can strengthen your portfolio in times when other equities are struggling. The dividend provides a tangible return on investment, which makes the stock more attractive to investors and less likely to lose significant market value. If the stock price does decline, the dividend softens the blow. And dividends can be reinvested to buy additional shares of that company "on sale," which can pay you back in spades when the stock price recovers.

- **Hedge Funds:** If you have heard of hedge funds, you might associate them with rich Wall Street bankers who summer in the Hamptons. You would be correct, but only partially.

  Unlike mutual funds, hedge funds are typically private partnerships with less government regulation. They are free to be invested directly in a variety of assets, such as stocks, bonds, real estate, commodities, etc., with the goal of earning a positive return with as little risk as possible. Toward that end, hedge fund managers use any number of sophisticated trading strategies, which, when executed effectively, can deliver higher returns than bonds at less risk than stocks. The success of these strategies is highly dependent on the skill of the manager, which is why hedge fund managers are often treated (and paid) like rock stars of the financial industry.

  Only accredited investors with a high net worth can participate directly in hedge funds, which gives them their exclusive cachet. But events of recent years have opened up similar opportunities for people of more modest means. Some advisors offer access to so-called funds of funds, pooling the resources of many investors to create a central fund that subsequently invests in hedge funds. These investments can perform well although it is important to be aware that their two-layer approach can result in two layers of fees.

- **Annuities:** An annuity is an investment that guarantees a stream of income either for life or for a specified period of time.

Annuities are a common choice for retirees who are concerned about outliving their retirement savings. For example, if you had saved enough to live comfortably through age seventy-five but kept going strong to ninety, you would be in serious danger of running out of funds. If you had purchased a lifetime annuity, however, it would continue to pay out long after your other accounts ran dry. In this way, annuities are like insurance against living too long.

Annuities can also serve the purpose of defending against investment losses. If you're approaching retirement and have a million dollars or more in your 401(k) or IRA, for instance, you have presumably moved some of that money to safer asset classes already. But as long as your funds are invested, there will always be some level of risk involved. Using at least a portion of those funds to purchase an annuity could protect you from whatever market crisis might be lurking around the corner.

To be clear, I have not mentioned these defensive strategies so you can constantly manipulate your portfolio in an effort to time the market. Rather, these are options that you and your advisor can consider together in response to long-term trends in the economy and your evolving needs.

DEFENDING YOUR FINANCIAL WELL-BEING WITH INSURANCE

So far in this chapter, we have discussed ways to shelter your investment portfolio from unpredictable and merciless market forces. That's certainly important if you hope to accumulate enough money to achieve major financial goals in your lifetime. But your investments are not the only assets that need protection.

While you might not think of them as assets, the cash in your checking and savings accounts as well as your home, vehicles, furniture, jewelry, electronics—everything you own—and even the income you expect to earn in the future are part of your financial universe. Like your investments, they are all at risk. And in a way, the threats against your everyday lifestyle are even more frightening than a crashing stock market.

While investment losses on paper might dampen your hopes and dreams for the future, a more personal and immediate catastrophe could wreck the way of life you and your family enjoy right here and now.

Death, disease, disability, auto accidents, fires—these are risks we live with every day, and they could strike without warning at any time. That, of course, is why we have insurance.

Insurance cannot stop you from getting sick, keep your home from burning down, or save you from a car crash. What insurance can do is prevent these tragedies from wiping you out financially, giving you and your family an opportunity to recover and move on.

In the next few pages, we will talk about some key categories of insurance coverage you will need to consider as you build a financial force field around your life.

Healthcare Insurance

Everyone needs healthcare insurance. There's no way around it. Just for the record: Do not even think about going without it.

Yes, the coverage has grown increasingly expensive. A study by the nonprofit Kaiser Family Foundation reported that the average annual premium for family healthcare coverage through an employer reached $15,073 in 2011, almost double the price tag from 2001. New medical technologies, expensive prescription drugs, rising administrative costs, and the American obesity epidemic are among many contributors to the sky-high costs for insurance.

As premiums have risen ever higher, many families (even those who are not struggling financially) begin to wonder whether they can get by with a bare-bones policy or even no coverage at all. At first, their rationale sounds reasonable: We are young, healthy people, and we only go to the doctor for annual checkups. Even if one of us broke an arm or needed stitches every so often, in the long run we would still pay a lot less for actual healthcare than what we are shelling out for insurance.

This argument might hold water—*if* the family could guarantee that minor medical care is all it would ever need. That is a huge *if*. No matter how strong and healthy you might feel today, no one is invincible.

No amount of eating right or working out can completely protect you from cancer or a car accident or a fluke brain aneurysm. With healthcare insurance, your costs to treat a major condition could be daunting yet manageable; without insurance, the numbers could be absolutely staggering. Hundreds of thousands, even a million, dollars or more spent on surgeries or chemotherapy could erase everything you have saved and shatter your family's dreams for the future.

Is good healthcare insurance pricey? Yes. Is it worth it? Without a doubt.

As with any insurance policy, your objective should be to get the most coverage you can for the most reasonable price. For most people, that means getting a group policy through an employer or a spouse's employer.

That might not be an option, however, if you are self-employed or work for a small company. Unfortunately, your premiums are likely to be even higher than if you worked for a big corporation or a government agency. Even then, comparison shopping is an option as it might reveal a policy that fits your budget and provides the protection you need. One caveat to all this is that changes related to President Barack Obama's healthcare reform bill are, as of 2013, still in development and might have significant implications for the way individuals shop for and obtain insurance.

Continuing healthcare coverage is also of chief concern for retirees. It used to be that many employers offered coverage to workers who retired from the company, but that practice is fading fast as the costs of providing insurance have become a huge financial burden for corporate America. Until Medicare kicks in at age sixty-five, an increasing number of retirees must foot the whole bill for healthcare insurance. Face the reality: Costs for ongoing healthcare coverage should figure prominently in your retirement savings plan.

LIFE INSURANCE

Ask yourself a simple question: "If I died today, would anyone be worse off financially?"

If the answer is yes, you should at least consider having life insurance.

Your income, especially if you are the sole breadwinner in the household, makes possible the way of life you know. If that paycheck suddenly went away forever because of your death, chances are it would have dramatic and long-lasting fallout for your family not just because of the emotional trauma but because your family depends on the money you make to live comfortably today and meet their goals for the future. Without your paycheck, could your spouse continue to pay the mortgage and all the bills? Could he or she continue to save for retirement and the kids' education? Could they carry on with a sense of normalcy, able to afford life's little luxuries such as eating out, going to the movies, or vacationing at the beach?

It is uncomfortable to imagine your loved ones struggling through the hardships that might result from your absence. Life insurance helps to allay those fears. It provides peace of mind in knowing that your family will be OK, at least financially, without you.

Life Insurance:
Term vs. Permanent

Term Insurance:
Coverage is for a contracted period or term, usually a specified number of years or up to a certain age. Generally, term insurance gives you the largest immediate payout for the lowest premiums. The downside is that you get nothing back if you outlive the policy, and if you want to renew, your premiums will be higher. There is also a chance you won't qualify for a renewal—if you contract a serious disease, for example.

Permanent Insurance:
As the name implies, coverage lasts your entire life as long as you continue to pay the premium. A portion of your premium goes into a cash fund that might appreciate on a tax-deferred basis.

If you die, your beneficiaries get the death benefit plus the cash value in the account. Or, while you are still living, you can borrow against the cash value or cancel the policy and get the money back (subject to some fees and restrictions). The bad news is that premiums for permanent life insurance, which includes variations called Whole Life, Universal Life, and Variable Universal Life, are typically far more expensive than term coverage.

Approach with Caution
Life insurance (especially permanent policies) can be complex and confusing. Before you purchase anything, consult with an unbiased advisor who is not selling insurance.

Many corporations provide their employees with free life insurance with a "death benefit"—payout amount—of twice their annual salary. It is a nice perk but probably far from what is needed to support a spouse and children for years to come.

A common rule of thumb is that adequate life insurance protection should cover seven to ten times your annual income although you should definitely make more thorough calculations before purchasing a policy. Speaking with an insurance professional or financial advisor will help you estimate what immediate and ongoing expenses your family would have to cover if your income were lost. A professional also can guide you in deciding whether a term or permanent life insurance policy, or a combination of both, would best suit your goals.

Even if you are not the primary earner in your home, life insurance is worth consideration. If you are a stay-at-home spouse, for example, you probably provide important services such as childcare, cooking, and cleaning that could create financial hardship if your family had to hire help to get by without you. A life insurance policy could offset those costs.

What if you are single and have no dependents? Life insurance might not be necessary, but do not rule it out automatically. If you died, you might leave behind credit card debt, student loans, and a car payment (not to mention funeral expenses) that would have to be paid off by your family. A small life insurance policy would ease their burden. Also, buying life insurance while you are young can help you lock in lower rates and guarantee coverage if you develop health problems later in life.

DISABILITY INSURANCE

Like life insurance, the purpose of disability insurance is to replace your income if you can no longer provide it. The difference is that you do not have to die for the disability policy to pay out. Disability insurance kicks in if an injury or illness renders you unable to do your job and earn a living.

Strangely, it seems more people are aware of and purchase life insurance than disability coverage. Statistically speaking, however, your odds of becoming disabled and not being able to work are much higher than the risk of dying prematurely. According to the Council for Disability

Awareness, as many as one in four adults will become disabled at some time before they retire, and the average long-term disability claim lasts about thirty-one months.

A lack of steady income can quickly take its toll on your finances. Imagine what might happen if you were diagnosed with an aggressive form of cancer and you had to leave your job. While health insurance hopefully would cover most of your medical costs, the bills at home would still need to be paid while you were not working. Without an income, you would have little choice but to burn through your cash savings and then start depleting your investment portfolio, perhaps drawing from retirement or college funds long before you had imagined. Either that or you would be forced to rack up an unmanageable mountain of debt. If and when you returned to work, it might be too late to get your plans for the future back on track.

Disability insurance is there to help you avoid such a financially crippling situation. As with life insurance, you might be covered by a group policy through your employer, but the coverage is often limited to 60 percent of your salary, not including bonuses or commissions. You might not even get that much if you earn a high salary and the policy is capped at a level below your wage. Moreover, your employer's coverage might only cover permanent, long-term disability, which is rarer than short-term, and might only pay out for a limited time, meaning the checks stop coming after several years.

These limitations can be overcome by buying additional coverage through your employer or purchasing a separate disability policy on your own. When you are

> ### Disability Insurance: Short-Term vs. Long-Term
>
> Short-term disability coverage is helpful if you miss work for six months or less although most policies do not start paying until you have used up all of your sick leave and/or vacation time from your job. If you have saved a substantial cash emergency fund to carry you through the crisis, you might not need short-term disability coverage beyond what your employer provides (often for free).
>
> The more important type of coverage is long-term disability, which picks up where any short-term policies leave off. Depending on the policy you choose, the payments could last for five or ten years or until you are sixty-five. While the latter option is not cheap, it is the safest way to go.

comparison shopping, the key factors to consider are how much of your income the policy will replace, how long you want to be covered, and how long the payments will last if you do file a claim.

HOMEOWNERS INSURANCE

If you have a mortgage, your lender requires you to have homeowners insurance. But you should have insurance even if you have paid off your house.

For most homeowners, the question is not whether to buy but how much. Surprisingly, a large percentage of people get this part wrong, and the consequences can be heartbreaking. Here are three mistakes you should try to avoid.

- *Not Insuring to Replacement Value.* Homeowners insurance is mandatory for mortgage holders, but what is required by the bank might be much less than you actually need. See it from the bank's point of view: It is only concerned with recouping the money it loaned to you (say $300,000), so it will require a minimum insurance policy of $300,000 on the home. Now imagine that your home burned to the ground. Would $300,000 in insurance money be enough to completely rebuild your home just the way you had it?

  If you bought the house during a real estate slump, the price you paid for the home could be considerably less than the construction cost. And if you have made any major improvements since you moved in, like renovating the kitchen or adding an outdoor living area, these things also add to the replacement value. An anemic insurance policy could leave you on the hook for tens of thousands of dollars if your home was wiped off the map.

  If you have no idea what your cost to rebuild would be, it might be time to hire an appraiser.

  By the same logic, consider buying replacement-cost coverage for the contents of the home (furniture, clothes, electronics, etc.). Basic policies offer to pay only the actual cash value (garage sale prices) for your stuff. But slightly more expensive coverage would allow you to go on a shopping spree to buy all-new things.

Renters Take Note

If you rent an apartment or a house, you are not required to carry insurance. But that doesn't mean you do not need it.

Add up the value of everything in your apartment: furniture, clothes, electronics, dishes, etc. Now consider that your landlord's insurance covers his building, not your possessions. If a fire or flood wipes out your belongings, you are on the hook to replace them.

This is a scary thought—unless you have *renters insurance*, sometimes called personal property insurance. A small premium can keep you covered.

- *Ignoring Natural Disasters.* Be aware that not all risks that threaten your home are covered by the standard homeowners insurance policy. To get protection against floods, earthquakes, and windstorms, you will need an additional policy. As with all insurance, the higher your odds of experiencing a loss, the higher your premiums will be. That means if you are bound and determined to live on a beach or overlook a fault line, your costs for insurance could be higher—a lot higher, in some cases. These extra policies are optional, but you forgo them at your peril.

- *Skimping on Liability Coverage.* The other, less-talked-about component of homeowners insurance is liability coverage—the part that protects you from lawsuits if someone gets injured on your property and decides to sue. True, it is probably a remote possibility. But it is worth insuring against tragic incidents that you might have never considered. What if your dog got loose and severely mauled a neighbor? What if your son's friend fell down your stairs and broke his neck? These are horrible accidents that might leave physical and emotional scars for everyone involved, but they do not have to ruin you

When It Rains, It Pours

A serious lawsuit could burn right through whatever liability protection you have as part of your home or auto policy. High net worth individuals, especially, should consider an *umbrella policy*. That is extra liability insurance that takes effect when your other policies are exhausted. A few hundred dollars per year could provide a million dollars or more of protection.

financially. A basic homeowners policy might provide $100,000 to $300,000 of protection. But the more money you have to lose in a lawsuit, the more liability insurance you should have.

AUTO INSURANCE

Buying auto insurance can be a lot like buying an actual car. There are so many bells and whistles to choose from, but the primary coverage areas break down into a few basic categories.

- *Liability.* This is the part that is required by law in most states. If you cause an accident, it will help pay for any damage you cause to other vehicles or property. It also protects you from paying the medical bills of other people injured in the crash and can shield you from lawsuits they might file. But, as with homeowners insurance, there are limits to how much your policy will pay before you have to cover the shortfall. Usually, a slightly higher premium can buy a lot more coverage.

- *Collision.* This piece pays for the damages your car incurs from an accident, regardless of who is at fault. If you are currently financing or leasing a car, collision insurance is usually required by the lender or car dealer. It is optional if you own the car free and clear. If you have an old clunker that is not worth much money, you might consider dropping collision coverage and putting those funds toward another type of insurance.

- *Comprehensive.* This coverage pays for damages to your car caused by something other than a collision, such as hail, vandalism, theft, or fire. As with collision coverage, you could probably go without comprehensive if your beat-up jalopy is not worth the extra premiums.

Picking up the Slack: UIM Coverage

A study by the Insurance Research Council estimates that as many as one in six drivers are on the road without liability insurance. If they crash into you, guess who pays for your damages? You do.

That is why it is smart to add *uninsured/ underinsured motorist* coverage to your auto policy. It will pay for repair work or medical bills when the other guy cannot. This coverage also protects you in the case of a hit-and-run.

LONG-TERM CARE INSURANCE

I saved this type of coverage for last because most people do not even need to consider it until they are middle-aged or approaching retirement.

As you enter your golden years, you likely envision the days ahead filled with travel, hobbies, and grandkids. Unfortunately, sometimes getting older also comes with some very expensive side effects. Serious health problems that require a stay in a nursing home or assisted living facility can devour a healthy retirement fund.

That's why your preretirement to-do list should include checking into long-term care insurance. This kind of insurance helps cover the costs of nursing home care, rehabilitation, adult day care and similar services, any of which can cost tens of thousands of dollars a year. Since many of the costs are not covered by healthcare insurance, long-term care coverage can make up at least part of the shortfall and protect your financial resources. Perhaps more importantly, it can save your grown children the immense financial burden of paying for your care.

Buying this type of coverage while you are still in your thirties or forties is usually unnecessary. That money could be put to better use. But long-term care insurance is worth considering once you reach your fifties because people who are relatively young (in retirement terms) and still in good health can qualify for much better rates. Past your fifties, extremely high premiums could put the coverage out of reach, or you might not qualify for coverage at all.

Alternatives to LTC Insurance

As costs for long-term care and premiums for long-term care insurance continue to rise, more middle-agers are reluctant to shell out big bucks for a policy they might never use. Well aware of these concerns, the insurance industry has begun offering an alternative to traditional long-term care coverage. Usually called a *hybrid policy*, this product combines a life insurance policy with a long-term care insurance rider. Essentially, this two-in-one policy could be used to pay for long-term care costs and/or provide a payout to your heirs when you die. The key advantage is that you are sure to use it for *something*.

Yet another option is to forego long-term care insurance altogether and simply earmark more of your savings to pay for the potential costs. You might hear this practice referred to as self-insuring. Your financial planner can help you arrive at the best choice for you and your family.

STRETCHING YOUR DEFENSIVE DOLLAR

When you take it in all at once, the list of recommended insurance policies might seem like preparation for a nuclear winter. How will you ever meet your investment goals if you are devoting so much money to a bulletproof insurance plan?

It is possible to do both if you take a tip from good defensive ball clubs: Put your primary focus on the most dangerous threats, but keep the whole floor covered. Ewing and Georgetown collapsed on Olajuwon when he got the ball inside yet somehow still managed to prevent wide-open shots from the perimeter.

Similarly, you should coordinate your insurance policies to give you optimum protection where you need it most. For example, if you have three young kids at home and your spouse does not earn an income, life insurance is critically important. If your daily commute takes you through forty miles of rush-hour traffic, make sure you have plenty of auto coverage to mitigate that increased risk.

You might be able to spend less in areas where your risks are decidedly lower. But do not make the mistake of ignoring entire categories altogether. Like defense in basketball, having some coverage in all areas is better than overloading one spot and leaving another completely exposed.

If you still have trouble fitting adequate insurance coverage into your budget, explore the possibility of accepting higher deductibles. When you agree to pay more out of pocket for damages before insurance takes over, you can save a bundle on your monthly premiums. As long as you have enough liquid funds to cover the deductible, this is a reasonable trade-off. Insurance, after all, is not intended to pay for minor expenses such as fixing a leaky roof; it is there for when there is no roof left to fix.

Finally, as in most industries, insurance companies compete for your business, so do not just buy the first policy that comes your way. Using the Internet to shop around and get multiple quotes, you might find the coverage you need for less money than you expected.

Brace Yourself

Up to now, this book has imparted many of the basic concepts and strategies behind financial planning. But many times a game plan that looks great on paper can be picked apart by the competition once the game really heats up.

Far from a leisurely stroll to a championship victory, the game of personal finance is more likely to be a dogfight. You will encounter problems. There will be setbacks that cause you to doubt your plan. But, equally, there will be fortuitous bounces of the ball that give you an unexpected leg up—if you can seize the moment. The next chapter focuses on how to deal with the snags, make the most of happy accidents, and stay on track toward your financial goals through thick and thin.

Chapter-Ending Three-Pointer:

1. Create an effective investment portfolio through diversification.
2. Identify lower-risk investments and their role in your investment strategy.
3. Plan to add or change insurance coverage as needed for health, life, disability, property, or liability.

Chapter Six

Sticking with the Game Plan

Keeping Sight of Your Goals through Challenges and Opportunities

Peach Basket Parables: Connecticut vs. Butler, 2011 NCAA Championship Game

For many NCAA Tournament champions, the season leading up to the championship goes pretty much as everyone expected. They go into the season highly rated in the polls, and then they pretty much dominate from start to finish, beating up on lesser opponents as praise gets heaped upon their marquee players, shaking off the rare loss after an off night, and eventually winning their conference title or postseason tournament. Come March Madness, they are in peak form and ready for almost anything an opponent can throw at them.

That is not always how it works out, though. Some champions are not predestined from opening day to win it all. They do not waltz gracefully through the Big Dance. Rather, they trip and stumble their way to victory. Throughout the season, they fight internal battles that spill onto the court and into the box score. And they second-guess themselves all year, until somehow, with remarkable timing, they find a way to capture lightning in a bottle.

The 2010–2011 Connecticut (UConn) Huskies had that kind of a season.

LOW EXPECTATIONS

That season started off under a blanket of dark clouds over Storrs, Connecticut. The Huskies had failed to earn an invitation to the NCAA Tournament the season before, and they started 2010 unranked in the national polls. Both snubs were ego busters for a school that had grown accustomed to winning. Though a relative newcomer to the roundtable of basketball royalty, UConn had become a regular national contender in recent decades. Coach Jim Calhoun, at the helm since 1986, had taken the team to the Sweet Sixteen twelve times over twenty years, winning two championships. Those teams included NBA-bound stars such as Ray Allen, Richard "Rip" Hamilton, Donyell Marshall, Rudy Gay, Caron Butler, Emeka Okafor, and Ben Gordon. In 2004, UConn became the first school in history to have its men's and women's teams win the NCAA Tournament in the same year. Come 2010, however, Huskies fans were desperate for something to believe in.

Deepening the gloom for them was the fact that the men's program was under NCAA investigation for recruiting violations. Two members of the basketball staff had already lost their jobs, and rumor had it that the NCAA might ban UConn from all postseason play (though, as it turned out later, Calhoun and his program would dodge a larger bullet and incur only some minor sanctions the following year).

Despite a lack of fanfare surrounding the 2010–11 team, the Huskies shot out of the gate eager to disprove their detractors. They jumped out to a 10–0 start, including winning the Maui Invitational Tournament in November. But the momentum dissipated as UConn's schedule transitioned over to Big East Conference play, which featured a steady stream of more powerful opponents. The Huskies finished the season a dreary 9–9 in the Big East, losing their last two games to finish in ninth place in the conference. As the regular season was ending in early March, no one in their right mind picked UConn to go all the way. Then everything changed.

THE TURNAROUND

Based on their regular season performance, the Huskies likely would have gone a second straight year without an NCAA Tournament berth. They did not deserve serious consideration. But teams that win their conference tournaments are automatically entered into the Big Dance, and that's exactly what UConn did.

Kemba Walker, the Huskies' All-American guard, caught fire and scored a tournament-record 130 points over a stretch of five games in five days. The late resurgence earned the Huskies a number four seed as March Madness began.

UConn won each of its first two games in the NCAA Tournament by more than ten points but had to fight tooth and nail to make it to the championship game, ousting Arizona by two points in a Sweet Sixteen matchup and beating Kentucky by one in a regional final. This Final Four was unique. It was the first ever to not feature a single number one or number two seed. Although UConn would ultimately face eighth-seeded mid-major Butler in the final game, its struggles were far from over.

BETTER OF TWO BADS

Butler University, a small school in Indianapolis with a fraction of the basketball clout as its goliath competitors, had nearly pulled off a shocking upset in the 2010 NCAA Tournament championship game, losing to Duke 61–59 when a last-second, desperation three-point shot barely missed what would have been a game winner for Butler. Now, for the second year in a row, the Bulldogs had accomplished the unthinkable and made it to the title game. Sadly for them, their dreams would be dashed yet again—but not because UConn played brilliantly.

The 2011 NCAA championship game will not be remembered for its crisp execution or spectacular shooting—far from it. Some reports called it the ugliest championship game ever played.

Both teams came out cold. After a forgettable first half, UConn trailed Butler in the low-scoring affair 22–19. Then cold turned to downright freezing. Choose your most jaw-dropping statistic:

- Butler had one stretch of 13 minutes and 26 seconds in the second half during which it made only one field goal.

- The Bulldogs shot a woeful 18.8 percent from the field in the game, the worst shooting performance in NCAA Championship Game history.
- Butler made only three two-point field goals for the whole game. Butler could not throw the ball in the ocean, but UConn was not much better.
- The Huskies made only 19 of 55 shots, shooting 34.5 percent for the game.
- They were 1–11 (9.1 percent) from 3-point range, the worst ever for a title winner.
- Star Kemba Walker had 16 points, but they came on 5-for-19 shooting (26 percent).
- UConn's final point total of 53 was its lowest scoring output of the entire season.

The 94 combined points by UConn and Butler were the fewest in a National Championship game since 1950 (and back then there was no shot clock, which usually meant fewer shots were taken).

You could credit good defense (which UConn did play), or blame the brickfest on frayed nerves. But the fact is neither team played like a national champion that night. Nevertheless, someone had to win, and UConn dragged itself to a 53–41 victory.

The general TV audience might have gotten more entertainment value out of watching paint dry, but UConn and its fans were no less ecstatic to claim their third title in twelve years.

COLOR COMMENTARY

- Former UCLA great Bill Walton, who sat courtside at the 2011 championship game, once scored 44 points in a title game—more than the entire Butler Bulldogs team scored that night.
- In 2011, UConn's Calhoun became the oldest coach (at sixty-eight) to win an NCAA basketball championship and one of just five to win three or more. The others are John Wooden, Bob Knight, Adolph Rupp, and Mike Krzyzewski.

RESILIENCE TRUMPS ADVERSITY

There are a couple of related lessons that emerged from the Huskies' rather drab championship season (if there is such a thing). First, winners are often far from flawless. They might start the season slow or go through a midseason meltdown. At times their chances of claiming a national title might even seem laughable. Yet they hang in there, keep their chins up, grind it out, and do whatever it takes to come out ahead.

Second, surprises are not always bad. Yes, good teams sometimes suffer embarrassing losses at the hands of an inferior team, or they lose a star player to an injury, dampening their chances of a title. But sometimes an unexpected gust of good fortune can sweep through a locker room and turn a spark into a roaring fire. These are the good surprises, like when Kemba Walker simply took over in the Big East Tournament and almost singlehandedly carried UConn into the NCAA Tournament.

Both of these concepts have a place in your financial life as well. You might start your saving and investing "career" with a 0–0 record, a clean slate with nothing but positive aspirations ahead of you. But it never stays that way for long.

Even if you implement all the advice from the early part of this book (building a strategic financial game plan with strong offensive and defensive elements), what looks great on paper will undoubtedly face resistance when deployed in the real world. You will come upon challenges—at home, at work, in the financial markets—that will knock you down and test your resolve to get back up. If you have been managing your finances for more than a few years, you have likely experienced this for yourself.

When things go wrong, it is natural to question your game plan. Some objective analysis is healthy and worthwhile, of course; it can help you make deliberate changes for the better. It's also easy to fall into a self-defeating spiral of negativity, convincing yourself that you don't have what it takes to succeed financially, or worse, that you don't deserve to.

Resilience is a word that is often used in sports. It describes the team or the player that, like a Timex watch, can take a licking and keep on ticking. They stay the course and they do not give up—ever. Resilience can separate champions from also-rans, and it's a central theme for this chapter.

Sometimes there are the good surprises, the unexpected windfalls that lift you up when you least expect it. They can have a tremendous positive impact on your long-term financial plan. If mismanaged, however, they can hurt you as much as they help. I will explain later in the chapter.

Sticking to your financial game plan can help you stay on course through these types of financial highs and lows. As time passes, you will need to reassess your position in life, and that's when you ask yourself if the financial goals and strategies you set in motion years ago still make sense. This process of re-evaluation becomes critical when you go through major life events, such as a career change or a divorce, or as you approach watershed moments, such as sending your kids off to college.

As every coach knows, how your team finishes out the first half of a game can have a powerful influence on the final outcome. Even if you're still behind, a strong push in the last two minutes of the half can change the tone, bolster your confidence going into the locker room, and allow you to carry the momentum into the second half. A similar sentiment applies to increasing your focus on financial planning as you prepare to enter each new phase of your life.

Managing Team Dynamics

The 2010–11 UConn team did not have a mediocre regular season because it was incompetent. It was because it had internal struggles to overcome—a young and untested roster, controversy among the coaching staff, and other problems—before it really hit its stride.

Likewise, issues facing your team—your family—continue to exert influence over your financial success. Your marriage, your kids, and even your own parents affect how, when, and where your money is spent or saved. As time goes by, it's important to recognize how those roles change. Family members and their impacts on your household finances might be dramatically different today than they were just several years ago. For that reason, it's smart to conduct a periodic review of your financial plan to ensure it makes as much sense today as it did then.

When you consider the typical progression of financial needs that modern families experience as they grow older together, it is easy to see how essential it is to keep spending, saving, and investing plans in concert with one another. Here are two examples of what I mean.

- *Kids in Transition.* When you think about it, parents really have two major financial responsibilities when it comes to their children. The first is to provide for them when they are young—feed them, clothe them, take them to the doctor, and pay for enriching activities. Obviously, that adds up to a huge financial commitment on your part that must be managed carefully. As children get older, however, the parents' role begins a slow transition from provider to teacher.

  You might start off young, giving them a small allowance and encouraging them to save it for something they want. When they hit their mid-teens and start driving, a debit card might take the place of the piggy bank. And by the time they head off for college or elsewhere, they should know how to pay their own bills and balance a checkbook.

  Your role as a money mentor to your kids is an important part of your overall financial plan. You're not only laying the groundwork for them to be successful in life, but you're also unburdening yourself of supporting them in the future (freeing up a lot of money for your other financial goals). Remember the old

> **Big Events, Deep Thoughts**
> It is good to keep a constant eye on your financial plan and progress. But it is especially important to re-evaluate your financial goals and strategies at key turning points in your life, when your income, expenses, tax status, and even your personal values might change. Here are a few examples:
>
> - Buying a house
> - Moving in with a partner
> - Getting married/divorced/remarried
> - Having a child
> - Changing jobs
> - Relocating
> - Sending kids to college
> - Paying for a child's wedding
> - Dealing with disease or death in the family
> - Retiring
> - Selling major assets
> - Receiving an inheritance

Chinese proverb: If you give a man a fish, you feed him for a day. If you teach a man to fish, you feed him for a lifetime.

Balancing the parental roles of provider and teacher, eventually leaving the former behind, is an important objective for any parent with designs on an empty nest.

- *Marital Changes.* Like the subtle changes in our aging faces, marriages tend to go through a maturing process over time. Your hopes and dreams as a couple, and the role that money plays in them, might have changed considerably since you were young newlyweds. For example, perhaps you have been inspired to make sizeable contributions to charity even if it means delaying your plans to buy a vacation property. There is nothing wrong with that, of course, as long as you and your spouse are singing from the same sheet music. But problems can arise when both parties drift through life with dramatically different plans and expectations. At some point, the discord inevitably comes to a head.

  That's why it's advisable to sit down every so often and talk things through, especially when you plan for any significant lifestyle changes. Meeting with a financial planner can help you formalize that process and arrive at a vision of the future with which you're both comfortable. The occasional powwow can do more than just keep your finances on track; it might just save your marriage.

  Of course, even with thorough financial planning, not all couples live happily ever after. Divorce is a sad fact of life in households everywhere. If you have been through one, you know there's no question that it changes your outlook on life and requires a careful review of how your finances are structured. Practically speaking, it could mean settling joint debt with your ex-spouse, establishing clear ownership of investments, and updating your estate plan and beneficiaries named on your accounts. On a deeper level, a divorce could trigger a profound shift in your worldview that makes you rethink your financial goals altogether.

  The same can occur when you remarry. With a new spouse comes an entirely new set of financial conditions—a different income level, different philosophies and goals on spending and saving, different assets and investments, different financial baggage such as debt, maybe even a different family structure with different children. To think that these things would not affect your personal finances would be ludicrous. If you are going to fulfill some of your own financial aspirations (and maintain a happy marriage), you will have to do it within this new context.

OVERCOMING SETBACKS

The family dynamics discussed in the previous section are examples of evolving financial challenges that involve natural progressions in your life that you can usually see coming and plan for in advance. Unless you are extremely lucky, however, you will also encounter your share of more immediate financial crises. These can seem to sneak up on you from behind, such as mounting debt, or explode right in your face, like an urgent health problem.

We have covered how defensive measures such as investment diversification, insurance, and emergency savings can help shield you from life's nasty surprises. But sometimes even the best-planned defenses are not enough to prevent all damage to your financial fortress. There will be setbacks, and how you deal with them can make all the difference in whether or not you fully recover.

Look at it this way. In basketball games, teams go through frustrating stretches when there's an invisible lid on the basket. The opposing team gets hot and makes a run, and your team is convinced the referees are secretly plotting against them. Does the coach lose his cool? Does he blow a gasket on the court and compound the damage? Or should he maintain his poise, call a timeout, and think his way through the problem?

As intense and vocal as Duke Coach Mike Krzyzewski can be at times, he seems to hold things together in tough stretches about as well as any head coach in the game. Coach K is not a perfect angel at courtside by any stretch, but just try to think of an instance where he has hurt his team's chances by losing his cool to the point where he becomes a detriment.

Krzyzewski touches on this subject in his book *Beyond Basketball,* in which he devotes a chapter to a discussion on poise. Coach K points out a common game scenario that gives a player every opportunity to lose his poise—when he's being double-teamed, which any of us can relate to when life's circumstances can seem to gang up on us.

"Being double-teamed creates quite a challenge, and it is hard to keep your wits about you," Krzyzewski writes. "On our teams, we continually use the expression with our post players that they must show 'poise in the post.' This means that if you get double-teamed, you must remain composed.

"Remember your training and make a choice. Ask yourself: What do I do? Do I pass the ball out to a teammate? Do I make a move to the basket? Do not panic. Make a play."

So, what do *you* do when you hit a sticky patch in your own life? Do you call a timeout (you can use as many as you want, no limits in life) and reassess?

You know the right answer, of course. It's the same with crises in your life. They will test your financial planning mettle to see whether you will cave or fight back. Here are a few examples of common financial predicaments that necessitate a cool head and a calculated counterattack.

- *Market Declines.* Like I've already said, making financial decisions based on emotion is never a good idea. Unfortunately, it is in the practice of investing where many people seem prone to panic attacks perhaps due to a lack of understanding about the market's long-term tendencies. They read the doomsday reports in the financial news, and they see their account balances falling. Therefore, they convince themselves to stop investing and sell off their holdings before the bottom drops out. It bears repeating that this reaction usually does more harm than good. While your advisor might recommend some fine tuning to your portfolio, in most cases where a well-diversified portfolio is already in place, the best strategy for investors is to keep chugging along, contributing to their accounts systematically, and putting themselves in a good position to experience the market upswing when it occurs.

  You still might face times when the losses truly are real, not the result of normal market fluctuations but actually deep cuts into your net worth that resulted from ill-fated, perhaps ill-advised, investments. In these cases, I suggest working with a professional advisor to review your current portfolio and develop a strategy to move forward. That might involve cutting your lifestyle expenses and making larger investment contributions in hopes of making up ground over time. It might not be easy, but it beats throwing in the towel on your financial goals.

- *Job Loss.* Layoffs in the workplace are no longer just a sign of bad economic times. At many companies, periodic right-sizing has become standard operating procedure. If you find yourself on the wrong end of a pink slip, lack of a paycheck can quickly eat into your savings and put the brakes on your investing progress. But there are ways to offset a layoff's potentially devastating effects and maybe even make lemonade out of lemons.

First if you are eligible for unemployment benefits through the government, don't be too proud to file. It's money you are entitled to as a taxpayer, and the partial income can keep you from accumulating debt while you're looking for a new job. To that point, don't be above taking a lower-paying job to hold you over until a better career move opens up.

A period of unemployment is also a good time to take a hard look at your household budget and cut unnecessary expenses, at least temporarily. I am talking about steak dinners and satellite TV—not health and auto insurance.

You might have no choice but to put your investment contributions on hold, but make a promise to yourself to get things rolling again when you find a job. If you're in danger of missing mortgage payments or not putting groceries in the fridge, look into selling off some of your liquid investments to cover the gap. Just stay away from your retirement and college funds as long as possible or risk paying early withdrawal penalties and taxes, not to mention the further delay to reaching your investment goals.

In a best-case scenario, you could use your time away from the job to learn a marketable new skill, transition to a more fulfilling career, or even start your own business, any of which could sow the seeds for greater financial rewards down the road.

- *Health Problems.* A life-threatening disease or injury can turn a family's world upside down emotionally, physically, and financially. Ideally, you will have good health insurance in place to help pay the high bills that go along with extensive medical treatment as well as disability insurance to provide income if you can no longer work. Even so, the out-of-pocket healthcare costs could be enough to make your bank account and investment portfolio sick.

  There is no way around paying, but a few strategic moves could help you stay above water until the worst is over. As with any major financial setback, adjusting your lifestyle to free up cash should be priority number one. You might also consider selling some assets—either material possessions or investments—to help pay off your bills faster.

  Avoid paying major medical bills with a credit card—a high interest rate will only prolong your financial misery. Instead, try working with the creditors (hospitals, labs, etc.) to negotiate a payment plan with favorable terms.

  If your expenses are unmanageable without tapping into your nest egg, consider your IRA or 401(k). You might qualify for a penalty-free withdrawal to pay for unreimbursed medical expenses that exceed 7.5 percent of your adjusted gross income.

- *Consumer Debt.* Some debts are unfortunate but unavoidable, such as the medical bills we just discussed. Other debt can actually be a good thing, like a sensible mortgage on an appreciating asset like a house. Then there are bad debts such as the consumer debts you took on when you did not really have to.

  In a perfect world, we could slap down cold hard cash for everything we bought. But in today's society, that's usually not realistic. Most of us find it normal and acceptable to use debt, whether with credit cards or loans, to finance big-ticket purchases such as furniture, cars, and vacations. Debt can be a useful tool if managed wisely. But consumer debt also can be its own disease brought on by an addiction to spending. A great many people, regardless of their income, go through life buying what they want, when they want thanks to credit. They don't stop to worry about the consequences until they're in way over their heads. As the bills become too large to ignore, every other aspect of their financial plan suffers.

They might spend years paying interest on purchases they have long since forgotten, robbing themselves of opportunities to put that money to far better use. To keep up with the payments, they might have little choice but to skimp on important things such as insurance, or they could raid whatever investment accounts they have built, hurting their chances for retirement or other long-term goals. Excessive debt might also lower their credit rating, making it difficult to qualify for future loans at reasonable interest rates. This is to say nothing of the emotional toll that severe debt can wage on your personal life and your marriage.

If you find yourself in this kind of mess, don't bury your head in the sand. Stop adding to your debts immediately, find ways to cut expenses, and start funneling the extra cash toward paying off your bills. Again, it might make sense to scale down your investment contributions or sell some assets in order to pay down debt, especially if the interest you are paying is higher than what you can expect your investments to earn.

There are books and limitless online resources covering debt management. I would encourage you to look there for more thorough advice. One word of caution, however: Be extremely careful about working with credit counselors, debt-management plans, or debt-settlement programs. Aside from reports of unscrupulous businesses preying on desperate consumers, even the most reputable organizations might charge high fees and interest rates to do a job that, with some elbow grease, you could manage on your own.

You're bound to encounter at least one of these or other financial stumbling blocks in your lifetime, and you probably will recognize trouble when you see it. Then again, maybe not. Money problems are not always tied to tragedy. Say you learn at age forty-seven that you're expecting a new baby just as your oldest is filling out college applications. It might be cause for celebration, but it's also a big wrench thrown in the gears of whatever financial plans you have made. Just like the negative scenarios we covered, it necessitates a financial timeout—a step back to collect yourself, reassess your goals, and adjust your strategies to meet them.

SEIZING OPPORTUNITIES

Thankfully, not every unexpected event in life has the potential to knock your financial goals off-kilter. There are good surprises that, if handled the right way, can put wind in your sails and push you to your destination ahead of schedule. If you will allow me to stray from college sports to the pros for a moment, I'll give you a great basketball example.

In early 2012, relatively few people outside of NBA scouts had ever heard of Jeremy Lin. Undrafted out of Harvard, he played a bit part for the Golden State Warriors his rookie year and was waived after one season before squeezing onto the New York Knicks' roster as a third-string point guard. Lin rode the bench early in the season, but his team had underperformed and lost several key players to injuries. Running out of options, Coach Mike D'Antoni took a chance on Lin in a game against the New Jersey Nets. Lin shocked the building as he exploded for twenty-five points and seven assists, outplaying all-star point guard Deron Williams and leading the Knicks to a much-needed win.

It is not uncommon for role players like Lin to come up big for one game and then fade back into obscurity. But that's not what Lin did. He started the next game against the Utah Jazz, turning in twenty-eight points and eight assists. And he did not stop. In his first five starts as an NBA player, Lin averaged more than twenty-seven points per game, including a thirty-eight-point barrage against the Lakers and a winning buzzer-beater against the Raptors, all of which carried the Knicks to a mid-season, seven-game winning streak.

New York (and much of the country) quickly developed a fanatical interest in Lin's story. He was front-page news in many major newspapers for weeks. TV ratings soared during Knicks games, and although he is Asian-American (born and raised in California), he became an international superstar to millions of basketball fans in the Far East. The phenomenon, dubbed "Linsanity," would eventually die down (Lin went out with a knee injury that March), but not before his extraordinary play rekindled New Yorkers' love of the Knicks and inspired underdogs the world over.

Every now and then, good things just come out of nowhere. It can happen in your life too, and chances are at least one of those unexpected gifts will involve money. The news might not make it onto CNN, but it could certainly be a big deal for your financial future—that is, if you manage your newfound funds appropriately. Whether it's a big bonus or a raise at work, an inheritance or an investment that goes through the roof, don't fritter it away. Put it to work to put yourself a step closer to financial independence. Here are some realistic scenarios involving a mound of money dropping into your lap and some advice on how to handle it.

- *Family Inheritance.* Coming into a large sum of money or assets that could be worth a lot can be a bittersweet occasion since it often follows the death of a family member. That and the financial and legal complexities that come along with a big inheritance can be a pain in the neck. Without careful planning, the money could disappear as quickly as it arrived.

  Before you start making big plans for the windfall, take some time to heal. If your benefactor was a parent or close relative, the strong emotions surrounding the inheritance could lead you to make choices you will later regret. When you're ready, meet with a tax accountant, an attorney, and/or a financial planner (one might refer you to the other). These professionals can help you minimize what you will pay to the IRS, get past any legal hurdles regarding your loved one's estate, and start planning to make meaningful use of the money.

  The fact that your loved ones left behind a nice inheritance says something about their financial planning skills, so a good way to honor their memory would be to make your own family's financial security a top priority. When you have the money in hand, consider paying off debts, shoring up your emergency fund, addressing any shortfalls in insurance coverage, or making a hefty contribution to your retirement fund or the kids' college savings.

Even when your plan for the future is in good shape, don't make the mistake of using what is left as mad money. Working with your advisor to invest the funds strategically can allow you to have some fun today while preserving the balance to last through the years and potentially enable all sorts of other financial goals.

- *Performance Bonus.* If it's been a banner year at work, a fat bonus check might not come as a surprise for those in corporate management. But it's still a windfall that, like an inheritance, could provide a great opportunity to knock out some financial concerns in one fell swoop.

  The same thought process should apply even if it's on a smaller scale. With a $10,000 bonus, for example, a good plan might be to put a third toward debt reduction, a third toward retirement, and treat yourself or someone else with the rest, not forgetting that taxes will lop a good chunk off the top. Making a substantial contribution to an employer-sponsored retirement plan like a 401(k) might be as easy as doing nothing since in many cases it will come out of your bonus check automatically. But if you have other plans for that cash, be sure to opt out of the 401(k) contribution for that pay period.

- *Pay Raises.* A substantial increase in your salary also presents financial opportunities, but making good use of a larger monthly paycheck is a different ballgame than dealing with a lump sum of many thousands. Even with a substantial pay increase, it's extremely easy for your lifestyle to absorb those extra funds. A nice lunch here, theater tickets there—before you know it, your spending routines have crept up unnoticed, and you've come to count on that pocket money.

Sure, you deserve to celebrate little victories like a raise. Life is too short not to. Just be careful that your raise doesn't disappear into thin air, leaving you wondering where it went. The best way to keep that from happening is to act immediately—as soon as the raise takes effect—to increase your investment contributions or fund other financial goals.

- *Investment Gains.* In a well-diversified investment portfolio, you are more likely to experience slow and steady gains than you are to hit the jackpot on a single asset. But big, quick run-ups can and do occur. This is especially true if you own individual stocks. If one of those companies introduces a revolutionary new product (think the Apple iPhone for instance), you could see your investment value skyrocket, which would provide you an opportunity to sell for a robust profit. Real estate assets might also appreciate considerably over the course of a year if, for example, an oil and gas company discovers a rich reserve under land that you own.

    I do not advocate speculating on investments that you hope might be big winners. But sometimes things just work out that way. In a case like this, the tax ramifications of selling should be your top consideration. If you have owned a stock for less than a year, for example, your sale will be subject to short-term capital gains taxes that could dampen your takeaway severely. And real estate sales could be subject to a litany of tax consequences depending on how long you have owned the property and what it was used for. Make these selling decisions carefully with the help of a tax accountant.

    If you choose not to sell your star investment, perhaps waiting to see how high it will go, consult your financial planner to find out how the added value in one asset class affects the overall asset allocation in your portfolio. A huge gain on one volatile stock, for instance, could create a risky imbalance that could be corrected by moving some of that money into more stable investments.

- *Found Money.* The next best thing to suddenly inheriting a large sum of money might be the realization that you already have more than enough. In other words, you might have saved for years for some specific financial goal only to find out later that you don't need quite as much. Sound improbable? Here's a real-life example.

When I was in my twenties, I was certain I would want to retire by age fifty-five, which seemed eons away at the time. By following many of the approaches I'm sharing in this book, I'm happy to say that I put myself in a position to do just that. Ironically, the closer I got to fifty-five, the less I really wanted to retire. I truly enjoy what I do, and I earn a nice living doing it. So I decided to stick around for a while, and in doing so, I opened up my financial options. I could keep saving toward an even nicer retirement, give more to charity, or dive into another personal interest. It was like a breath of fresh air to realize I had met a huge, lifelong financial goal before I even needed to.

OK, so maybe loving your career enough to keep working into your retirement years is not your thing. Have kids? If so, here's another possibility. Suppose you have been building a college savings fund for your daughter since she was wearing diapers. Then, during her senior year in high school, she earns a full scholarship to a top-notch university. You might as well have pulled up a couch cushion and found $50,000 (or however much) just lying there.

Such opportunities are not as rare as you might think. If good fortune rolls your way, think long and hard about what you will do with that money.

• *Low Interest Rates.* Admittedly, "low interest rates" does not sound as exciting as a five-figure bonus check. But consider this: Over the course of many years, low rates could put even more money in your pocket. How? Refinance your home.

Suppose you bought a house with a $250,000 mortgage at a 6 percent interest rate over thirty years. Under these terms, the monthly payment would be about $1,500. After thirty years, you will have paid almost $540,000 for the house (about $290,000 in interest alone). Let's say after you've owned the home for five years, you notice that interest rates have dropped quite a bit, so you decide to refinance. With your good credit, you're able to refinance the remaining principal on the loan ($232,000) at a new interest rate of 3.5 percent for thirty years.

Your monthly mortgage payment would drop to just over $1,000, and you would reduce your total interest paid by about $70,000 over the life of the loan. The refinance would knock $500 off your monthly expenses, enough to give your investment portfolio a potent shot in the arm or bring some other big financial goal within reach—all this for the few hours of paperwork it took to refinance.

Alternatively, you could opt for a slightly higher mortgage payment and reduce the loan term from thirty years to twenty or even fifteen—a move that would pay off later when you own your home outright at an early age.

This is a realistic example of the opportunities homeowners have seen in recent years (2010–2013) as mortgage rates have hovered at historically low levels. However, the decision to refinance is not always a no-brainer. It becomes less attractive as rates rise, and there are closing costs to consider. Nevertheless, it's worth comparing your current interest rate to what's currently available.

There are no limits to the things that can go wrong in our financial lives, a reality that hit home for countless millions during the recent recession. But it's uplifting to remember that good surprises, like the scenarios just mentioned, can help to balance out the bad.

I didn't include them in this book so you would count on them happening to you. They might not. It's best to plan for the worst and be pleasantly surprised when a windfall comes your way. Even so, potential windfalls are worth thinking about because, if and when your lucky day comes, a judicious reaction can do wonders for your financial fortunes while imprudence can amount to a golden opportunity wasted.

MAINTAINING THE MOMENTUM

If given the choice, any basketball team would opt to end the first half of a game with the lead. Ideally, it would be sitting pretty with a double-digit lead. If that describes your financial position as you approach middle age, then my hat is off to you, though it's not time to let your guard down. Overconfidence has been to blame for many late-game collapses.

Perhaps you got off to a slow start toward your financial goals, but you have managed to put a solid plan in place and make encouraging progress in recent years. In that case, you're exiting the first half with something almost more valuable than being ahead. You have the momentum, that intangible energy that headstrong teams use to take back the lead and surge ahead. Your mission as you enter the second half is to keep that momentum rolling.

Even if you've struggled mightily early in your life, piling financial mistakes on top of misfortune, don't give up hope. An experienced coach would remind you there is still a lot of game left to be played. And with the right mix of grit and focus, you too can emerge victorious.

We'll discuss the possibilities as we head back into the locker room for a halftime strategy session.

CHAPTER-ENDING THREE-POINTER

1. Identify previous financial setbacks and/or potential roadblocks in your personal or job situation.
2. Think about possible unexpected financial events that might help your family reach your goals.
3. List current economic or financial conditions that are beneficial to attaining financial objectives.

HALFTIME

CHAPTER SEVEN

HALFTIME ADJUSTMENTS

A Mid-Life Reassessment of Financial Needs and Goals

PEACH BASKET PARABLES: LOUISVILLE VS. UCLA, 1980 NCAA CHAMPIONSHIP GAME

Before the Houston Cougars brought us Phi Slama Jama, the Louisville Cardinals were the Doctors of Dunk. The 1979–1980 Louisville team was led by the high-flying Darrell Griffith, who went by the name of, what else? Dr. Dunkenstein.

Griffith was heavily recruited in high school by top basketball colleges all over the country, but he chose to stay in his hometown of Louisville. At the time, he promised local fans that he would bring them an NCAA championship. It took him until his senior year, but the Doctor delivered.

In helping Louisville win its first national title, Griffith played a role in cementing the great basketball tradition that coach Denny Crum had started back in 1971. Louisville had been to the Final Four once prior to Crum's arrival in 1959, but it was Crum who came along and built Louisville into a perennial powerhouse. In thirty seasons coaching the Cardinals, Crum amassed 675 victories at a winning percentage of nearly 70 percent, making him a beloved basketball icon in Kentucky and across the nation.

It might come as no surprise that Crum cut his teeth under the tutelage of another basketball legend, UCLA's John Wooden. Crum played at UCLA his final two seasons in college and later served in assistant coaching roles under Wooden for another eight years. He was part of three championship teams with the Bruins.

By the time he was hired for the head job at Louisville in 1971, Crum was no stranger to the NCAA's biggest stage. He proved it when, in his first season, he led the Cardinals to the Final Four. Which team knocked them out? UCLA, of course. The next time Louisville made it to the Final Four was in 1975. And again, the Cardinals bowed to the Wizard of Westwood and his unbeatable Bruins. It seemed Crum's mentor was becoming his nemesis.

THIRD TIME IS THE CHARM

In that 1979–1980 season, when Crum's Doctors of Dunk were leaping over every opponent in their path, Louisville got yet another shot at UCLA. This time, it was the Cardinals' first trip to the NCAA Championship game. And this time, they were the favorites.

Number two seed Louisville was heading into the game with a 32-3 record and hoping to cap off its stellar season with the only trophy it had yet to win. UCLA, on the other hand, was no longer the monster it once was. The Bruins had been lucky to get an eighth seed in the tournament after a mediocre (for them) 22–10 season. Wooden had retired after his last win in 1975, and UCLA was now helmed by the journeyman Larry Brown.

The Bruins might have been the underdogs that year, but they did not play that way. They matched the Cardinals blow for blow in the first half, forcing poor shots and careless turnovers. UCLA surged to finish the half up by two points. It seemed the basketball gods had cast a cruel curse upon Crum, and he would never defeat his alma mater.

A WELL-TIMED WAKE-UP CALL

Crum, whose normally calm and collected demeanor earned him the nickname Cool Hand Luke, was anything but cool in the locker room. He chose the right moment to explode, berating his players like an angry drill sergeant and going so far as to call them chokers.

Whether it was a shrewd psychological ploy or simply a case of overwhelming frustration, only Crum knows. But he later admitted that the halftime chew-out had been so uncharacteristic for him that he felt the need to apologize to his players. Nevertheless, the speech achieved the attitude adjustment Crum was looking for. The Cardinals woke up in the second half, playing with greater focus and urgency.

Still, UCLA gave Louisville all it could handle, and the Bruins led by four with four minutes to play. That's when Louisville's superior talent and conditioning finally won out. They scored the last nine points of the game, including an eighteen-footer from Griffith to reclaim the lead once and for all. Dr. Dunkenstein's twenty-three points earned him the Most Outstanding Player award, and Crum finally shook the Bruins off his back.

COLOR COMMENTARY

- Louisville's Doctors of Dunk are often credited with popularizing one of the most common celebrations in all of sports, the high-five.
- One of the Cardinals' most frequent high-fivers was forward Wiley Brown. Ironically, Brown had only four fingers on his right hand as his thumb had been amputated at age four. He wore a prosthetic thumb developed by his doctors, but on the day of the championship game, the thumb went missing. Brown realized he had left it on the breakfast table at the hotel, and a team assistant was able to fish the thumb out of the garbage in time for the game.
- In 2013, Louisville overcame another player's physical ailment en route to its third NCAA championship. Backup guard Kevin Ware suffered a gruesome compound fracture of his leg during the Cardinals' Elite Eight victory over Duke. While Ware watched from the sideline, his team played brilliantly in his honor to take down Wichita State and Michigan for the title as Coach Rick Pitino became the only NCAA coach to win championships with two different schools.

Finding Your Second Wind

Every team needs a pep talk at halftime, especially when an important game is on the line. For a team that's playing well, it could be a mid-game reminder to keep up the good work. Or, as in Louisville's case, the pep talk could be more of a tongue lashing to "stop lollygagging and get your head in the game."

At halftime, a coach's words tend to sink in deeper than they do during the pregame meeting. That's because now it is no longer about scouting and practicing. The situation has become real. The team has experienced its opponent in the flesh. All of the players' drilling and conditioning has been put into play, and only now do they truly understand what they're up against. At intermission, the slate is no longer clean. And the end is in sight.

Unlike basketball, life has no set midpoint defined by a time period. Who knows how long you will live? For most of us, however, there does come a time when we feel we have reached a turning point, a new beginning where there is an opportunity to refresh as well as reflect on our accomplishments, take stock of new challenges, and make or accept significant changes in our lives.

For many people, that turning point comes around the time their kids are leaving high school or transitioning from college to the working world. That in itself can be a major social and financial change for families, but it often coincides with other personal revelations. For example, in those years when your kids are turning into grownups, you're probably hitting middle age and your parents are growing elderly.

When you were in your twenties and thirties, these days seemed far away. But time tends to slip by. Whether suddenly or gradually, you realize the game will not go on forever. The first half is over, and it's time to think carefully about how you're going to see your way through to ultimate victory, however you define it. Take it slowly and protect your lead? Or claw your way back into a game you're losing?

Like a basketball team at halftime, you now have the benefit of clarity. All those financial assumptions you were forced to make in your earlier years—about your needs for retirement, college savings, etc.—are now in plain sight. You can adjust your game plan, this time with much more certainty and confidence than you have ever had before.

In this chapter we'll discuss some of the key financial concepts and strategies worth considering as you regroup, renew your focus and motivation, and lead your team into the second half.

CONDUCT A MID-LIFE MONEY CHECKUP

Before you can make changes in your game plan, of course, you have to take stock of what has happened so far and where you stand today. What has gone right and what has gone wrong? Perhaps, more importantly, what are the reasons for your results?

In basketball, you might be ahead at halftime, but is it truly because of your own great performance or simply because the other team was ice cold? If you're trailing, is it because of a flawed game plan or poor execution on your part, or did the ball just not bounce your way? When you can answer these questions honestly, you can decide if (and how much) your game plan needs to change and what your goals for the second half should be.

The trouble is it's often difficult to step back and self-analyze when you're embroiled in the action of the game. Even subconsciously, you might convince yourself what feels comfortable is fine when the cold, hard truth might be something quite different.

When it comes to reviewing your financial progress, I strongly suggest you work with a professional financial planner who can view your situation with complete objectivity. Together you should conduct a head-to-toe checkup of the many factors that contribute to your financial well-being and your plans for the future. These and other questions are important to address.

- Am I saving enough to meet my retirement goals?
- Where is my money invested, and how have these accounts performed over the years?
- Do I have sufficient savings for emergencies or other short-term needs?
- How much debt (and what types) am I carrying?

- Is my cash flow situation sustainable given my savings goals, expenses, and liabilities?
- How much money do I make, and how do I expect that to change in the next decade?
- Am I adequately covered by the right types of insurance? If so, do I have too much?

Once you have a firm grip on the state of your financial health (whether you're ahead or behind and why), you can go about redefining your goals and your approach to the next phase of your life. The following sections discuss some specific and common halftime changes that could have a place in your retuned game plan.

Shed Financial Baggage: Changes to Consider

Seeing a child off to college for the first time can be a proud and tearful moment. At the same time, some parents are also giddy with the excitement of having the house to themselves, perhaps converting their kid's bedroom into a home theater or a personal gym.

At this midpoint in your life, there's a similar opportunity to clean house and make over your finances. Upon thorough review of your investments and obligations, you might find that certain expenses you've gotten used to paying are no longer necessary. And you will almost surely uncover ways to de-clutter your personal balance sheet and put a new shine on your financial plan as you head toward retirement. Here are a few possibilities.

- *Stop Saving for College.* If your child is headed off to school with a fat 529 account or other savings plan in place, it's time to ask whether you've done enough. Some parents continue to sock away college funds even after Junior's freshman year just in case he wants to get a master's or go to law school. But such generosity can backfire if the account is significantly overfunded. Any leftover money in a 529 account can be held over for future educational expenses or transferred to another recipient (often your next child in line for college), but withdrawing it outright for non-educational expenses would cost you a 10 percent penalty on the earnings plus income taxes. If you're facing the possibility of oversaving for college, consider whether those funds could do more good in another part of your financial plan.

- *Cut Back on Life Insurance.* Watching your kids become financially self-sufficient is gratifying not just because you're proud of them, but also because you're off the hook for supporting them. If they have a good job and a bright future, you know they would get by if you were no longer around. Once you reach that level of confidence in your own children, it might be time to scale back on life insurance. If you're unmarried or have a high-earning spouse, you might no longer need life insurance at all. Keep in mind, however, that life insurance might still serve a strategic role in your estate plan.

- *Decrease Disability Insurance.* The thought process used to decrease life insurance coverage applies here as well. When the kids can take care of themselves, you probably don't need as much protection as you had when they counted on your income to support them. Unlike life insurance, however, you might still need the money that disability insurance will provide if you're unable to work because of illness or injury. Plus, your likelihood of incurring a life-altering disease like cancer goes up with every new gray hair. While spending less on disability coverage (for which you would receive a lower payout) might be an option, I would recommend against canceling the policy altogether unless you have the financial wherewithal to both retire comfortably and cover major medical expenses.

- *Sell Bad Investments.* Some people tend to hold on to losing or stagnant investments for years without a good reason. Maybe it's wishful thinking that the dog will finally have its day. Or it's a case of portfolio neglect and lame investments have been forgotten like junk in the back of the closet. A thorough mid-life review of your portfolio could be just the time to clean house. Taking a loss on an underperforming stock or fund could produce a nice deduction on your next tax return. But even if you would be selling at a net gain, consider whether the proceeds could be put into an investment that would grow faster for the same level of risk or less.

- *Pay Off Debts.* As we've discussed, lingering credit card debt or other high-interest obligations can put a severe drag on your financial progress in other areas. The last thing you want is to lug those chains into retirement, a time when you might be watching your pennies even closer than before. The money you save by reducing college savings contributions or insurance payments could help you attack your debts and coast into retirement light on your feet. Don't forget auto loans or financing on home furnishings and other purchases. These also count as bad debts that are best paid off as soon as possible.

- *Accelerate Mortgage Payments.* While carrying a mortgage offers the benefit of tax-deductible interest, owning your home free and clear can be a great source of relief as you creep toward retirement. Whether it makes sense to make extra payments and pay off your mortgage early depends on several factors: how high your current interest rate is, how much you need the current tax deduction, and what kind of investment returns you're expecting in your retirement fund. If your mortgage interest rate is more than you would expect to earn on your investments, paying off your house early could be the right move. Plus, there is the intangible emotional benefit of living debt free that appeals to just about everyone.

Those are just a few examples of how your halftime financial analysis could present opportunities to inject new energy into your second-half effort. Of course, you can count on the opposition to come back strong as well, so it's important to think two steps ahead and plan your counterattack now. We'll talk about that next.

ANTICIPATE EMERGING CHALLENGES

A good basketball coach makes adjustments in his own game plan to correct the mistakes of the first half. But a great coach also anticipates changes the other team will make and directs his team accordingly.

Share Your Game Plan

When a head coach gets ejected from the game, he needs to know his assistants can take over and lead the team. Similarly, your loved ones need to be in tune with your financial plan in case you are suddenly not around. Your halftime financial checkup is a good time to make sure your spouse (and perhaps your grown kids) are aware of the major components of your plan.

Let them know where to find important paperwork such as estate planning documents, insurance policies, and investment account statements, or show them how to access the information online. Discuss the purpose of each account and how much you contribute each month. Share important phone numbers and passwords. And make it clear what your spouse and kids should do with this information if they find themselves in charge.

If you are the one who is uninformed, ask your spouse to bring you into the loop. Make a list of questions, write down or type up the answers, and keep them somewhere you know you will remember.

In real life, there is no one in the opposite locker room plotting against your financial success, but there will certainly be new challenges that arise to take the place of old ones. No matter how old you are or how much financial stability you have built, there is always something threatening to pull the rug out from under you. In your forties or fifties, you would be wise to look out for these slippery slopes and think about whether you will be prepared to handle them.

- *Boomerang Kids.* As your child donned the college cap and gown, you said a silent, "Thank goodness." It's time for her to get a professional office job somewhere while you kick back and enjoy the newfound wealth of an empty-nester. Not so fast. These days, it's entirely common for graduates to turn right back around and move in with Mom and Dad. In tough economic times when unemployment rates are high, young job seekers might have an incredibly hard time breaking into their chosen career fields, rendering their university degrees next-to-worthless until more jobs open up. Other graduates decide that an advanced degree is their only ticket to the good life. Either way, they need a place to stay while they sort things out, and the weeks can stretch into years.

As a loving parent, you probably are inclined to help. But think carefully about whether you're really supporting your kids' causes or simply prolonging their immaturity. Do not let your parental instincts blind you to the fact that you've got an adult freeloader in the house who is quite likely siphoning off your financial resources and delaying your retirement. If you do take your kids in, consider charging them for rent, groceries, utilities, or other expenses they can cover with a part-time job—the rest of the time should be spent looking for a career in their field. To give them a push in the right direction, try helping with things such as training courses that will pay off later or a sensible vehicle they will need in order to go on job interviews. But be sure to set limits on how much and how long you're willing to continue supporting your kids. The faster you can get them on their feet and out on their own, the better off your financial prospects will be.

- *Aging Parents.* Your parents supported you when you were young. But it's usually not until later in life when it dawns on you that you might have to return the favor. A 2011 study by MetLife found that a quarter of all adult children in America provide some type of personal care or financial assistance to their elderly parents. And you thought you were free of dependents when your kids finally moved out!

Protect Your Parents from Predators

Some people will do anything to make a buck. That includes dodgy pitchmen who prey on the elderly by offering unsuitable financial products. Well-to-do old folks make attractive targets; they have money to invest but might have lost the critical eye they once possessed.

The bait could range from dubious high-return investment plans or annuities with excessive commissions to outright scams selling fraudulent securities.

If you think your parents could be at risk, you can help by offering to review their financial statements, checking up on any unfamiliar companies (start with the Better Business Bureau), and blocking telemarketers by adding your parents' phone number to the National Do Not Call Registry.

In all earnestness, caring for an elderly parent can be one of life's greatest callings. It can also demand some significant sacrifices whether it's from your personal time, your bank account, or both. If you're unprepared for that eventuality, your financial goals could pay the price.

For most adult children, there comes a time when (maybe suddenly, maybe gradually) they come to the uncomfortable realization that their parents have gotten old. When that day comes for you, add several important items to your to-do list. First, find out what types of financial arrangements your parents have in place (retirement funds, long-term care insurance, estate planning, etc.) to support themselves and to hand down their assets prudently. This is not always an easy conversation to have, especially if your parents consider it none of your business. You do not necessarily have to have a formal meeting. You can work it into casual conversation by asking how you can be prepared to help them in an emergency. Where do they keep their financial accounts and insurance policies, and would you have the ability to work with those institutions if something happened? You might even broach the subject by asking for advice on how to handle your own finances.

Better Health Equals Greater Wealth

I am not an expert on diet and exercise, but I can tell you that living a healthier lifestyle can have a major positive impact on your financial well-being. This is especially true as you pass middle age and become more susceptible to injuries and diseases. Clearly, the cost of healthcare is one of our nation's most pressing concerns. So preserving our good health also saves money and lots of it. Avoiding just one surgery or ongoing treatment plan could keep tens of thousands of dollars in the bank. A Cambridge University study found that people can add fourteen years to their lives, on average, by doing these four things regularly:

- Not smoking
- Exercising daily
- Drinking in moderation
- Eating plenty of fruits and vegetables

Once you have a general idea of your parents' financial health, think carefully about whether you will need to pitch in for their care some day. That might mean helping with medical bills, paying for an assisted living facility, or taking one or both of your parents under your roof. The potential impact on your financial assets could be profound, especially if you're a member of the so-called sandwich generation, which must provide for parents and children at the same time. If you see yourself playing this role in the future, it is best to start earmarking that money now.

Finally, if you have siblings, you will need to discuss with them how to share the responsibility of caring for your parents. Perhaps you have always been the responsible one who has seen the most financial success, but does that mean your less-prosperous siblings should be excused from carrying their weight? On the other hand, will they resent you if you volunteer to foot the full bill? These are sensitive issues that, if not handled with great care, can tear families apart.

- *Your Own Vulnerability.* Your parents may be the elderly ones, but let's face it—you're not getting any younger either. And, if you're like most people in their forties and fifties, you can feel the spry and flexible days of your youth slipping away (if they're not already long gone). You might still feel healthy as a horse, but chances are good that at some point in the future—be it fifteen or thirty years from now—you will require the services of an assisted living facility, nursing home, or hospice care.

Now is the time to start seriously considering long-term care insurance, which we discussed earlier, as a means to cover yourself against the potentially astronomical costs of long-term care. Though there is the risk of never needing it (as with any insurance), locking in relatively affordable rates while you're still in good health can help you maintain the coverage through your retirement. If you wait much beyond sixty, the premiums will be sky-high if you qualify for coverage at all.

At this point, let's say you've given your financial game plan a good halftime assessment, purging unnecessary expenses that might be dragging you down, freeing up cash, and thinking ahead to the foreseeable challenges of the future. With all of these factors at the surface, you're in the right frame of mind to start thinking more seriously about the biggest goal of all—retirement—and what it's going to take to get there.

GIVE RETIREMENT A CLOSER LOOK

At the beginning of the basketball season, a talented team might have championship dreams, but it dares not look that far ahead. It knows that if it consistently works hard and wins one game at a time, the tournament awaits at the end. Until then, it tries not to clutter its focus with visions of cutting down nets.

Duke's Coach Krzyzewski had a ploy he used at least once with his players to get them focused on the games at hand and to discard thoughts of games just left behind.

In 2005–06, the Blue Devils finished the regular season 27–3 and won the Atlantic Coast Conference title to go along with a number three ranking, but all was not well. Duke had suffered back-to-back losses to Florida State and North Carolina late in the season, and Coach K reasoned that his players had been too distracted. They were losing focus with the postseason about to begin, and he needed to get the Blue Devils back on track.

Krzyzewski got his team off campus to a banquet room at a nearby hotel for a relaxed team meal, after which he showed the tape of the loss to North Carolina. He conducted a thorough analysis of the game using a chalkboard to draw two columns, one for the game's good plays and the other for the bad plays. "The motivation behind this was that we wanted to get a really good look at who we were as a team at that particular time," Krzyzewski writes in *Beyond Basketball*.

Once the game analysis was done, Krzyzewski had his team managers bring out two large cardboard boxes, one labeled "Preseason NIT" and the other "Regular Season." He then instructed his team to fill the boxes with everything representative of what had occurred so far that season, including tapes of the games, team and individual trophies, scouting reports, and each player's written list of memories and frustrations from the season sealed in envelopes. The boxes were then closed and Coach K declared that the team was now 0–0, its regular season a thing of the past. He said it was time for a fresh start.

"At the end of our season," Krzyzewski told his team, we will open these boxes, return your envelopes to each of you, and collectively remember and recognize all that we have done together. But for right now, it is on to the next play."

Keeping an uncluttered mind was probably a way of life during most of your young adult years, knowing that the possibility of a happy retirement awaited you somewhere far, far down the road. It seemed silly to make specific plans with so many years left between you and a life of perpetual leisure. Your approach to retirement planning was pretty straightforward: save, save, save so that one day you would have the good problem of figuring out what to do with all that money.

Well, Father Time has done what he does best. What was once a fuzzy little dot in the distance has grown so close and so clear that you can almost reach out and touch it. You might still have ten to fifteen years left until retirement, and you're probably far from finished building your nest egg. But be warned: the time will fly by like Dr. Dunkenstein on his way to a thunderous jam. Now is the time to start turning those hazy visions of retirement into lucid, strategic plans. What follows is a handful of important questions to contemplate. The answers are interdependent, meaning your conclusions in one area will likely affect all of the others.

WHEN DO YOU WANT TO RETIRE?

A financial planner might have asked you this question many years ago, and you probably pulled a "why not" number out of thin air. Maybe it was sixty-five if you were going with conventional projections or fifty-five if you were feeling especially self-confident that day. But even if you put some serious thought into it at that time, setting what you thought were reasonable and attainable goals, those goals need to be refined now that retirement is actually creeping onto your radar screen.

For a growing majority of investors, retiring completely (with no income-producing job) before the age of sixty is not realistic. People are living longer as medical technology improves. Federal budget issues are putting entitlements such as Social Security and Medicare at risk. A struggling economy has robbed the nest eggs of many investors and put the kibosh on raises and bonuses at work. In other words, retiring early—and staying retired—is harder than it used to be. It's going to require either substantial wealth or living on a shoestring budget through your golden years.

Working a bit longer might not be so bad. For most professionals, the forties and fifties are peak earning years. Staying on board in the workforce provides an opportunity to bolster your retirement fund with bigger contributions (especially if you have jettisoned some expenses that are no longer necessary, as we discussed earlier). Also, if your employer offers a pension, make sure you understand how your years of service will affect your payout. If a few more years on the job will give you a larger guaranteed income stream through retirement, it's probably worth sticking around for.

An increasingly popular alternative to full retirement is a phased or transitional approach in which you gradually taper off your workload. Many professionals make a move from full-time work to a consultant-type role in which they're able to continue using their career knowledge and skills to earn an income while enjoying a more flexible lifestyle.

Your qualified retirement accounts and when you are able to access them should also factor into your timing. If you're planning to retire before age fifty-nine-and-a-half, for instance, make sure you'll be able to do it without incurring early withdrawal penalties from your IRA or employer-sponsored plan. (There are ways to access the funds penalty-free, discussed in more detail in chapter 8.) Ideally, you would have another source of funds to tide you over until then.

Finally, Social Security should also play a role in your decision. You can begin taking payouts as early as age sixty-two although the benefit amount will be reduced. If you wait until what the Social Security Administration calls your "full retirement age" (between sixty-five and sixty-seven, depending on when you were born), you'll get a larger monthly benefit, presumably because you'll receive it for fewer years. You can estimate various payout scenarios at the US Social Security Administration website, www.ssa.gov.

WHAT DO YOU WANT TO DO?

So much about financial planning for retirement revolves around how you want to live the rest of your life. After all, figuring out how much money you're going to need depends on what you're going to buy.

When you were twenty-seven and made your first contribution to your 401(k), you might have been a sun-worshipper envisioning your retirement in a beachside bungalow. But over the years, you developed a love of fine art, and now your wish list includes traveling through Europe to build your personal collection. Maybe your idea of paradise is a golf course in Hawaii, a snowy ski chalet in Vail, or a simple suburban home where you can watch your grandkids grow up. Perhaps you'll turn your favorite hobby into a small business or launch a charitable organization. Maybe it's a combination of all these things.

No two definitions of retirement are exactly the same, so no one can tell you exactly how much you need to save. However, you probably have

---

Can You Count on Social Security and Medicare?

For decades, retirees have looked forward to the day they could claim a monthly paycheck from Social Security and get affordable healthcare insurance through Medicare. After all, they were entitled to these services as American taxpayers. But as high unemployment rates and a wave of aging baby boomers puts unprecedented strain on these programs, it becomes less likely that retirees of the future will get their due.

In 2012, the Social Security Administration reported that its trust fund will run dry by 2033 because it is paying out so much more than it is collecting in tax revenue. Medicare is also on the rocks—it expects to scrape the bottom by 2024. At that point, the government will be able to pay only a portion of promised benefits, depending on how many tax dollars it takes in at the time.

What does it all mean? If you are in your sixties as of 2013 (the time of this writing), you probably will get most of what you've been promised. But if you're still twenty years or more from retirement, plan to get by without 100 percent of your Social Security and Medicare benefits. If the government somehow fixes the problem, you'll be in for a nice surprise.

a much clearer idea of your wants and needs now than you did when you first started saving. You can look closely at your current expenses and make realistic estimates of how they will change if you pursue your ideal retirement scenario.

You can start writing things down and crunching the numbers. Will you move or build a new home upon retiring? How much is the cost of living in that new location? Where do you want to travel, and how high-end will you go? Will you work some in retirement or live a life of leisure instead? Do you want to leave a substantial inheritance to your kids, or is it enough to give them whatever is left?

These questions and others can help you make calculations that are much more concrete than the guesses you made years ago. Even as you near retirement, your answers are not set in stone, but the shifting sands of possibility are becoming more like moldable clay.

Are You Saving Enough?

As decisions about when and how you want to retire come into greater focus, so does an understanding of your financial capacity to meet those goals. While you will never be 100 percent sure about how much money you need, you have to give yourself a target to shoot for.

One way to come up with that big number is to compare your life in retirement to your life today. Say your annual household income today is $100,000. Use that as a benchmark. If you want to continue living a similar lifestyle after you stop working, you'll need roughly $100,000 per year to do it. Now let's assume you'll live for another thirty years after you retire. Does that mean you need to have $3 million (30 x $100,000) in the bank at the time you retire? No.

Remember—just because you'll quit your job someday doesn't mean your investing career will come screeching to a halt. Even if you stop contributing to your accounts when you retire, you can still expect to receive at least a modest return on the assets you've invested. That investment return provides you with income during retirement.

For example, a $1.5 million nest egg earning a conservative 4 percent per year would supply you with an income of $60,000 per year. Add to that amount whatever you expect to receive from Social Security. In this example, that could be around $25,000 per year, giving you a total annual income of $85,000 before you ever withdraw a dime from your principal amount.

Of course, there are other variables at work—inflation, taxes, etc.—that make these calculations more complex. That's why I recommend working with a financial planner or at least running the numbers through a comprehensive retirement calculator.

With a better handle on what you'll need to retire in ten to fifteen years, you can start fine-tuning your investment portfolio today and decide whether you need to ramp up your contributions. If you're running up against a serious shortfall, there are ways to play catch-up, a topic we'll cover in the next chapter.

ARE YOUR ASSETS IN THE RIGHT PLACES?

Knowing how much you need to save for retirement tells you more about how your current portfolio should be structured. Have you already met your goal? You have the luxury of playing it safe and focusing on defense. Need to make up ground? A more aggressive offensive approach might be in order.

In every stage of the game, the types of investments you own in your retirement fund and other accounts determine how quickly your money can grow and how much risk you are taking in pursuit of that growth. For a reminder on the basics of asset allocation, I would suggest reviewing the initial discussion of that topic in chapter 4.

With years of savings under your belt and retirement within reach, the stakes are higher than ever. You might be tempted to protect your hard-earned funds by making conservative bonds a larger piece of the pie, but be careful not to go too far. Even if you're in your early fifties, you probably still have a decade or more until full retirement—plenty of time to continue growing your wealth and pushing through any slumps in the stock market.

A common rule of thumb is that you should subtract your age from 120 to get the percentage of stocks you should have in your portfolio. If you're 55 years old, for example, 120 minus 55 equals a recommended allocation of 65 percent stocks. Though depending on your risk tolerance and goals, the big number could go as high as 130 or as low as 100.

Suffice it to say that in your early fifties, it's still too soon to eliminate all risk from your portfolio. You not only need growth to continue working toward your retirement goal but also to provide income and outpace inflation even after you're in retirement. As always, appropriate diversification is the key to achieving growth while keeping risk in check. So for a greater degree of protection on the equity side, you might lean toward stock funds that are traditionally more stable, such as large-cap domestic stocks. Meanwhile, higher-risk stocks such as small-cap domestics and international stocks might play a diminishing role in your portfolio.

Your financial planner might also help you with asset location—that is, organizing your investments across different types of accounts in order to minimize the tax consequences on your portfolio. For example, a common strategy is to use tax-deferred accounts (IRA, 401(k)) to house assets that trigger high taxes, such as income-producing bonds and high-dividend stocks. Meanwhile, more tax-efficient investments such as index funds would be held in taxable accounts outside of your qualified retirement plan. When executed correctly, this type of strategy can result in a more efficient portfolio with higher overall returns.

GET BACK OUT THERE

It's the championship game and halftime is almost over. This is the time when inspiration happens. The coach has finished drawing plays on the board and pointing out mistakes. He looks his players in the eyes and, with a solemn stare, he shows them his level of absolute commitment. He asks the same from them—to dig deep within themselves and find the heart of a champion, to play like it's the last game of their lives.

As you wave a final good-bye to your youth and soldier on toward retirement, you're probably acutely aware of the weight on your shoulders. How you perform financially in the next decade or two will have a tremendous and lasting impact on the rest of your life and the lives of your loved ones. The pressure to execute flawlessly can be overwhelming, especially if you're entering the second half in a hole. That's why the next chapter is devoted to further discussion about retirement planning and finding the will to pull off a spectacular come-from-behind victory.

CHAPTER-ENDING THREE-POINTER

1. If you're nearing your financial halftime, review any changes to your financial goals.
2. Review expenses, insurance, and savings plans that can be reduced or eliminated.
3. Be specific on your retirement age, necessary income, location, and activities.

THE SECOND HALF

CHAPTER EIGHT

PLAYING NOT TO LOSE IN RETIREMENT

Putting the Odds in Your Favor as You Make the Transition

PEACH BASKET PARABLES: THROUGH IT ALL, KENTUCKY KEEPS WINNING

In less time than it takes to play a college basketball game, you could drive from the University of Louisville to Lexington, Kentucky, home of the exalted Kentucky Wildcats. The former has had its share of NCAA glory, including most recently a 2013 NCAA Tournament championship, but the bright red Louisville Cardinals have often lived in the shadow of the team known throughout the Southeast as Big Blue.

Even set against the magnificent accomplishments of John Wooden's UCLA Bruins, Kentucky is by many measures the most dominant basketball program of all time. Going into the 2013–14 season, the Wildcats had the most wins (2,111) and the highest winning percentage (.762) of any college program in history. They have had an astounding fifty-seven seasons with twenty or more victories. They have appeared in the most NCAA Tournaments (fifty-two), won the most tournament games (111), and reached the Sweet Sixteen and Elite Eight more times than any other school. They have won eight NCAA titles, second only to UCLA's eleven.

Perhaps what is most impressive about Kentucky's supremacy is that it has been remarkably consistent over a span of nearly eighty years. Remember, ten of UCLA's championships came under Wooden in the course of only twelve seasons. By comparison, the Wildcats' eight championships have come in five different decades under the leadership of five different coaches.

How do they perform at such a high level year after year? Rival fans have their suspicions, but there's no denying that Kentucky's program has mastered the art of building (and rebuilding) winning ball clubs even as the game itself has changed.

REVERED AND REVILED

Kentucky's rise to greatness began with the man whose name now adorns the Wildcats' home arena, Adolph Rupp. The Baron of the Bluegrass coached Kentucky for an incredible forty-one seasons, from 1930–1972, winning more than 80 percent of his games and bringing home four NCAA championships.

Despite his winning legacy and the adoration of Kentucky fans, however, Rupp's reputation has been tarnished by allegations that he was an obsessive taskmaster and a bully. He was also on the wrong side of one of the seminal moments in basketball's history of racial tension. Rupp's all-white team lost the 1966 NCAA championship to Texas Western's group of five black starters. Understandably, the drama of the game was heightened by the fact that it occurred around the peak of the civil rights movement in America. The game's political impact is debatable, but it is widely recognized as a turning point in basketball when more Southern schools started actively recruiting black players.

Even Rupp eventually conceded, dressing Kentucky's first black player in 1970. Since then, and mostly since Rupp's departure, the Wildcats' program has evolved with the sport and has long been a top destination for the finest young athletes of any race. Incidentally, Kentucky's 2012 championship team started five black players.

Never Down for Long

Through the years, the legality and principles behind Kentucky's dominance have been called into question on multiple occasions. After being found guilty of several NCAA rule violations, Rupp's team sat out the entire 1952–1953 season. Amazingly, it returned the next season to go undefeated at 25–0 but skipped the NCAA Tournament out of protest when three of its players were declared ineligible.

Kentucky coaches who followed in Rupp's footsteps have had their own run-ins with NCAA administrators. Allegations of recruiting violations, payments to players, and other infringements tainted the terms of coaches Joe Hall in the seventies and Eddie Sutton in the eighties. As a result, the Wildcats were hit with various recruiting penalties and bans from postseason play. Yet they have always rebounded to championship form within a few short years.

Then there is the controversy surrounding the "one-and-done" phenomenon, referring to star high school players who attend college for only one year to satisfy NBA rules before going pro. Kentucky has drawn criticism for shamelessly recruiting one-and-done players. Indeed, three of Kentucky's freshman starters from the 2012 championship team declared for the NBA draft after only one season with the Wildcats. Rival fans called them hired guns and bemoaned the lack of team loyalty or commitment to education. Yet those complaints could be dismissed as sour grapes as Kentucky still manages to pull together winning teams from a fresh crop of starters every year.

The Greatest Comeback

Big Blue always seems to bounce back or stay on top; it seems the program is due for a dry spell or deserving of one.

Perhaps it's not a coincidence that, among all of its records, Kentucky also holds the record for mounting the biggest-ever comeback in an NCAA game. Under Coach Rick Pitino in 1994, the Wildcats were losing to Louisiana State by 16 at halftime. And that was before things got bad. Early in the second half, LSU went on an 18–0 run to increase its lead to 31 points with fifteen minutes left in the game.

It was a seemingly insurmountable deficit, but Kentucky somehow flipped a switch and turned a horrible blowout loss into an unforgettable performance the Wildcats scored 24 of the next 28 points, raining 3-pointers and capitalizing on LSU's complacency with steals and fast breaks. Miraculously, they clawed their way out of the cavernous hole, winning 99–95.

The Wildcats didn't go all the way that season. They were upset by Marquette in the second round of the NCAA Tournament. But it doesn't change the fact that the people at Kentucky have managed to forge a tradition of basketball excellence through generations. They simply know how to win under any circumstances.

COLOR COMMENTARY

- More evidence of the tightly knit basketball family tree: Adolph Rupp, Kentucky's winningest coach ever, played ball at Kansas under the legendary Phog Allen, who earlier was coached by James Naismith. Kentucky's current coach (as of 2013), John Calipari, also earned his stripes at Kansas as an assistant coach under Larry Brown.
- Adolph Rupp's 1966 team, the one that lost to Texas Western, was nicknamed Rupp's Runts because no player on the roster was taller than six-foot-five. That team's brightest star was Pat Riley, who later became one of the NBA's greatest coaches.
- Adolph Rupp died late at night on December 10, 1977. Just a few hours earlier, his beloved Kentucky Wildcats had defeated his alma mater, the Kansas Jayhawks.

CARRYING THE TORCH

In over a century of Kentucky basketball, Wildcats fans have just about seen it all: blowouts, nail-biters, glorious championships, and low-down dirty scandals. Through it all, the program has remained one of college basketball's most-revered and feared opponents. For decades, Kentucky's challenge has not been to build a competitive program. Rather, it has been to protect and add to its treasure trove of collective basketball wisdom. It's done it by learning from the successes and mistakes of the past and imbuing each year's team with the pride, work ethic, and sense of responsibility required to wear Kentucky blue.

People entering their retirement years can learn a thing or two from Kentucky. No, you Louisville fans, the lesson is not that cheaters actually can win. The lesson to be learned is that even those who make mistakes can achieve—or return to—greatness. While every generation and every individual faces unique challenges in retirement, it's important to learn from and take comfort in the fact that millions of retirees who came before found a way to make it work.

Kentucky has continued its winning ways despite the dramatic evolution of the game of basketball. You too can be successful even though your financial circumstances are probably much different than those of your parents and their parents.

In this chapter, we dig deeper into the topic of retirement planning, this time focusing more on your actual transition away from work. We discuss how you can mount a comeback win of your own even if you're still short of retirement funds. And we'll cover some important decisions you'll need to make to get your retirement off to a good start.

One side note before we move on: If you looked at the table of contents, you might have noticed that The Second Half section of the book is shorter than The First Half. This is intentional because most people spend about two-thirds of their lives preparing for retirement and one-third of their lives in retirement. By definition, two halves should be equal in size, but this book is an exception.

PLAYING CATCH-UP

If you're on the cusp of retirement, one of the big questions you're probably asking yourself is, "Do I have enough?" As we discussed in the last chapter, making a fair number of calculations will help you answer that question, but you might never be absolutely certain that what you have saved will carry you through another twenty or thirty years. If you're feeling insecure, it could be that you just haven't managed to contribute as much to your accounts as you once thought you could. Or maybe you were hit by a few years of bad investment returns just as retirement was coming into view. Either way, you may not be quite as confident about retiring as you would like to be.

In that case, it's time to kick your savings into high gear and fight to finish the game strong. Kentucky didn't pull off history's greatest comeback against LSU by being meek, did it?

If you're not already maxing out your contributions to your IRA and/or employer-sponsored retirement plan, do it now. You can save even beyond the annual limits of these plans by making what the IRS calls "catch-up contributions." Investors fifty years of age and older can make extra contributions of up to $5,500 per year in a 401(k), 403(b), and certain other employer plans. Similarly, if you're fifty-plus, you can add an extra $1,000 per year to your traditional IRA or Roth IRA (amounts are per 2013 tax laws). These bonus contributions might not make up your entire shortfall, but they should definitely be part of your comeback plan even if you only do it for a few years leading up to retirement.

Playing catch-up might only add ten to twenty thousand dollars to your nest egg ("I'll blow through that in a few months," you might say). But don't think of it that way. Remember, that extra principal can be invested to grow and provide you with additional income throughout retirement. Every little bit counts.

So how will you find the money to invest more when you have not even been saving enough to this point? My first piece of advice is the simplest: spend less. Earlier we discussed various ways to analyze your household spending, such as cutting back on everyday purchases and freeing up cash to invest. You might have gone through this process years ago, but little extravagances have a way of creeping back into your life. Crunch the numbers again.

Beyond that, we've already discussed shedding financial baggage such as bad investments and unnecessary insurance coverage. You might find some large chunks of cash that could be put to better use in your retirement portfolio.

You also could consider selling off some physical assets. Not that hawking knickknacks at a yard sale is going to put your retirement fund over the top, but chances are you're holding on to some big-ticket items that could provide a substantial boost if converted to cash. "Like what?" you ask. I'll give you a few examples: the diamond necklace you haven't worn in years, antiques cluttering your attic, the boat you took out once last year, the vacation home that's too far away, and the original artwork that hangs unappreciated in the guest bedroom.

Like any come-from-behind win, making up a retirement shortfall in a small amount of time might take extreme focus and personal sacrifice, but the rewards await you.

What to Do with Your Money at Retirement: Weighing the Options

When it finally comes time to bid adieu to the working world, there is at least one thing you will need to decide on before you grab your gold watch and dart for the exit. You will need to know what you are going to do with all that money you have saved for retirement. I am not talking about how to spend it. I am talking about how you will set up your financial accounts for safekeeping as you enter your nonworking (or at least part-time working) life.

This is not usually an easy decision as the options are numerous and come with some complex rules. Here are a few directions you might consider:

- *Take Early Withdrawals.* You know the golden rule about not touching your retirement funds until at least age fifty-nine-and-a-half lest you face the dreaded 10 percent penalty? Well, there are a couple of exceptions to that rule if you want to retire earlier. There is a little-known provision in many employer-sponsored retirement plans, such as 401(k), 403(b), the federal government's TSP, and others, that allows you to make penalty-free withdrawals if you leave the company during or after the calendar year in which you turn fifty-five. To take advantage of this option, you have to stop working for that employer and take withdrawals directly from that plan. In other words, you lose the penalty-free privilege if you roll the funds into an IRA.

> ## Should You Take an Early Retirement Package?
> In the corporate world, no one is safe from the threat of downsizing. That is especially true for seasoned managers who, despite their years of experience and body of knowledge, are often viewed as expensive liabilities when it comes time for company streamlining.
>
> Aside from the blow to your pride, being labeled expendable actually could work out well if it means you will get an early retirement package. Rather than conduct an outright layoff, many companies offer to buy out older employees with a polite "golden handshake." The deal might include a robust severance payout, stock options, or extended healthcare benefits that go beyond a typical severance package.
>
> For high-level managers and executives, there could be six or seven figures at stake, so weigh your options carefully.
>
> Will taking the package provide the boost you need to truly retire? Or are you betting that you'll be able to pocket the money *and* continue to earn a living somewhere else?
>
> If you refuse the deal, are you in danger of being let go the old-fashioned way and leaving with a comparatively meager severance package?
>
> Like investing itself, the choice of whether to accept early retirement must be based on calculated risks.

If you already have your retirement funds in an IRA, there is still a way to get at them before you turn fifty-nine-and-a-half, but it's a bit trickier than doing it through an employer's plan. At any age, you can set up what is called a Series of Substantially Equal Periodic Payments (SOSEPP). Essentially, the IRS gives you permission to withdraw a specified amount penalty-free from your IRA every month. But there's a catch. You must keep taking the payments, and only those payments, for five years or until you turn fifty-nine-and-a-half, whichever comes later. If you withdraw more or less than your specified payment, the plan is "busted" and you will owe taxes and a 10 percent penalty on everything you have withdrawn.

The SOSEPP strategy can work well if, for example, you retire at fifty-five and want to take early IRA distributions to carry you to your true retirement age. But the potential for missteps with this course of action is high, so take extra measures to make sure you understand exactly what you're doing. Once you pull the trigger, there's no changing your mind—not without throwing a lot of money away.

- *Cash Out Completely.* Remember that feeling of elation when you turned sixteen and got your driver's license? You wanted nothing more than to jump behind the wheel and cruise around town. "Not so fast," said your dad. "No freeways and no friends in the car until you've been driving for six months."

  A similar feeling of newfound freedom might hit you when you turn fifty-nine-and-a-half, the age when the IRS unlocks the sacred vault that has held your retirement funds for so long. You might be tempted to withdraw it all at once if only to take pleasure in holding a million-dollar check in your hands before investing it elsewhere.

  But remember—just because you're safe from the 10 percent early withdrawal penalty doesn't mean the distributions come scot-free. You will still have to pay income taxes on withdrawals, which means cashing out all at once would trigger an enormous tax bill the next April.

  One of the next two options is usually a smarter move.

- *Leave Your Funds Alone.* When you retire, whether it's early or otherwise, your employer's retirement plan might allow you to leave your funds in the plan. As long as you're happy with the investment choices your plan offers, it's not such a bad option. Your money can continue to grow, tax-deferred. If you wish, you can leave it untouched until you're required to start taking distributions at age seventy-and-a-half. On the other hand, there are a few good reasons to sever ties completely with your former employer and move your retirement funds elsewhere. Read on.

- *Roll to an IRA.* By the time you reach retirement, you probably have various taxable investments beyond the walls of your employer's retirement plan. And as you work to simplify your financial affairs, bringing your retirement funds under the same roof as your other assets can make your life easier. You can accomplish this by conducting a rollover from your employer's plan to an IRA. A rollover allows you to work with the management company of your choice and gives you access to a universe of investment choices not offered through the plan you had at work.

The safest way to move your money from one place to the next is to conduct a trustee-to-trustee transfer of funds in which you never have a check in your possession. This guarantees that you will not procrastinate and miss the sixty-day window to open an IRA and deposit the funds, which would result in taxes and penalties.

Once your IRA is established, you can choose to set up regular withdrawals or continue to let it grow.

- *Buy an Annuity.* I mentioned annuities briefly in chapter 5 as one possible way to defend your investments against major losses as you near retirement. But the more common use for annuities is in retirement itself. As a reminder, when you buy an annuity, you are paying up-front for the right to receive a guaranteed stream of income in the future. You might think of it as buying a pension for yourself. Depending on which type of annuity you purchase, the checks could keep coming for the rest of your life or for only a specified number of years. With any luck, the annuity eventually will pay you more than you put into it.

Pondering Pensions: Take the Lump Sum or a Lifetime Annuity?

If you are eligible for a pension from your longtime employer, you might be given the option to receive all the money at once (a lump sum) or receive equal pension payments over your lifetime (an annuity). There are many factors to consider (your age, health, and marital status among them), but a big part of the decision might come down to your confidence as an investor.

By taking the lump sum instead of an annuity, you're betting that you can make better long-term use of that money on your own versus some plan administrator holding on to it and doling it out over time. You accept the risk of managing the money or hiring someone to do it for you, but you give yourself the opportunity to achieve at least modest investment growth and counteract the effects of inflation.

Rather than continually tapping into an IRA, which might one day run dry, many retirees choose annuities for the peace of mind of knowing the funds will keep coming as long as they need them.

There are downsides to annuities, of course. The first is complexity. There are enough clauses and stipulations involved to make a lawyer blush. You have to be extremely careful to understand the limitations and potential penalties to which you are agreeing. Annuities can also be burdened by high commissions and fees that make them expensive to buy, and they could continue to nip at any investment returns your account might produce.

Keep in mind there are several different types of annuities that offer varying levels of risk and reward as well as fixed or variable payouts. Be sure to work with your financial planner to determine which type might meet your needs.

- *Mix and Match.* There is nothing that says you have to choose only one of the options above. In fact, most people find that a combination of these choices and others works best. For example, you could take early withdrawals from your 401(k) and, several years later, roll the remaining funds into an IRA. You could buy an annuity upon retirement using a portion of your nest egg yet keep a substantial chunk in your IRA to maintain growth, diversification, and liquidity.

Work with your planner to decide which approach makes the most sense for you. I've said this before and it's worth repeating: Planning is key. This brings us back to former coach Bob Knight, whose book about the power of negative thinking is not so much an endorsement for cynicism as it is a wakeup call for being prepared to handle crunch times. For most of us, impending retirement is crunch time.

"I wanted to plan every game as though it was against a good opponent because it was," Knight says. "I felt every time we played, the real opponent was the game itself—how close could we come to playing it perfectly?"

Few, if any of us, play a perfect game preparing for retirement, but that's OK. What's important is doing the right thing when you still have time to make something of it.

HOW TO INVEST DURING RETIREMENT (RE-EVALUATING RISK TOLERANCE)

Put yourself in the coach's shoes: Your team is deep into its Final Four semifinal game, and you're sitting comfortably atop a fifteen-point lead. Only a few minutes of basketball stand between you and your first trip to the NCAA Tournament championship game. What do you do? Pull your star players and give the well-deserving reserve squad its moment in the spotlight? Or implement stall tactics to run out the clock? If you do either, there's the chance (however slim) that your opponents could pull off some last-minute miracle and get back in the game. Your other option is to keep your best players on the floor, continue attacking, and eliminate any chance of a comeback. But this could also backfire. What if your MVP sprains an ankle in the final minute? You'll still win today's battle, but you're severely crippled heading into the championship game.

Coaches have to make these difficult decisions all the time. So do retirees. A strikingly similar risk/reward scenario faces investors as they seek to keep their financial assets secure and growing while avoiding the potential for devastating losses that could haunt them later.

Assuming you have substantial savings in place as you exit the working world, your investing career will continue long after your office has been redecorated by your replacement. Your portfolio needs to be built to pay off today and stay healthy for the long haul. Generally speaking, your investing objectives during retirement should be threefold.

1. Preserve your principal by avoiding excessive investment risk that could put a crack or a gaping hole in your nest egg.
2. Provide income, such as bond returns and stock dividends, to support your living expenses so you withdraw less (perhaps none) of your principal.

3. Achieve investment growth, which can at least counteract the corrosive effects of inflation and at best buy more income-producing assets.

Achieving and maintaining a good balance among these strategies gives you the best odds for long-term retirement bliss. And for most successful retirees, this three-pronged approach manifests itself in the form of a mixed investment portfolio of stocks, bonds, and alternative assets whether they're in an IRA, taxable accounts, or both.

Gone are the days when you snubbed your nose at conservative bonds and dove fancy-free into risky small-cap stocks. You have got to play it safer these days, but it doesn't mean you should eliminate risk from your portfolio altogether. In fact, don't be surprised if your financial advisor recommends that 50 percent or more of your portfolio should stay in growth-oriented investments, including stocks, at the time you retire.

What did you say?! I thought stocks were way too risky for retirees!

Stocks do not have to pose an extreme risk to your principal. The stocks of large, stalwart companies still play an important role in your portfolio because they throw off dividends (read: your greens fees) every year and typically achieve enough modest yet predictable growth to keep you ahead of inflation. A smaller dose of more aggressive stocks might even be acceptable if you have plenty of time for them to meet their potential. Meanwhile, conservative bonds anchor a considerable portion of your principal in place and produce income you can count on.

Even in retirement, a change in strategy—even a slight one—is worth thinking about when it comes to handling your investments. That brings us back to Rick Pitino, an advocate of change and keeping your eyes open to ways to improve yourself.

In his book *Rebound Rules: The Art of Success 2.0*, Pitino writes, "Doing the same things over and over can work for a while. It sets a winning foundation for your team or company—but do not wait for it to stop working before changing it up."

Case in point for Pitino was when he returned to college coaching at Louisville after coaching in the NBA with the Celtics. The college game had changed in just the four years between the time he left Kentucky in

1997 and then returned to college ball for the 2001–2002 season, this time with Louisville. Pitino quickly discovered that college teams had become better at handling full-court pressure and defending the three-point line.

"We could not continue to attack teams in 2002 the same way we did in 1997, and we could not rely on getting open three-pointers the same way we did [earlier]," Pitino says. "We had to break our mold and make it better."

As with everything in investing, your specific asset allocation should be based on your risk tolerance and personal goals. These things are ever-evolving, of course, so don't hesitate to scrutinize them yet again now that you've actually entered retirement and have a clearer view of the variables in play.

Your portfolio might lean toward the aggressive side (a higher percentage of stocks) under certain circumstances:

- You can already count on Social Security, a pension, or other income to cover most of your living expenses.
- You want to leave behind a sizeable inheritance for your heirs.
- You are comfortable knowing that even safer stocks could lose significant value if another severe market downturn came along.
- You are relatively young—still in your sixties or early seventies—in good health, and still likely have a decade or more for down markets to bounce back.

Other circumstances might lead you to take a more conservative stance:

- You are content to draw down your principal and end your life with little or nothing left. By the way, there's nothing wrong with that approach except the risk of living longer than you anticipated.
- To support your lifestyle, you need a lot more income than Social Security or a pension can provide.
- You're getting into your late seventies or beyond and might not have the decade or more it could take to recover from a major market meltdown.

So far in this chapter, we've talked about where you should stash your retirement funds and how to invest them wisely. But to state the obvious, these decisions are also dependent on how much money you plan to spend during retirement.

How Much to Take Out

I would venture to say that 99 percent of the financial literature you read focuses on ways to save money, put more away, and grow your investments. Well, it's time to get to the other 1 percent—the fun part—where we finally get to talk about using all that money you've been working so hard to accumulate.

You've earned the right to enjoy yourself, but it's not quite as simple as living carefree (or carelessly) from here on out. You have to make sure your money will last as long as you need it. After all, nobody's bank account is bottomless, and yours might be shallower than you realize. To avoid running out of funds prematurely, you'll need a drawdown strategy, a plan to take out a little money at a time throughout the years. The question is—how much?

I've already touched on the topic of planning your lifestyle during retirement, estimating the costs for how and where you'll pass the time. It matters greatly because, simply put, the more money you're going to spend, the more income you will need to draw from your retirement accounts. Once you've taken a thorough tally of your estimated monthly expenses, you can extrapolate years into the future.

Even with a solid understanding of how much retired life is going to cost each year, drawing money from your accounts can seem dangerously presumptuous when you don't know how many years you're going to live or how much inflation will work against you. Thankfully, many smart financial professionals have wrestled with these problems as well, and they have come up with some pretty good solutions.

One in particular is especially prevalent in the financial planning community. It's called the 4 percent rule, and it goes like this: You withdraw 4 percent of your nest egg during the first year of retirement and then increase that dollar amount by the rate of inflation every year.

Sticking to that system, there is a high probability, based on historical market performance, that your savings should last at least thirty years and probably longer.

The 4 percent rule was developed in 1994 through extensive research by William Bengen, a financial planner in California. Bengen's calculations were based on the assumption that 50 percent stocks and 50 percent bonds would comprise a retirement portfolio, and they would be held in a tax-deferred account such as an IRA. This system also assumes that you don't care to leave behind a substantial inheritance.

Put into practice, the plan might look something like this: You have $2 million in your IRA when you retire at age sixty-five. In the first full year of retirement, you withdraw 4 percent of the total—$80,000. The inflation rate that year is 3 percent. So the next year you withdraw $82,400. Assuming inflation stays the same, the following year you take out $84,872, and so on. Meanwhile, investment returns continue to add value to your principal, so you're not chipping away at the account balance as quickly as it might seem. According to Bengen, at this rate you shouldn't scrape the bottom of the barrel until you're at least ninety-five years old, and there is a good chance you would still have plenty left.

Is this a foolproof system? Of course not—there is no such thing. And, as you would expect, financial experts far and wide have stepped forward to proclaim a new and better rule of thumb. Nevertheless, the 4 percent rule could serve as a good starting point to help you determine the specific drawdown rate that's right for you. Any of the variables we've discussed (the age you retire, your costs of living, whether you have a pension, how much you want to leave behind, etc.) could lead you to decide that your withdrawal rate should be higher or lower. And that percentage certainly could be adjusted as the years pass, the markets fluctuate, and your needs change.

How to Minimize Taxes on Distributions

As multiple Kentucky basketball coaches have learned over the years, trying to get ahead can hurt you later if you're not playing by the rules. That's the way it is with taxes.

Social Security: Keep What You Can

With Social Security, what's yours is yours, and no one can take that away, right? Well, sorry to burst your bubble.

Social Security payments *are* tax-free for people who have little to no other income, but that's not going to be you (right?) because you have built a healthy nest egg upon which to draw in retirement.

Depending on how much income you take in (from pensions, annuities, dividends, bond income, your consulting gig, etc.), between 50 percent and 85 percent of your Social Security benefits could be taxed. The specific income limits vary by year and your filing status (look them up at www.ssa.gov), but suffice it to say you shouldn't count on keeping *all* of your Social Security money.

If the opportunity arises to stay below the income limits in a given year, carefully timing an IRA distribution or an invoice to a client could spare some of your Social Security from the tax axe.

Taxes are a fact of life, even retired life. As the IRS sees it, just because you're no longer drawing a paycheck doesn't mean you don't have income. The money you pocket from investments is taxable too. Paying taxes might be unavoidable, but you can pay less and stretch your dollars further by taking retirement income from the right places at the right times.

Different types of investments are taxed in different ways, so your drawdown strategy should include a close look at the tax ramifications of taking distributions from each account.

One common approach is to deplete your taxable investment accounts first before you start dipping into tax-deferred accounts such as your 401(k) or IRA. Why? Because when mutual funds, for example, are held in an outside investment account, the income or dividends they provide might be fully taxable either at your income tax bracket or the capital gains rate. It makes sense to cash out those investments first and eliminate the annual tax headache they create. Meanwhile, the money in your IRA or 401(k) can continue to grow, tax-deferred.

Once you've spent down your taxable accounts, your tax-deferred accounts are next in line. Keep in mind that the law requires you to start taking distributions at seventy-and-a-half.

Finally, if you have a Roth IRA, it is usually advisable to spend that last. Those distributions are tax-free. Since you have already paid taxes on the principal, there is no rule that requires you to withdraw the funds at a certain age. Furthermore, your Roth can be passed on to your heirs, who could choose to keep the money in the account and continue to watch it grow.

Ultimately, an approach like this could result in much more after-tax income over the course of your retirement compared to what you might achieve if you accessed the money without regard for tax consequences. But tax planning advice never comes without a big caveat, so here it is: Your circumstances are unique, and they might very well warrant a different approach than the one I have outlined here. In any case, unless you take great pleasure in dissecting the IRS codebook, you would be wise to work with your financial advisor and/or tax planning accountant to ensure your strategy is sound.

How to Handle Healthcare Insurance

Earlier, we discussed the critical need to maintain good healthcare insurance coverage or risk getting wiped out financially by a major injury or disease. That need for insurance does not go away during retirement; it might be more essential than ever as your likelihood of needing medical treatments increases.

OK, I got it, stay insured. Moving on.

Staying insured during retirement can be easier said than done. If you've spent your whole career working for companies that offer affordable health insurance benefits, you might be unprepared for the sticker shock that awaits you when you try to get your own coverage. Thus, maintaining adequate medical insurance should not be an afterthought in your retirement plan. It needs to be a focal point.

Medicare can take much of the weight off your shoulders when

> ### Medicare vs. Medicaid
> These oft-confused programs are actually quite different. While Medicare is available to virtually all Americans when they turn sixty-five, Medicaid is a special federal- and state-run insurance program specifically for low-income individuals and their families.

you turn sixty-five. So it's best to examine your health insurance options in two separate timeframes: before sixty-five and after.

- *Before age sixty-five.* Aside from a lack of savings, the high cost of private health insurance is one of the big reasons more people don't retire earlier. If you're hoping to skip out before you're eligible for Medicare, start doing your homework. Some employers still offer full medical benefits to retirees (a sweet deal), but those offers are becoming rarer every year as companies fight their own battles against rising healthcare costs. Your next best bet will likely be CO-BRA, the law that allows you to stay on your employer's medical insurance for up to eighteen months after you leave. Though with COBRA, you must foot the bill for the entire premium (your employer might have paid half while you worked there).

  If the first two options are not available, going it alone might be the only alternative. And obtaining a comprehensive individual policy can be an extremely expensive proposition—so expensive that it might make you wonder if this retirement thing is all it's cracked up to be.

  If you find yourself in this position, start shopping around. As mentioned earlier, recent changes in healthcare legislation might affect how and where your shopping process actually occurs.

  If you are in relatively good health, choosing a high-deductible plan could help keep your premiums in check. You'll pay more out of pocket for routine doctor visits, but you'll be shielded financially if a major disaster lands you in the hospital.

- *After age sixty-five.* You're in for some well-deserved relief once you reach sixty-five because that's when Medicare comes into play. It's not exactly free insurance—you paid for it up front throughout your working life in the form of FICA taxes that came out of your paycheck. And you will likely continue to pay some additional premiums to get all that Medicare has to offer. But assuming you're retired and don't have affordable insurance through an employer, Medicare should cost far less than what you would pay for a private policy.

Medicare is a veritable alphabet soup of options. It breaks down like this:

Part A: This is the base Medicare policy and covers you if you're hospitalized. Assuming you paid FICA taxes for ten years or more, you're automatically enrolled in this program and don't pay any more for it.

Part B: This optional policy covers a much wider variety of medical services (doctor visits, health screenings, physical therapy, etc.). As such, you will have to pay a premium for it. It's a bargain compared to private insurance, but current laws require more affluent retirees to pay hefty surcharges for the coverage. Sound unfair? Write your congressman.

Part C: This is where Medicare can get confusing. Part C, called "Medicare Advantage," allows you to access alternative plans offered by private insurance companies approved by Medicare. These plans cover everything you would get from Parts A and B but might also offer additional coverages and benefits. They also might have different rules for out-of-pocket costs or for which healthcare providers qualify as in-network. It's worth researching to find out if Part A+B or a Part C plan would work better for you.

Part D: This is Medicare's prescription drug program. There's a monthly premium for this as well, and you will have to meet a deductible before your prescription drugs will be fully covered up to a certain amount.

Medigap: This type of policy, bought through a private insurer, covers the gap between Medicare and any additional needs you might have. In other words, it's health coverage above and beyond what Medicare provides. You also can use a Medigap policy to cover expenses you have under Medicare, such as annual co-pays and deductibles. Be aware, however, that Medigap is not compatible with Medicare Part C. You cannot have both at the same time.

It is important to remember that even after you're sixty-five and Medicare helps out, controlling your healthcare costs will be a challenge. A 2012 study by Fidelity Investments estimated that an average sixty-five-year-old couple retiring today would need $230,000 to cover its medical costs throughout retirement. And that number does not include costs for long-term care services, which can be frightening if you don't have long-term care insurance.

To top it off, Medicare is on the brink of insolvency and will likely reduce benefits for future retirees. So if you're reading this well in advance of retiring, keep making those investment contributions.

CHOOSING WHERE TO LIVE

Maybe you won't pack up and skip town the day after you quit your job, but you're probably at least considering relocation as part of your retirement adventure. If you're not, maybe you should. Moving to a new abode is not always about settling down in your dream destination. It can also be about saving money. A change of scenery could add years of vitality to your retirement funds.

Take a look around your current home. With your kids out on their own, do you really still need five bedrooms, three baths, and a lawn big enough for a polo match? Even if your mortgage is paid off, there's homeowners insurance, property taxes, utilities, and maintenance costs to keep up with. All in all, downsizing to more modest living arrangements could save a small fortune in housing expenses over the years, not to mention making life simpler for you. If you can't bear the thought of leaving behind the home where you raised a family, keep in mind that the memories will travel with you wherever you go.

As long as you're thinking about moving, you should also consider how state and local tax laws could impact your retirement costs. Hint: retirees do not flock to Florida just for the warm winters and golf courses. They also know that Florida is one of seven states that doesn't impose an individual income tax, which allows retirees to stretch their dollars further, especially if they take some part-time work.

But do not limit your tax-savvy strategies to the Sunshine State. Other state laws might work more in your favor. For example, if much of your income will come from Social Security, you might want to make sure you live in one of the thirty-six states that doesn't tax those benefits. If you worked in the public sector and will receive a government pension, there are ten states that don't levy a tax on that income.

Tax laws can also vary from city to city. Once you've decided on moving to a general region, you might focus your house-hunting in the specific municipality with the most attractive sales and property tax rules.

MAKE YOUR FREE THROWS COUNT

There is an old truism in basketball that every coach has experienced firsthand: free throws win—or lose—ball games. In the box scores of countless close games, you can look back and find that the outcome might have been different if only the losing team had made a few more free throws. It had its chances—easy opportunities to rack up points with the clock stopped and no defenders in sight. But it missed too many, and that was the difference in the game.

Remember the mention of Kentucky's epic comeback win vs. LSU earlier in this chapter? In the final twelve minutes of that game, LSU *missed* eleven of twelve free throws. Had it made just half of them, usually a given at this level of play, it probably would have won and would not have been on the wrong side of college basketball history.

In many ways, you have free throws available to you in retirement too. You have opportunities to avoid withdrawal penalties, minimize taxes, keep your costs of living in check, and make the most of Social Security and Medicare. It's easy money if you plan carefully, yet many retirees fail to take advantage and watch their savings wither away like LSU's thirty-one-point lead.

The more you're able to seize these opportunities as they come along, the less you will have to rely on miracles come crunch time. And your biggest financial concern at the end of your life will be what to do with all the money you will leave behind.

Chapter-Ending Three-Pointer

1. Assess your life expectancy and determine the best way to withdraw retirement income from your accounts.

2. Plan to have your income tax planning in retirement be confirmed by a tax expert.

3. Balance retirement location and housing with personal goals and expense budget.

CHAPTER NINE

LAST-SECOND SHOTS

Planning to Leave a Financial Legacy for Your Family

PEACH BASKET PARABLES: DUKE, CHRISTIAN LAETTNER, AND THE SHOT

As much success as the Kentucky Wildcats have had over the years, they would tell you there's one crushing defeat—now more than twenty years old—that still haunts them like an irksome ghost in the attic.

For Wildcats fans, it is a dark, deplorable moment they wish could be purged from the record books, yet they are forced to relive it year after year on various NCAA Tournament highlight shows. For basketball purists not in love with Big Blue, the moment in question is perhaps the most memorable two seconds college basketball has ever experienced.

To either group, it is known simply as The Shot.

If you've watched much NCAA basketball, you've undoubtedly seen replays or at least heard about The Shot. It is included on any credible list of great moments in college basketball. The footage has been repackaged and replayed in commercials for everything from insurance to overnight shipping, and of course, it's part of every March Madness promotional montage.

The Shot has been covered, analyzed, and revisited by the sports media for two decades, some would say *ad nauseam*. So why write about it again? Because omitting it would be basketball blasphemy. Besides, as far as we know, it's never been written about in a book about financial planning. So here we go.

A MASTERPIECE IN BLUE AND WHITE

It was March 28, 1992. Kentucky Wildcats vs. Duke Blue Devils. It was not a championship game, not even Final Four. It was the East Regional Final (the Elite Eight round of the NCAA Tournament) played in Philadelphia. *Sports Illustrated*, *The Sporting News*, *USA Today*, and many other media have called it the greatest college basketball game ever.

From the beginning, the stage was set for an epic thriller. It was a blockbuster matchup of two national powerhouse teams featuring star-studded rosters (Duke's Bobby Hurley, Christian Laettner, and Grant Hill; Kentucky's Jamal Mashburn) and two of the game's most prominent coaches (Duke's Mike Krzyzewski and Kentucky's Rick Pitino). Duke, the number one seed, was the defending NCAA champion—it had beaten Kansas in 1991. Kentucky, ranked number two, was seeking a return to power after a ban from postseason play the previous two years.

Kentucky jumped out to an early lead, but Duke fought back to take a 5-point lead into halftime. The Blue Devils appeared in total control when they led by 12 points midway through the second half. That is when the Wildcats clawed their way back with a furious run. Both teams performed exceptionally well in a see-saw battle for the ages, making big shot after big shot. With the game tied 93–93 in the final seconds of regulation, Hurley narrowly missed a buzzer-beater to win, and they were headed into overtime.

The tension only heightened in the extra period, but neither team cracked. Despite the smothering defense by both sides, the incredible plays kept coming, back and forth, to the very end. There were five lead changes in the final thirty seconds, keeping fans across the nation riveted.

- Thirty seconds left: Laettner, draped in defenders, contorts his body and makes an amazing jump shot off the glass. Duke up by two.

- Twenty seconds left: Jamal Mashburn is fouled on a drive and completes a three-point play. Kentucky up by one.

- Fourteen seconds left: Mashburn fouls out when he hacks Laettner on the shot. Laettner sinks both free throws. Duke up by one.
- Three seconds left: Kentucky's Sean Woods lofts a running floater in the lane that ricochets in. Kentucky up by one.

Wildcats fans erupted. On any normal night, Woods's amazing shot would have sealed the game. By the time Duke was able to call timeout, the game clock had wound down to 2.1 seconds. The Blue Devils would have to in-bound the ball on the baseline and move it all the way up the floor for a desperation heave. In other words, no chance, right? Not in two seconds plus a tick.

INCONCEIVABLE, NOT IMPOSSIBLE

"We are going to win." That is what Krzyzewski said to his Blue Devils as they gathered for their final timeout. Then he drew up a play that the players recognized. They had rehearsed it in practice, and they had even tried it in a game once (though it had not worked). Instead of telling them what they were going to do, he asked his players for their consensus. In doing so, he planted the confidence in their minds.

He asked Grant Hill: "Can you make a seventy-five-foot pass to the free-throw line?"

"Yes," Hill answered.

Krzyzewski then asked Christian Laettner: "Can you catch it and get off a good shot?"

"Yes."

When Hill took his position on the baseline, he was surprised to find that Kentucky had not put a defender on him. He could attempt the Hail Mary pass uncontested. The Wildcats opted instead to double-team Laettner, who had not missed any of his nine shots so far.

It would not have the same ring to it, but the famous play might as well be called The Pass because Hill's was perfect. He threw it like a football, and it floated the length of the court while time stood still (the clock would not start until the inbounded ball touched a player). As millions of viewers held their breaths, Laettner fought his way to the free-throw line. Wildcat defenders lunged to intercept the pass, but the six-foot-eleven Laettner rose above them to make a clean catch. The clock started, and thus began the longest 2.1 seconds imaginable.

With his back to the basket, Laettner took a single dribble to his right, pivoted back to his left, and with 0.3 seconds to go, launched a fadeaway jumper over the outstretched arm of a scrambling defender.

Swish. Duke wins, 104–103.

Jaws dropped. Fans went wild. Some players embraced. Others collapsed. Tears flowed.

For Laettner, it was the perfect ending to a perfect night. He was 10-of-10 from the field and hit 10-of-10 free throws for 31 points. He was a memorable player already, but on that night, his name was permanently etched in the annals of basketball greatness. Duke went on to win its second straight national championship, the first team to repeat since UCLA in 1973. It would be Krzyzewski's second title of four through 2013. He was en route to becoming the winningest coach in NCAA men's basketball history.

Duke is not the only team to boast a long tradition of elite teams, a who's who of player alumni, a famous coach, and a legion of diehard fans. Most of the schools mentioned in this book also qualify. But Duke always will have something the others wish they had. It will always have The Shot.

COLOR COMMENTARY

- There is another, less glorious side to the story of Laettner's perfect game. Kentucky fans protested that Laettner should have been ejected in the second half when, in a moment of adrenaline-fueled combativeness, he intentionally stepped on the chest of Kentucky's downed Aminu Timberlake. Laettner received a technical foul, but had the referees reacted with a harsher punishment, The Shot might never have happened.

- In 2009, seventeen years after The Shot, Laettner appeared in a TV commercial for Vitamin Water in which he is shown reliving his moment of glory every time he throws away some trash. His neighbor witnesses this childish behavior, rolls his eyes, and hollers, "Give it a rest, Laettner!" The neighbor is former Kentucky coach Rick Pitino.

LEAVING YOUR LEGACY

After college, Laettner went on to a respectable if not distinguished NBA career. But he will always be best remembered for his time at Duke. The Shot was just one of his many great accomplishments. He is the only player in history to be a starter in four consecutive Final Fours. He holds NCAA Tournament records for most games played, most points scored overall, and most free throws made. And he was the only college player picked for the Olympic gold medal-winning Dream Team of 1992, arguably the greatest team ever assembled in any sport.

Not all of us can leave behind an on-court curriculum vitae like Laettner's, but most of us want to be remembered one way or another for the right reasons after we're gone. And we want not just to be remembered but also be remembered fondly, if only by our loved ones and the generations that follow them. We also want to feel confident that they will carry on and prosper without us, that they will be successful in life, raise happy families, and so on. As the years in retirement go by, you start to think more seriously about your exit plan and what you need to do to ensure that everything turns out the way you hope it will.

There are two main parts to the legacy you will leave behind. The first part is relationship-driven—how you will be remembered as a person, a professional, a parent, a spouse, and a member of your community. Your actions throughout your life, the friendships and family bonds you have forged and nurtured, and the wisdom and experience you have passed to others will largely determine whether people remember you with a smile. By the way, if you feel like you have fallen short in these areas, it's never too late to set things right.

The second part is asset-driven—all your worldly possessions that will remain after you have passed on, including money, property, and personal belongings. This exhaustive collection and compilation of everything you own (as well as debts you owe) is called your estate. And somebody will have to do something with all of it whether you are leaving behind a business empire or your prized collection of NCAA Final Four videos. Your likely goal, as you're thinking ahead to your final departure, will be to ensure that these assets are passed down to your heirs exactly as you desire—without paying too many taxes or triggering undue strife within the family. This is the process of estate planning, and it will occupy most of this chapter.

As you're reading, keep in mind that the two parts of your personal legacy—relationships and assets—can and do overlap. The way you feel about certain people will affect how you distribute your assets, and how you distribute your assets will affect the way people feel about you. We will explore these ideas in more depth.

One more thought before we dive in. This chapter is called Last-Second Shots because it relates to the idea of setting up your final play (perhaps a brilliant one) before the big buzzer of life sounds. That does not mean you should wait until the last second to plan. Remember, Duke had devised the play and practiced The Shot well in advance of that classic game against Kentucky. The sooner you consider the eventualities, the more prepared and confident you will be when the clock nears zero.

UPDATE YOUR ESTATE PLAN

Earlier, we touched on some basic aspects of estate planning that should be put in place well in advance of retirement. These include drafting a last will and testament, which allows you to control how your assets will be handled after you die. You can also choose who takes care of your minor children if both you and your spouse perish. If you don't spell out your wishes, the state government makes those decisions for you. You also might establish a revocable trust with the goal of keeping your estate out of probate court and/or entrusting a third party to manage your financial assets until your kids are old enough to handle the responsibility.

If you have had these legal instruments in place for decades, congratulations on being ahead of the curve. It's possible that the simple estate plan you laid out long ago will be all you need. But it's not likely. Most retirees, especially affluent ones, find that their financial affairs have grown more complex through the years and their visions of how to bequeath their assets have matured as well. After all, estate planning in your thirties or forties is more of a contingency plan for the "what-if" scenarios, but in retirement, it becomes a question of when your plan will take effect. With the inevitability of death feeling a lot more real, it is natural to want to make a more comprehensive estate plan while there is still time.

WHO GETS WHAT

The first step in estate planning before any legal documents are drawn up is to think carefully about how you want your wealth and possessions to be distributed when you die. In the simplest terms, that usually comes down to deciding who gets what.

Who gets what's left of your retirement savings and other investments? Who gets the proceeds from your life insurance (if you still have a policy)? Who will take over the family business? Who will inherit your home? That piece of land in Florida? The antique sewing machine?

If you're married, your first thought might be that everything will be left to your spouse. That's standard procedure for most couples. However, consider this: Unless your partner is decades younger than you, there is no telling which of you will expire first or how long the surviving spouse will keep on living. In estate planning, it's essential to think beyond the bounds of your marriage to whomever is next in line to receive your assets. And those decisions are best made jointly before either you or your spouse passes away.

For some people, choosing the beneficiaries of their estate can be a no-brainer. Longtime couples with only one beloved child, for instance, might simply choose to leave the whole enchilada (and all the side dishes) to Junior. For most families, however, it's not that simple. Multiple children, prior marriages, strained relationships, and other intricacies of your family history all come to the fore and require you to make difficult choices about who is more worthy of your benevolence.

For example, let's say you have two children. Do you split your assets evenly between them? Do you leave more to your golden child who you know will manage the money responsibly? Or do you give extra to the child who needs it more? And what about grandchildren? Should you earmark part of your savings for them? Would that be unfair to your child who is unmarried and has no kids?

What if you want to give a substantial sum to your favorite charity? Will your kids feel cheated?

Add another layer of complexity if you have family members from multiple marriages. Is the stepchild you have grown to love just as deserving as your own children from your first marriage?

Tough choices. So tough, in fact, that many retirees would rather ignore the problem altogether. Unfortunately, when heirs are left to settle the estate on their own with no clear instructions left by the deceased, things can get extremely ugly. Otherwise responsible adults, convinced of their entitlement, can be reduced to fighting like spoiled brats. Disagreements over estate issues can drive a wedge between close-knit relatives, setting off a bitter family feud that lasts for years whether it's fought in the courtroom or the dining room. Amid their quarreling, they fail to realize that they're dishonoring the memory of the loved one they lost. It's the stuff of soap operas, but it happens in the real world all the time.

You might insist that your own family would never be so petty. But consider that such infighting is not always driven by greed for more money. It is more about what the inheritance might represent: a parent's love, approval, or trust. Whatever piece of the estate each child receives could dramatically impact their sense of self-worth. They will fight to get what they believe is rightfully theirs even if its value is trivial from a financial perspective.

There is no guarantee that drafting a clear estate plan will prevent these family squabbles. But at least your heirs will know exactly what you wanted to do with your estate, and they will have little choice but to accept the outcome and move on. Thus, by planning carefully and making your wishes clear, you're not only contributing to the financial security of your descendents, but you're also helping to preserve harmony and happiness among your surviving family.

An even more proactive way to defuse potentially divisive estate issues is to discuss your intentions with your family in person. That way, you're able to explain the decisions you've made in advance, and there will be no shocking surprises at the proverbial reading of the will, which, by the way, only happens in the movies.

When it comes to your material belongings, you might consider letting your heirs decide among themselves who gets what while you're still around to act as a moderator. For example, if one child feels strongly that she should inherit your precious wedding ring, you might placate your other daughter with something else of significant value. In some cases, the kids might agree to terms on their own in a way you would not have considered had you made the list yourself. For example, one child says to the other, "You can have the grand piano—I have nowhere to put it. I'll take Dad's boat since you don't like the water. We'll call it even."

It might feel a bit macabre, allowing your kids to place dibs on your stuff while you're still healthy as a horse, but it's a practical way to prevent some nasty arguments the day after your funeral.

Once you've carefully considered how you want to divide your estate among your heirs, the next step is to find the best way to execute that plan without giving too much away to old Uncle Sam because, as we'll discuss in the next section, estate taxes can be a killer.

DEATH AND TAXES

You've undoubtedly heard the old saying, usually attributed to Benjamin Franklin, that there are only two certainties in life: death and taxes. Well, sometimes those two things occur simultaneously. That is to say, when you die and pass your assets on to your family (other than your spouse), the federal government imposes estate taxes, helping itself to a potentially huge chunk of what you intended for your children and grandchildren.

Think that's bad? It gets worse if you live in one of twenty-two states that levies additional taxes on your estate. Often called inheritance taxes, they can cut even deeper into your remaining assets. Critics

> **Do Not Die in New Jersey**
> In a 2011 *SmartMoney* magazine article titled "Estate Taxes: The Worst Places to Die," New Jersey took first honors because it imposes both an inheritance tax and an estate tax (there are subtle differences between the two) for a combined rate of 54.1 percent. Maryland, the only other state to have two death taxes, claimed the runner-up spot.

generally refer to either or all of these tolls as death taxes, and they have been the subject of heated debate among politicians for many years.

Because estate taxes, and taxes in general, are a polarizing issue in government, they can and do change depending on who's calling the shots in Washington and in your state capital. The tax rates rise and fall as do the limits on how big your estate can be before it gets hit with these taxes. Consequently, it would be unwise to offer specific tax-planning advice in this book when the rules can oscillate from year to year and from state to state.

Here is a high-profile example that illustrates the point. George Steinbrenner, billionaire owner of the New York Yankees, died in July 2010 at age eighty. Had he died in 2009 or 2011, federal estate taxes would have lopped $500–600 million off the top of his vast estate. But boy, did George's family luck out. Under President George W. Bush's sweeping tax legislation of 2001, the estate tax expired in 2009. Everyone expected Congress to put a new tax in place for 2010, but it didn't reach an agreement in time. As a result, anyone who died in 2010 paid absolutely no federal estate taxes. And the Steinbrenner heirs saved enough money in taxes alone to fill Yankee Stadium with dollar bills.

That is an extreme case, of course, and I'm not encouraging you to time your own death strategically. The point is, tax laws are always changing, so you cannot assume that what applies to you today will still be in effect when your time is up.

Regardless of current estate tax laws, there are ways you can reduce your taxable estate and ensure that as much of your money as possible finds its way into the hands of your loved ones. We'll cover some of the basics next, but if you think you might be subject to estate taxes, be sure to work with a professional—an estate planning or elder law attorney and a financial planner or CPA who specializes in this area—to explore the dozens of available strategies.

Give Now to Save Later

Yes, estate taxes threaten to chop your family's inheritance in half when you die. But "when you die" is the operative phrase because the estate tax is not triggered until you have passed away and the assets are transferred to your heirs. That's why tax-savvy retirees often give away a lot of their money long before their date with destiny. They aren't just being generous. They're being crafty.

Now before you get the bright idea to move a huge sum of money into your daughter's bank account, don't think that the IRS is not aware of this little trick to avoid estate taxes. The IRS also imposes taxes on any large gifts you make.

The gift tax takes effect when you transfer a significant amount of money or property to any individual without being fairly compensated for it. For 2013, the gift tax exemption threshold is $14,000, meaning you can give up to $14,000 to one person before incurring a tax (the gift tax rate mirrors the estate tax rate). Keep in mind we're not just talking about cash. You could also give away stocks, real estate, jewelry, or anything else to reduce the size of your estate. But the same rule applies. If that property is worth more than $14,000, there will be tax consequences.

If you have a multimillion-dollar estate, $14,000 might not sound like much of a reduction. Consider, however, that you can gift that amount to as many people as you wish, and you can do it year after year. Plus, your spouse has his or her own $14,000 limit, effectively doubling the amount you could give away annually.

You can also make certain types of gifts tax-free regardless of the amount, such as paying directly for someone else's medical care or education expenses or donating to charities or political parties.

Here is a simplified example of how it all can add up. Let's say you have an estate worth about $6 million, and the estate tax threshold is $5.12 million (as it is for 2013). To avoid estate taxes and leave as much money as possible to your three children, you need your estate to squeeze under the $5.12 million bar. You and your wife can each gift as much as $14,000 to each of the three kids, each year, tax-free. That amounts to giving away $84,000 per year. Do that for ten years ($840,000), and you have already transferred a big chunk of your estate tax-free. On top of those gifts, let's say your grandson gets into Yale. You pay for four years of his tuition for a total of $160,000, not subject to the gift tax. Unfortunately, one of your daughters is diagnosed with a serious disease, and you pay her doctor bills for a few years, totaling another $40,000. Finally, you make a $20,000 donation to your favorite nonprofit organization, the World Wildlife Fund.

Through your generous gifts, you not only have shown love and support for your family and made a sizeable contribution to a meaningful cause, but you also have reduced the value of your estate to less than $5 million, thereby avoiding the shrinking effect of estate taxes and leaving even more to your heirs when you pass away.

Like almost every investing or tax planning decision, you have to be careful because there are potential downsides to this type of approach.

First is the possibility that your successful avoidance of estate and gift taxes could produce some negative tax side effects in other areas. For example, if you gift long-held shares of stock to your family members and they wish to sell them, they might be stuck paying hefty capital gains taxes figured using your original cost basis, which is the price at which you purchased the stock. If, on the other hand, they received the stock as part of an inheritance when you died, the cost basis would be stepped up to the fair market value on the date the assets were transferred, possibly resulting in far fewer capital gains taxes.

Another concern about gifting is giving away too much too early. In other words, don't be so anxious to dole out your estate and escape taxes that you don't leave enough for yourself to enjoy your own retirement. Run the numbers carefully, taking your age, expenses, and life expectancy into account. And leave plenty of financial padding to fall back on in case you stick around longer than you thought.

Make no mistake—this is complicated stuff, and we have only scratched the surface. Again, consult with a tax expert and an estate planner before you put a gifting strategy into action.

LET'S TALK TRUSTS

We've established that the idea behind gifting is to minimize estate taxes by reducing the size of your estate before you die. But for many retirees, especially those with multimillion-dollar estates, gifting is only part of the solution.

First, the idea of making five-figure handouts right and left might make you uncomfortable, and that's OK. It's your money, and you're entitled to hang on to it until the very end if that's what you want. Second, even if you enjoy doling out large gifts, your estate may still be too large to scoot beneath the exclusion limit for estate taxes when you die.

Thankfully, there are other ways to spare your heirs from the IRS guillotine. Chief among them is the estate planning tool known as a trust.

There are many types of trusts, but they all share the same basic definition: a trust is a legal entity you set up to house certain assets and is held by a trustee (a third party) for the later benefit of the recipients—usually your heirs or a charity.

Think of a trust as an empty box that you fill with property such as investment assets, your home, your collection of fine wines—virtually anything you want. When you die, the trustee (it could be a family member or a financial institution) is required by law to distribute the contents of the box exactly as you specified in the document.

The right type of trust can offer some important estate planning benefits for you and your heirs (only one of which is tax savings) that cannot be accomplished through a simple last will and testament. Here is a quick rundown of the advantages:

Trust Terms

Revocable trust: Allows the grantor to modify the contents of the trust or terminate it altogether.

Irrevocable trust: Cannot be modified or terminated without the permission of the beneficiary.

Living trust: A trust that you establish and manage while you are still alive.

Testamentary trust: The alternative to a living trust, created by your will when you die.

Grantor: The person who establishes and funds the trust.

Trustee: The person or entity responsible for managing the trust and distributing the assets and income as specified by the grantor.

Beneficiary: The person or entity that receives the assets or income from the trust.

- Trusts give you complete control over who manages your assets when you die or become incapacitated. You can put someone you know in charge, such as a sibling or a trusted advisor, or choose a corporate executor, which is a firm that specializes in these matters. Appointing a professional will cost extra, of course, but could save your family the headache of administering your estate.

- Trusts allow you to put specific conditions on how and when your assets will be made available to your beneficiaries after you die. For example, you could stipulate that your grandson must graduate from college or turn thirty years old before he gets access to the money in the trust. You could also specify that the money is parceled out in installments over many years, not in a huge lump sum.

- As I mentioned earlier, a living trust, which takes effect while you are still alive, can prevent your estate from passing through probate court in some states. Probate can be costly. As much as 5 percent of your estate could be eaten up by fees for court time, attorneys, appraisals, accountants, etc. It can also be time-consuming. Depending on the complexity of your estate, it could be months or even years before your heirs get access to it. Finally, information on probate proceedings is available to the public's prying eyes, something prominent figures might want to avoid.

- Certain types of trusts can create a shelter and protect your assets from creditors or lawsuits. For example, if you're a doctor and you are sued for malpractice, you might be able to avoid a financial disaster if your assets reside in a properly structured trust.

But let us get back to the topic at hand: estate and gift taxes. There are literally dozens of trust provisions (and trust me, you don't want the full laundry list here), but a few are especially worth mentioning when it comes to protecting your family's inheritance from Uncle Sam's sticky fingers. We'll discuss those next.

Life Settlements:
Sell Your Insurance for Cash?

It used to be that when you had a life insurance policy you no longer needed, you had two choices: You could let it lapse by no longer paying the premiums, or (with some policies) you could accept the surrender value. Today, there's a third option. You can sell your policy to an investor who will likely pay you more (sometimes much more) than any surrender value you could get from the life insurance company. This is called a *life insurance settlement*.

How do investors make money on this deal, you ask? They keep paying the premiums on the insurance policy, and they pocket the proceeds when you die, usually coming out ahead. Yes, they are profiting from your death, and you are not alone if you think that sounds a little grisly. Nevertheless, it's a legitimate business in which many reputable companies operate. And it can be a viable option for retirees who could use the extra money for living or medical expenses.

Like any financial transaction, you can and should shop around for the best offer and work only with licensed professionals.

USING TRUSTS TO MINIMIZE ESTATE TAXES

I'll start by pointing out that your basic revocable living trust will not do a thing to reduce taxes on your estate. Its main purpose is to avoid probate. To steer clear of excessive tax, you will need a different type of trust designed specifically with tax avoidance (the legal kind) in mind. Here are some of the more popular variations.

- *Dynasty Trust.* Like the basketball dynasties of UCLA, Duke, and Kentucky, you want to pass along your wealth to future generations. If you have an especially large estate, the family fortune might even be preserved to fund the future exploits of your grandkids and their grandkids. But estate taxes can curtail your legacy profoundly. Normally, large estates (the amount above that year's threshold) are taxed every time the assets are transferred from one generation to the next. So a mountainous fund that might have lasted forever could be hacked down to a nub after two or three handoffs.

  Enter the dynasty trust. If, when you die, your assets are housed in a dynasty trust, they are still subject to estate taxes if applicable. So there are no immediate tax benefits for your children. But the real benefit kicks in when they die because the estate now can pass to their heirs—and the generation after that and so on—free from estate taxes. Moreover, the assets in the trust, such as stocks or real estate, can continue to appreciate through all of these years. Your great-grandchildren could actually inherit more—not less—than your kids did.

There are limits to how much tax a dynasty trust can actually avert thanks to the IRS's solution of generation-skipping taxes. But your heirs would still be far better off than if there had been no trust at all.

- *Inheritor's Trust.* An inheritor's trust is similar to a dynasty trust in that it protects future generations from paying estate taxes. But it's different because, as its name implies, it's set up by the person who will be inheriting the money, not by the grantor—presumably you.

  In this type of arrangement, your adult child could come to you and say, "I have set up an inheritor's trust. All you have to do is amend your estate plan so your assets will be bequeathed to the trust, not to me directly."

  A quick visit to your estate planning attorney could seal the deal.

- *Life Insurance Trust.* As we discussed in earlier sections, you might have decided by now that you don't need life insurance at this point in your life. Your kids are grown and self-sufficient, you have little debt, and there is plenty of money in your accounts to take care of your spouse if you die first. (In this case, see the sidebar about life settlements.)

  But there could be another reason to have life insurance, and that is to pay your estate taxes. If your estate is large enough to take a tax beating when you pass away, it might be worthwhile to consider a life insurance policy large enough to pay off the IRS and save your heirs the trouble.

  It's not quite that simple, of course. The proceeds from your life insurance policy will be considered part of your estate and will be taxable—unless the policy is held in an irrevocable life insurance trust (ILIT). With an ILIT, technically, the trust owns the life insurance, not you. And the trust gets the proceeds when you die, keeping the funds separate from your taxable estate. You can even stipulate in the trust that your heirs are required to use the life insurance payout to pay estate taxes.

ILITs can be especially helpful to your beneficiaries in cases when a large chunk of your estate is tied up in illiquid assets that you do not want to be sold. A common example is passing down ownership of a family business. If you died without a trust and your family owed millions in estate taxes, it might have no choice but to liquidate the business just to pay the taxes. But if it could use your life insurance proceeds to pay off (or at least pay most of) the taxes, it could keep the business alive as you intended.

- *Family Limited Partnership (FLP)*. While this estate planning tool is not the same thing as a trust, I'll mention it here because it often is used for similar purposes—reducing estate and gift taxes. An FLP is a legally formed holding company, a partnership consisting of family members. It's created and managed by a general partner, typically a parent or grandparent who wants to transfer significant financial assets to his or her heirs. The other family members in the partnership are called limited partners, limited because they can own a percentage of the assets but have no authority to make buy-and-sell transactions.

That is where the savings opportunity comes into play. Since limited partners have little control over their money while it's in the partnership, the IRS deems those assets to be less valuable than cash. When a general partner transfers his assets to a limited partner, effectively making a gift within the partnership, the gift taxes on that transaction are much less than if Dad had simply handed his son a million dollars in cash.

You can read about trusts and other estate planning tools until your face is as blue as the Duke locker room, but you're still going to need the help of an attorney to get legal documents drawn up. You should consult an expert, with a clear plan of exactly what you want to accomplish with your money, and allow them to navigate the intricacies of estate law on your behalf. Don't be surprised if they recommend more than one type of trust. Depending on the complexity of your estate, you could wind up with a network of separate legal entities with each serving a specific purpose. As long as they are established skillfully to work in concert and not conflict, trusts can bring your family members some much-needed good news at an extremely difficult time in their lives.

IF THE GAME GOES ON

Duke's perfectly executed play and Laettner's miraculous last-second shot put them on top to win the game. In your parallel version of crunch time, drawing up the right final play can help you go out a winner, financially speaking. More to the point, it can give your loved ones a leg up in their quests for success.

Luck, good or bad, and however you define it, could always enter the picture whether it's a basketball game or the timing of your death relative to tax laws (remember George Steinbrenner). Just do not mention luck around Krzyzewski if the topic happens to be the last few seconds of the 1992 Duke-Kentucky game.

"A lot of people say that we were lucky that day," Krzyzewski writes in *Beyond Basketball*. "I say luck favors those who have spent their preparation time building effective systems of communication and trust in one another. That way, when a crisis occurs for you, within your family, your team, or your business, it can turn into an opportunity to shine."

Imagine for a moment that the circumstances in that classic game had been slightly different. What if Kentucky had been up by two points instead of one when Laettner released The Shot? That incredible jumper only would have tied the game, resulting in yet another overtime period. And given five more minutes to play, who knows, maybe Duke would have run out of gas and The Shot would be all but forgotten.

Yes, the concept of overtime, even double or triple overtime, has its place in financial planning as well. If the game drags on longer than you ever thought possible, you must find the means to carry on with grace and pride.

CHAPTER-ENDING THREE-POINTER

1. Review your estate planning documents and update as needed.
2. Consult with a qualified estate planning attorney.
3. Communicate your overall plan to family members to reduce unexpected surprises.

CHAPTER TEN

OVERTIME

Managing Your Finances during Old Age

PEACH BASKET PARABLES: CINCINNATI AND THE LONGEST GAME EVER

There's something special about overtime games, contests in which two teams are so evenly matched that a winner cannot be declared in regulation, which for a college basketball game is forty minutes. An extra period is needed, or deserved, one might say, by the players who have matched each other point for point. In any sport, whether it's extra innings in baseball or overtime in football, the intensity reaches a new level for the exhausted players and nervous fans.

Overtime means another round of physical punishment for players, many of whom are already running on empty. It becomes more than a battle of basketball skill. It's a question of stamina and mental toughness. Every possession is critical, and a single lapse in concentration could cost you the game.

KINGS OF THE CLOCK

Perhaps no other NCAA program is more familiar with going the extra mile than the University of Cincinnati.

While mention of the Cincinnati Bearcats might not command the instant respect associated with the Bruins, Jayhawks, or Blue Devils, there was a period when the program was as dominant as any in the country. From 1959–1963, Cincinnati reached the NCAA Final Four five straight years, and the Bearcats appeared in the championship game three years in a row (only UCLA has done better).

Ironically, the Bearcats' first title came the year after the graduation of their most famous player, Oscar Robertson, who went on to achieve legendary status in the NBA as one of the best all-around players of all time.

Utilizing a slow-paced, half-court game, new head coach Ed Jucker led Cincinnati to the championship in 1961, beating Ohio State in overtime. The Bearcats bested Ohio State again in 1962 (the only back-to-back championship rematch in tournament history). And in 1963, the Bearcats fell to Loyola in another overtime title game. For the record, the NCAA championship game has gone to overtime a total of only seven times in seventy-five years (as of 2013).

After that splendid stretch under Jucker, Cincinnati's championship days were over but not the program's propensity for forcing games into extra minutes. In terms of sheer longevity, there was one overtime game in 1981 that topped all others.

THE LONGEST GAME

It was a regular season meeting between Cincinnati and Bradley University on a cold December day in Peoria, Illinois, when an NCAA Tournament berth was still only a twinkle in both teams' eyes. There was little drama to speak of that night—no epic showdown of big-name players, no trophies at stake, not even conference bragging rights. It was a relatively unimportant, early-season game on the packed schedule leading up to March. At least, it started out as no big deal.

The Bearcats and Bradley Braves played a fairly routine game through the first thirty-nine minutes. But with forty-five seconds left in regulation, Cincinnati surged from four points down to tie the score at 61–61 and force a five-minute overtime.

That's when things got really interesting. Both teams slowed the game to a crawl, attempting to score once and play keep-away to protect their lead—a common strategy in the pre-shot clock era. But the get-ahead-and-stall technique did not work for either team. Each scored only two points in overtime, and the score was tied 63–63 when the first extra period ended.

The same scenario played out again in the second overtime—just one basket for each team—leaving the score at 65–65. By the end of the third overtime, the scorekeeper must have been nodding off because not a single basket was made in that five-minute period. It's not that the players were not trying to win. It's that each team was all too eager to wait for the last shot, attempting buzzer-beaters to win the game instead of building a sizeable lead. As luck would have it, none of those last-second shots were going in. So the game continued.

The fourth overtime ended at 67–67 and the fifth at 71–71. Both teams scored another bucket in the sixth overtime to leave it knotted at 73-all.

It was getting very late on a Monday night, and thousands of exasperated spectators were undoubtedly considering calling in sick to work the next morning. As it turned out, Bradley fans probably wished they had left earlier. By the seventh overtime, two of Cincinnati's starting forwards had fouled out. Reserve Doug Schloemer found the ball in his hands with two seconds left, and he sank a fifteen-foot jumper from the wing to put the Bearcats up 75–73. With a final desperate shot, Bradley's Terry Cook almost took the game to an eighth overtime, but his eighteen-footer at the buzzer bounced off the rim.

The marathon game was over after seventy-five minutes of play, nearly the length of two full regulation games. It was, and as of 2013 still is, the only seven-overtime game in NCAA Division I history. Bradley's Donald Reese and Cincinnati's Bobby Austin, who each played seventy-three minutes that night, share the NCAA record for minutes played in a single game.

Purely for its "wow" value, the story earned a few column inches in the sports sections of major papers the next day, but the news faded quickly. The Bearcats didn't even make the NCAA Tournament that year, and on the whole, it was a rather disappointing season. But the Cincinnati players who ground out those seven overtimes will always own a part of something special. They participated in—and won—the longest game in history.

COLOR COMMENTARY

- Ed Jucker, who coached Cincinnati to its two championships, holds the record for the highest winning percentage (.917) in NCAA Tournament play. It's a rather misleading statistic, however. Jucker coached for only five seasons. In the first three, his team went to the championship game, winning it twice. In the last two, he didn't even make the tournament.

- One of Jucker's most promising freshman basketball players during the 1950s left the Bearcats after only one season—not to go to the NBA but to play professional baseball. It's a good thing too. That player was Sandy Koufax, one of Major League Baseball's greatest pitchers ever.

- The longest game in NBA history took place in 1951, when the Indianapolis Olympians defeated the Rochester Royals in six overtimes. Incredibly, the final score was 75–73, exactly the same as the Cincinnati-Bradley game.

A TEST OF ENDURANCE: YOUR EVER-EXPANDING LIFE EXPECTANCY

College basketball players begin every game with a reasonable expectation of how long it will last—two halves of twenty minutes each. They are trained to pace themselves throughout the game, to put forth maximum effort without tiring too early. If they play it just right, they have a little something left in the tank for those crucial final minutes.

Every now and then the game lasts longer than anyone expected. Forty minutes of playing time extends to forty-five, fifty, or longer, and the players' ingrained system of energy rationing is thrown for a loop. The key players are exhausted, having just fought tooth and nail (and failing) to pull out a victory in regulation. Yet the coach asks them for more, and they are faced with a choice: dig deeper or give up. True competitors never choose the latter.

> **Looking After Mom or Dad? Caregivers See Here**
> Though this chapter speaks directly to aging retirees, much of this advice could be helpful for adult children as their parents grow old and need help with their finances.

When you first got serious about retirement planning, you also had a realistic expectation about how long the game would last. But sometimes life goes into overtime. When you left your job two decades ago, for example, you might have planned to make your financial resources last through age eighty. But as your family toasts your good health on your seventy-fifth birthday, you become worried that your funds might expire before you do.

Outliving your savings is an unfortunate predicament that can befall even the wealthiest retirees. After all, spending too much too fast is not hard to do when you're unsure about how long you're going to live.

Consider how the life expectancies of Americans have changed in the last forty years. In 1970, the average life expectancy at birth was 70.8 years, according to the US Census Bureau. Today, thanks to advancements in healthcare and general improvements in our standard of living, the average American can expect to live well past seventy (seventy-five for men and eighty for women).

That might not seem like a huge change until you consider the increase in the total bill for retirement. For example, in 1970, the average person retiring at age sixty-five might have needed only enough savings to last six to seven years. Today, someone retiring at sixty-five could expect to live twice that long in retirement, close to fifteen more years, which means they would need twice the savings.

Those simple projections don't even account for the fact that your life expectancy actually increases as you grow older. In other words, your life expectancy at birth might be seventy-eight, but that average calculation includes statistics of people who died prematurely, say from childhood diseases or car accidents. The census says that people who make it to age sixty-five have an average life expectancy of nearly eighty-four. The average person who reaches seventy-five lives to be almost eighty-seven. Indeed, the older you get, the longer you will live!

All that is to say that your life expectancy is a moving target. And it's important to continue to adjust your financial aim even well after you've retired to make sure you're doing the right things to make your money last.

A Tale of Two Retirements

In many cases, the "right things" look much different in your late seventies than they did in your early sixties. Because if you're like most retirees, your lifestyle can change dramatically as your aging body demands it. Over the course of ten to twenty years, for instance, your idea of travel might go from a transatlantic cruise to a trip across town. You might drive a lot less, eat less, play less golf, and see the doctor more.

Obviously, changes like these can have a major impact on how and where you spend your money. So much so that it doesn't really make sense to lump all of your post-work years under the generic umbrella of retirement. From a financial planning perspective, it's more realistic to break it up into two phases. There are what you might call your active retirement years, and then there are, well, the twilight years. Strip away the sugarcoating, and the second phase of retirement could simply be called old age.

Planning for these later years—the overtime of your life—requires some special considerations. Certainly, it's still important to maintain a careful investing and withdrawal strategy to avoid draining your accounts prematurely. And, as we discussed at length in the last chapter, you will want to have a practical estate plan in place to ensure your assets are distributed as you would like with minimal taxation and fees. Now is the time you might also be thinking about different insurance plans, moving in with family or to an assisted living arrangement, or special tax concerns for the elderly.

Research and cautious decision making in all of these areas can help you live out your days with comfort and dignity and make life easier for your family both emotionally and financially. We will spend some time discussing these ideas in the next few pages.

START WITH PRECISE READINGS

Imagine for a minute that you're cruising down the highway in your car. You started with a full tank of gas, the wind in your hair, and a carefree spirit of adventure. But now, you're on a desolate stretch of road with no civilization in sight when your low-fuel light comes on. The gauge is almost at E, and you're not sure when you'll pass the next gas station. Salvation could be just over the next hill, or it could be thirty miles away. The anxiety-induced questions start coming: How much gas, precisely, is left in the tank? How many more miles will it take you before you have to hitchhike across the desert? What can you do to conserve fuel and get more miles out of every precious drop?

Thankfully, modern automakers have eased the worries of many motorists by creating more sophisticated sensors and gauges. Most new cars tell you how fast you're burning fuel (your current MPG) and how many miles you can drive before you run out of gas. These metrics are not perfectly accurate, but they're much more informative than your basic dropping needle.

What does all this have to do with your finances? Well, ideally, you could coast through retirement without giving a second thought to how much money you have left. But as the years go by and you watch your savings dip ever lower, you might feel a bit like that anxious driver, wondering whether you will have enough in the tank to carry you to that great refueling station in the sky.

Alas, even the wealthy have to watch their wallets or risk running dry. Remember, financial security is not about how much you start with. It's about how much you spend and how much you keep. So as you creep ever closer to your final destination, it's more important than ever to take frequent readings of your financial well-being.

There is more to it than just guessing and hoping. The closer your accounts get to the dreaded E, the more you need to know precisely how much money you still have, how much longer it will last, and what you can do to influence those factors.

Fortunately, just as cars today have more accurate gauges to keep drivers informed, you as a retiree have more advanced tools and services

---

Stay Alert to Fight Fraud

Exercise caution for salesmen pitching unsuitable financial products. There is one breed of fraudster that is even worse: identity thieves. They steal your personal information and use it to drain your bank account, use your credit cards, or apply for a loan in your name.

Identity theft can happen to anyone, but elderly retirees might be especially vulnerable. Why? Because con artists like to take advantage of old folks who might be lonely, overly trusting, uninformed, or suffering from diminished mental capacity.

Quick tips:

- Never give your Social Security number to someone over the phone or through e-mail unless *you contacted them.*
- If a bank or credit card company e-mails or calls and asks you to verify your private account information, it could be a scam. Call the company's real customer service line and ask if the request was real.
- Always equip your computer with antivirus and antispyware software, and keep it up to date.
- Do not click on pop-up ads or unfamiliar alerts in your web browser. You could be downloading malicious programs that raid your computer.
- Monitor your financial statements and review your credit report once a year (it is free) to look for suspicious activity.
- Shred any sensitive financial statements before throwing them away.

Take it upon yourself to educate yourself (or your parents) about the dangers of identity theft. If you feel you need extra help, some financial companies now offer identity theft monitoring services as well as insurance protection against the costs that might result from an attack.

---

available to manage your financial resources. Easy access to your account information online, web-based calculators, and objective advice from a professional financial planner allow you to figure out exactly where you stand and to fine-tune your spend-down strategy.

WHAT IS YOUR BURN RATE?

One key piece of information that needs re-evaluating is the rate at which you are withdrawing your retirement funds to support your lifestyle. In other words, how fast are you burning through money?

I remind you of the 4 percent rule, which offers a basic strategy of withdrawing 4 percent of your retirement funds per year and keeping the rest invested in a diversified portfolio. It might have been a great plan when you were sixty-five, but things might look different with a decade or more of retired life behind you and a better, though still not certain, estimate of how long you will live.

Perhaps your expenses have increased unexpectedly over the years, necessitating larger withdrawals to keep yourself out of debt. This is especially common as age takes its toll and necessitates more frequent and costly healthcare. If that is the case, it is time to hit the reset button and build a new strategy based on the realities you're facing today.

Even if you have been unfailingly consistent about withdrawing only the amount you planned, you might find reasons to decrease your burn rate. Maybe you're still running marathons at age seventy-seven, which is a pretty good sign that you're going to be around for a quite a while and you had better save some money for your nineties. Another less cheery possibility is that your investment portfolio suffered throughout your early retirement years and now you have less money than you thought you would at this point in your life. Either way, you would be wise to make some new calculations about how quickly you're depleting your funds.

The idea is to be versatile, even as you age, so you can stay ahead of the game, which brings us back to Bob Knight and his years at Indiana. Many of us know and have even witnessed the darker side of The General, such as when he angrily grabbed a player by the jersey during a game or when he stuffed an opposing fan who was giving him a hard time into a trash can. Still, Knight was loyal to his players, a brilliant teacher and tactician, and not above doling out compliments to his players.

One of Knight's favorite players was six-foot-seven Bobby Wilkerson, a member of the squad in the mid-seventies that lost only one game during a two-season stretch that included the 1976 national title. An exceptional jumper who was wiry-strong, Wilkerson could play just about any position on the floor—big guard, point guard, small forward. He even jumped center on occasion, filling the role of Mr. Versatile for the Hoosiers.

"Bobby was not a great shooter, but he recognized that and still had some big scoring nights," Knight said, writing in his book *The Power of Negative Thinking*. "And he led that [1976] team—maybe the best-passing team that ever won a national championship—in assists. All that does not even mention his greatest strength: defense."

If you don't have billions in the bank, the best method to ensure independence and a high quality of life through your final days, even if you're not a versatile, six-foot-seven basketball stud like Wilkerson, is to analyze (and re-analyze) your assets, return rate, spending, and life expectancy.

So what should you do if you find yourself running out of money too quickly? There are two simple solutions: either spend less or make more. Since that's probably not the answer you were looking for, let's talk about a few more specific ways to accomplish these objectives.

IF YOU FORESEE A SHORTFALL

I have discussed a three-pronged approach to investing during retirement: preserving capital, producing income, and achieving investment growth. These basic tenets apply just as much in the late stages of life as they did when you first retired. In fact, they apply to financial planning beyond your investment portfolio as well. If you think about it, making money, protecting what you have earned, and investing it to make more money are the underlying reasons for all financial planning. They have been with you your whole life. Now you simply need to apply them in a new context— the context of growing old.

If your calculations tell you that you're using up your retirement funds at an unsustainable rate, it could be that your once-balanced approach to earning, spending, and investing money has fallen out of whack. Whether that's due to lax money management or unfortunate circumstances beyond your control, you'll need to realign your financial behaviors to address the problem you face today.

Here's a list of concrete actions you can take to get back on track. They range from relatively easy tweaks in your spending habits to significant life changes.

Spend Less

- *Get Back to Budgeting Basics.* Find ways to cut spending on everyday items you can live without, such as cable TV, expensive meals, or the country club membership you rarely use.

- *Get Rid of Spare Cars.* If you aren't gallivanting around town quite as often, can you and your spouse get by with one vehicle? It could be an opportunity for sizeable savings on insurance, maintenance, registration, and gas, not to mention the cash you would get from the sale of the extra car.

- *Use Senior Discounts.* You've earned them, so don't be shy about asking for special rates at the movies, golf courses, or restaurants.

- *Travel on the Cheap.* You're retired, which means you're not restricted to vacationing at peak times when young families flood the airways and beachside resorts. Exploring in the off-season can cut your travel expenses in half.

- *Examine your Insurance.* Take yet another look at life insurance and disability insurance to see if they still make sense for you, and get competing quotes for homeowners and auto insurance. It could be that the provider you have been with for years no longer offers the best deal.

  Shop around for health insurance too. You don't want to skimp on good coverage because healthcare costs can suck the life out of your retirement fund. But if you're a meticulous comparison shopper, you might dig up a policy that supplements Medicare effectively for less money than you're paying now.

- *Downsize Your House.* Moving from your big, mostly empty house into a simpler home or condo could produce a windfall of cash plus savings on utilities, maintenance, property taxes, and other expenses.

- *Stop Being So Generous.* OK, I know that sounds bad. But if, for example, you've been spoiling the grandkids with ponies and new cars or supporting an adult child who is still "finding himself," now is probably the time to be a little more selfish and hang on to more of your money.

Make More

- *Sell Some Valuable Possessions.* Chances are you have thousands of dollars worth of stuff lying around that you really don't need. And in this era of eBay and Craigslist, it's easier than ever to find a buyer who is willing to pay good money for your cast-offs.

- *Get Cash for Using Credit.* You have to spend money to live, so why not put purchases on a card that gives you something back? Many credit cards pay you cash rewards of 1 to 2 percent of every purchase you make, which could add up to meaningful money if you use the card often. You must have the discipline, however, to avoid overspending and pay off the balance every month.

- *Make Money from a Hobby.* We've all heard the advice about turning your favorite pastime into a business. But can anyone really turn a decent profit selling homemade candles or wildlife photography? It might be easier than you think. Again, today's Internet resources can be incredibly effective in helping you create a storefront, identify a market for your product, and sell and ship to buyers all over the world. There are hundreds of small businesses you can run without ever leaving your house. It might not create a huge stream of income, but if you can bring in some extra cash by doing more of what you already enjoy, it's just icing on the cake.

- *Get a Real Job.* Maybe it is not as appealing as running a hobby business from your house, but if you're physically able to work outside the home and could use the extra money, consider a more traditional part-time job. For executive types with decades of business experience to share, some light consulting work could pay handsomely. There could also be opportunities to combine a job with a personal interest or desire to serve the community, such as teaching at a local college or working at a museum or charitable organization. For those who have trouble finding work, various job placement agencies specialize in helping retirees find part-time work. While some seniors might view returning to work as a retirement failure, others choose to see it in a positive light—a new life experience and an opportunity to stay active and engaged in the world outside.

- *Consider a Reverse Mortgage.* If you own your home outright or have considerable equity built up, you might qualify for a reverse mortgage. This is essentially a loan against your home equity. But unlike an actual home equity loan (a different product), you do not make monthly payments, and the loan does not have to be paid back until you die or move out. You can choose to receive the money as a lump sum, a stream of monthly checks, or a line of credit you can dip into as needed. How much you can borrow depends on your age, interest rates, and the value of your home.

  If you die while living in the home or if you need to move out, the loan has to be repaid in full, which is usually paid from the proceeds of the sale of the house. That means your children will not inherit that money, but the tradeoff makes sense if it's necessary for you to maintain quality of life in your remaining years.

  Until recently, reverse mortgages had a bad rap: predatory sales tactics by unscrupulous lenders put some homeowners in hot water. But regulations and oversight surrounding these loans have been cleaned up in recent years, and today, they can be a viable option for cash-strapped seniors. Nevertheless, it is still a complex financial arrangement that you should approach with extreme caution. Your financial planner can help you wrap your head around the details and decide if it's the right move for you.

Tune Up Your Investments

- *Clean House–Again.* In chapter 7, Halftime Adjustments, we talked about conducting a spring cleaning of your investment portfolio to weed out consistently poor performers. Ideally, this portfolio review process would be conducted every few years throughout your investing lifetime, but in reality, most investors do it far less often. Now is as good a time as any.

  Take a close look at the mutual funds, bond funds, and other investments in your portfolio, and compare their performance to funds in the same category (long-term bond funds, for example). Morningstar.com has great tools for this. If a fund you've been carrying for ten years has given you next to nothing in return for your loyalty, it's time to kick it to the curb. Replace it with an investment that is likely to be more productive.

Keep in mind that even investments that report positive returns could be losing money quietly after you factor in expenses and management fees. Be sure to look at your net return (post-expenses) when evaluating your current investments, and carefully consider the fees of any new investments you make.

- *Increase Stock Holdings.* If there is one message that cannot be overemphasized in this book, it's that stocks are not just for young up-and-comers. At any age, it's important to maintain some degree of growth potential in your portfolio, and that means an ongoing exposure to equities (stocks). Granted, you have probably been counseled from day one to reduce the volatility in your portfolio gradually as you age, creating a more dependable income stream through bonds. That is generally sound advice, but it's also a common mistake to overcorrect by being too conservative in retirement. With little to no capital appreciation, you'll burn through your funds faster and continue to lose purchasing power because of inflation.

  If, in the latter half of your golden years, you find that you're spending your way to destitution, a larger—perhaps 15 to 25 percent—allocation to growth stocks could pump life back into your deflated nest egg. There is certainly risk involved in this approach, but a financial professional can help you reshape your asset allocation and identify growth-oriented investments with as little downside as possible.

- *Up Your Interest.* Ever since the financial calamity of 2008, the Federal Reserve has presided over a steady decline in interest rates, and as of mid-2013, rates were sitting at incredibly low levels. It's been great news for people who refinanced their homes at 3.5 percent APR but bad news for people who count on

---

An Annuity for Old Age

We talked about annuities in earlier chapters as one way to arrange a steady and guaranteed income throughout retirement. If you did not purchase an immediate annuity in an earlier phase of retirement, there is a special type of annuity designed for seniors who have a growing fear they might outlive their savings. It is aptly named a longevity annuity, or sometimes called an advanced life delayed annuity.

Here's how it works: as a supplement to investing in stocks and bonds, you can put a portion (perhaps 10 to 25 percent) of your retirement savings toward a longevity annuity. You choose payments to begin at a certain age, say when you turn eighty years old. Until then, the money will be kept in a managed investment account to continue growing. At age eighty, you'd start receiving regular payments from the annuity that would continue for the rest of your life.

The upside: since you do not start the longevity annuity until late in life, you will get more bang for your buck compared to other annuities. The downside: if you die before you reach that designated age, the insurance company keeps your money and nothing goes to your heirs.

---

interest-bearing investments for a big chunk of their retirement income. Short-term certificates of deposit (CDs), for example, are currently being outpaced by the rate of inflation, thus doing investors more harm than good.

In such a low-interest-rate environment, moving a larger percentage of funds into dividend-bearing stocks can be a good idea. They can produce more income than the paltry returns of CDs or money market accounts. But again, investing too heavily in stocks at your ripe old age would be a mistake. Work with your financial planner to explore other income-producing options that might yield more than you're getting now. Some choices could include buying municipal bonds instead of treasuries, moving money from a basic savings account to a high-yield checking account, or purchasing longer-term CDs at a higher interest rate, taking your life expectancy under consideration, of course.

Low rates will not last forever, and they might be on the rise as you're reading this, in which case your retirement income strategy could change again. The takeaway here is to remain cognizant of how interest rates affect the staying power of your nest egg and to take action to make the most of the current situation.

Trim Your Taxes

After a lifetime of squeezing its share from your income, the IRS figures it's time to give you a break when you get old. That doesn't mean you're free from taxes altogether—you still could owe on investment income and Social Security—but you can take advantage of some senior-friendly tax policies to keep more money in your wallet.

- *Higher Standard Deduction.* If you're over sixty-five and don't itemize deductions on your tax return, which is likely if you no longer have a mortgage, you qualify for a higher standard deduction amount than a younger taxpayer. If you happen to be blind, the deduction is even higher. The money you save on taxes will not buy you a yacht, but it's worth your time to check a few boxes on your return and keep a few hundred dollars more.

- *Medical Expenses.* All taxpayers have an opportunity to deduct medical expenses from their taxes if they qualify. But most do not because only expenses that exceed 7.5 percent of your adjusted gross income can be deducted. That little piece of tax code looks a lot more applicable for aging retirees, who often have major medical costs and claim less income than they did in their working days. Add up your costs for health insurance, including Medicare, long-term care insurance, prescription drugs, any nursing home care, and most other out-of-pocket healthcare expenses, and you might find that thousands of dollars of it are deductible. One thing to note: These savings are only available if you itemize deductions on your return, which precludes taking the higher standard deduction mentioned earlier.

  If you operate a small business, the rules are different, allowing you to deduct healthcare insurance premiums without itemizing on your tax return.

- *Investment Expenses and Advice.* In the same way senior citizens become eligible to deduct medical expenses, they might also qualify to deduct expenses required to manage their investments. Those expenses might include attorney and accounting fees, financial planning fees, and even subscriptions to investing magazines. If it all adds up to more than 2 percent of your adjusted gross income, the excess is deductible.

- *Credit for the Elderly and Disabled.* I've included this here because you might come across a mention of this tax credit somewhere else and wonder if it applies to you. The title is rather misleading. It should be called Credit for Low-Income Elderly and Disabled. There is an IRS formula to determine whether you have too much income to qualify, but suffice it to say that if you are living much above the poverty line, you're not eligible. Still, it could be worth looking into if you're "permanently and totally disabled" (the IRS's words).

- *Free Tax Assistance.* Seniors who don't have a professional tax accountant at their beck and call can get free tax advice through the IRS Tax Counseling for the Elderly (TCE) program or AARP's Tax-Aide program. These free services are not sufficient to help you navigate the tax labyrinth of a complex investment portfolio, but they can help you file a relatively simple tax return.

WHEN TWO BECOME ONE: DEALING WITH THE DEATH OF A SPOUSE

If you're married and getting on in years, you've undoubtedly pondered an unsettling question: Which one of you is going to die first? Unless there's a freak deadly accident, one of you will die before the other. Statistically speaking, women tend to live a few years longer than men, but that's only an average. Being ready—financially prepared, that is—for either scenario is one of the best things you can do for each other.

As I have mentioned elsewhere, make sure both of you are at least generally aware of how your finances are structured, which accounts are where, and what is supposed to happen when one of you dies. For example, will there be a life insurance payout or an estate plan that takes effect?

Sorting all this out before one of you passes away spares the surviving spouse the burden of unraveling those mysteries alone.

Of course, even if you and your spouse are very familiar with your financial situation, it's not the same as being truly prepared for life without your partner. Aside from the emotional avalanche that's likely to follow the loss, living alone might be one of your last and greatest financial challenges.

While taking time to grieve is important, it will also be necessary to keep your financial affairs organized so you can carry on with some sense of normalcy. Before too much time passes, gather up important information such as your estate plan (if you have one), insurance policies, statements for banking and investment accounts, pension and Social Security documents, etc. It's time to make a new financial plan for the rest of your life as a widow or widower.

You'll need to recalculate your cash flow needs based on your new reality. Living alone could completely reshape your everyday expenses for housing, food, healthcare and medications, transportation, and recreation.

Your spouse's death might also prompt changes to plans you had made for the future. All of these changes combined are bound to make a difference in how much money you need to withdraw from your retirement savings.

It helps to know that if you have reached the full retirement age according to Social Security rules, you will continue to receive your spouse's full Social Security benefit under the Survivor's Insurance Program. You might also be entitled to continue receiving all or a part of your spouse's pension, if there is one. Expenses could be much lower as well. You will need to fund only your own health insurance and out-of-pocket medical costs from now on. So from a financial standpoint, you could actually end up better off than when there were two of you and spend the rest of your days free from worry. That's a best-case scenario, and it's surely how your departed spouse would have wanted it.

Unfortunately, many widowed spouses are not so lucky. They find themselves lost without their life partner. They lack the emotional and practical support a spouse once provided, such as help with shopping, cooking, or home maintenance. When it comes to money, even if they have enough, they might feel overwhelmed by the idea of suddenly managing the household finances after decades of entrusting that job to their partner.

If the adjustment to living alone seems too much to bear, it might be time to consider an alternative living arrangement.

CONSIDERING A HOME AWAY FROM HOME

Some senior citizens have the good fortune to remain spry and self-sufficient until the day they drift off comfortably to an eternal sleep. The majority of elderly folks, however, are going to need some help taking care of themselves in their final years. When that day comes, they and their children face some difficult decisions, not the least of which is whether to move to some sort of specialized elder care environment.

I use the term elder care in the most general sense because there are many options available that offer varying degrees of comfort, privacy, freedom, and professional assistance. At the low end of the spectrum, you could have basic services provided at home without having to move. At the highest end, you have skilled nursing homes with on-site medical facilities and twenty-four-hour supervision. Somewhere in between lie the less invasive assisted living communities, and of course, there is the option of moving in with a family member.

Clearly, there are emotional intricacies that weigh heavily in the decision to move: a parent's desire to remain independent and a child's sense of responsibility to help even when Mom doesn't think she needs it. But any of these elder care arrangements also promise to have a major impact on your retire-

> **Leave a Little for the End**
>
> According to the National Funeral Directors Association, the average cost for a funeral in the US was $7,755 in 2010. That covers basic expenses such as transporting the deceased, preparing the remains for viewing, facility rentals, a casket, and a vault. Add to that the costs of a burial plot, headstone, flowers, hosting a meal for the family, and other traditions, and your loved ones will be hit with a five-figure farewell bill.
>
> Want to leave a nice parting gift for your family? Before you go, think about earmarking some easily accessible funds to pay for your own send-off. Better yet, make the funeral arrangements in advance.

ment finances (and likely your family's finances), which is why it's important to mention them here.

Ideally, the decision should be discussed by the family, considering all the angles with an open mind. What level of care is most appropriate? A doctor should be consulted on this one. What location is best? How much is it going to cost, and where is the money going to come from? Are there siblings who could help? How will these decisions affect the personal lives and financial security of everyone involved?

By the way, if you or your parents have long-term care insurance, now would be a good time to review the policy in depth to understand what types of care will be covered, to what extent, and for how long. The two main components of a long-term care policy are the daily benefit, which is the maximum amount the insurer will pay for services per day, and the benefit period, which is how long the policy will pay for your long-term care services. Be sure to keep these numbers in mind when comparing the costs of various facilities.

Granted, it's often the adult children who do most of the decision making on behalf of their elderly parents. But if you are a senior citizen reading this book, I would bet you still have the presence of mind to make these decisions proactively on your own. Even at this late stage in life, thorough financial planning gives you an opportunity to improve your quality of life, go out on your terms, and, equally important, avoid placing excessive stress on the people you love.

FORGET ABOUT THE SCOREBOARD

No one is really sure who said it first, but there's an old maxim in sports that goes like this: "I never lost a game. I just ran out of time."

Surely that's how the Bradley Braves felt after losing the longest basketball game in history. While Cincinnati celebrated the seven-overtime victory in the opposite locker room, Bradley players were left to ponder what might have happened had they just had a few more seconds to get one more rebound, one more steal, one more all-important basket.

Despite the loss, Bradley's coach, Dick Versace, called the game an "incredible performance." He said his boys "played like men" and "handled themselves beautifully in the clutch." In a game like that, it's almost impossible to declare a true winner and loser. Versace was happy just to have been a part of it.

If your life has reached the overtime period, it's probably human nature to look back and wish you had done some things differently with your money. In fact, I would be surprised if you hadn't made a few financial blunders along the way. Nobody shoots 100 percent, not even from the free-throw line.

But that doesn't mean your financial plan was a failure. Far from it. You and your family are much better off for having planned at all. Unlike millions of others who merely watch from the sidelines, you fought the good fight and left your last drop of sweat on the floor. Instead of trophies, you have a lifetime of happy memories and maybe even a financial legacy to show for it.

Perhaps you don't regard yourself as a champion. But like those Bradley Braves, you can get on the bus with a smile on your face, knowing that the true joy was in playing the game.

CHAPTER-ENDING THREE-POINTER

1. Reduce your expenses as you age and potentially become less active.
2. Prepare the surviving spouse for managing the money after the other's death.
3. Seek professional advice in areas that are difficult for you to decide.

POSTGAME ROUNDUP

Being Your Own Superstar

Why We Admire Elite Athletes

In our sports-obsessed culture, we tend to put athletes on a pedestal. As early as middle school, gifted athletes are treated differently as part of a special club. In high school, they are showered with applause and featured in the hometown newspaper. If and when they reach the elite collegiate and professional ranks, we bestow upon them an exalted, almost superhuman status. It's certainly not fair to people who excel in academic fields or other nonsporting activities and receive relatively scant recognition, but sports fanaticism is a curious reality of our society.

Why do we admire and respect athletes so? Cynics would say it's because we envy the fame and fortune that outstanding athletes can achieve (an argument that could spur an interesting "chicken or egg" debate). That might be part of it, but I believe there is a better, more wholesome reason. True sports fans, the ones who know the game, see beyond the glamour of sports stardom and appreciate the rare blend of talent and determination found in high-level athletes. Unlike some of the instant celebrities we see on TV, the extraordinary athletes we cheer for (and against) have trained for countless hours over many years to sharpen their skills to a fine point.

Most, if not all, of them have spilled buckets of sweat, overcome painful injuries, persevered through frustrating slumps, and dedicated their existence to being the best at what they do. They did all this in pursuit of a dream, and against long odds, they succeeded in achieving greatness. That's why we hold them in such high esteem and why so many sports fans, deliberately or not, point to famous athletes as role models for their kids whether or not those athletes label themselves as role models.

That is not to say all sports figures are role-model material. Some clearly let success go to their heads. Others, such as former NBA star Charles Barkley, don't like being labeled role models. But every now and then, exceedingly rare players come along who are not only incredible athletes but also remarkable people as well. They put up dazzling individual stats, but they are seemingly committed to something bigger than themselves. They make others around them better. They are leaders on the court or on the field and in the locker room, and they take advantage of their position in the spotlight to do good things in the community. These are the superstars who are the most fun to root for and who perhaps one day will earn themselves a piece of immortality in a hall of fame. Many of them go on to share their wisdom as they become coaches, and eventually, they leave the game better than they found it.

Your Shot at Glory

The world of elite sports is one most of us can only witness as spectators. But I believe there are superstars in our workaday world too. They do not drive Lamborghinis, and you have probably never seen them on TV. Some are attorneys or doctors or CEOs, but most of them have normal-sounding jobs such as marketing director or operations manager. Others are happily retired. So why do I consider them superstars? Because like the most successful athletes, they have followed their passion, worked extremely hard to meet their goals, dealt with setbacks effectively, and succeeded in building a wonderful life for themselves and their families. That's not something everyone can claim. In fact, it's pretty rare.

Is it possible to accomplish all these things without a good financial plan to build and preserve wealth? Maybe, but I wouldn't try it. That would be a little like going into the NCAA championship game and just winging it.

Money isn't everything, but it's a major factor in your success. Money makes it possible for you to live in comfort, to eat well and take care of your body, to experience the joys that life has to offer (the ones that are not free), and to open doors of opportunity for yourself and your family. If you make and keep enough of it, money allows you to stop working so hard one day, live independently, allay many of the fears of old age, spend more quality time with your loved ones, and help them move on once you're gone.

Money cannot buy happiness, but money can be an enabler of happiness. Therefore, financial planning plays a central role not just in building wealth but also in making your dreams come true.

Do the Work, Reap the Rewards

No matter where you are in your financial journey, you can achieve your own personal vision of greatness by following many of the lessons in this book. Like an aspiring basketball player who religiously sticks to a grueling workout, you have to practice and practice until good financial habits become a part of who you are. In summary:

- Look inward to understand why you feel the way you do about money—making it, saving it, and spending it.
- Learn about the external forces in our economy and investment markets that constantly push and pull on your net worth.
- Set realistic financial goals for your future, both near-term and long-term, and put a system in place to achieve them.
- Fight the incessant pressure to amass material wealth and avoid accumulating harmful debt.
- Start saving for retirement the day you enter the workforce or as soon as you possibly can.
- Build and keep a cash reserve—enough to cover several months of expenses in case of an emergency.
- Diversify your portfolio across a wide range of investments and adjust your asset allocation as you get closer to your goals.
- Know the history of the stock market's upward march through time and thus avoid making damaging emotional decisions when times are tough.
- Defend your financial assets—and your family's way of life—with the right types of insurance.
- Plan your transition to retirement with the utmost forethought and prepare to live longer than you thought possible.

- Devise an estate plan that will carry out your wishes and take care of your family when you pass away.
- Revisit your financial plan year after year, knowing that vigilance, assessment, and adaptation comprise the never-ending cycle that will carry you to success.

It's a lot to take on. And if you're new to the financial planning process, it can seem like an overwhelming challenge, sort of like a high school basketball team taking on the Kentucky Wildcats.

But unlike that high school team, you actually have a chance—a good chance—of winning this game of financial strategy. It will take a champion's pedigree: guts, skill, determination, resilience, and at times, humility. But just as no superstar can do it all on his or her own, you're going to need help.

I cannot stress enough the importance of bringing an expert guide along on your quest for victory. In fact, over the course of your life, you will likely benefit from the services of a variety of specialists: a general financial planner, an investment advisor, a tax accountant, and an estate planning attorney among them. While you could conceivably meet your financial goals without these professionals, your odds of success increase dramatically with their advice in your ear.

Like a team of specialized coaches, these experts can help you break down the most overwhelming challenges into manageable tasks: objectively identify your strengths and weaknesses, scout the competition in your path, design effective offensive plays, and build an impenetrable defense.

In a financial sense, they can help you become a superstar, if only in the eyes of your biggest fans (the ones who matter most).

All the while, you make your own transition from player to coach, from learner to leader. Like the greatest of sports legends, your experiences—both the magnificent triumphs and the devastating defeats—can educate and inspire a new generation of players. It's your opportunity to achieve the sweetest victory of all: Creating a life full of glory not just for yourself but also for the generations who come after you and leaving the game better than you found it.

Here is to your championship in the making.

An Uncertain Future

Earlier, I covered the basic concepts of basketball's motion offense as they relate to investing. The main idea was that, when executed well, an offense that allows players to read the situation before them and make choices will fare better more often than one that operates in a rigid, predefined pattern.

As an investor, it makes perfect sense to save and invest habitually and stick with what is working. You must also possess the foresight and flexibility, however, to adjust your plan when necessary. As I wrap up the final pages of this book, I am convinced that advice is more pertinent than ever.

Few other times in America's history has the future of the financial world been more in question. Today it's spinning in one direction, but tomorrow it could reverse its course completely. To avoid being caught off guard and suffering expensive consequences, investors need to be prepared for whatever confronts them. I'll explain what those circumstances might be, but first, a final basketball analogy.

Imagine your team has just won a big game that has earned you a spot in the tournament championship. You have a few days to rest up and prepare for the final contest, but there's one problem: You still don't know which team you'll face in the battle royale. All you know is that your opponent will be the winner of two teams who will play each other in the semifinal game. Those two teams have dramatically different strengths and weaknesses, so your game plan will differ substantially depending on which team you play.

How does your team, sitting idle for the time being, get ready for the final standoff against an unknown challenger? What you certainly *do not* do is nothing. You have got to stay in shape and keep your mind focused and your skills sharp. And while it's too early to settle on one game plan, you can start making plans to take down whichever contender comes your way. You can scout the competition, learn about the tendencies of both teams, and make a Plan A and Plan B. When the matchup is set, you'll be ready to pull the trigger on the most appropriate strategy.

Given the current condition of financial markets around the world, I believe that most investors should be thinking in these terms and making alternative game plans of their own.

What Is Going On?

The US recession technically ended in mid-2009, and much of the commotion about America's pending financial collapse gradually faded away. Stocks have recovered most of what they lost during the crisis, and housing prices have started to rise again in some parts of the country. To the American consumer with a well-paying professional career, it might feel as though the financial world is on the mend. But while the 2008–2009 crisis is behind us, we are still struggling to escape its long, dark shadow.

The US economic recovery has been weak and extremely slow. As of 2013 unemployment remains high and job growth is anemic as are wage increases. Rock-bottom interest rates designed to spur economic activity are also dragging down Americans' savings growth. Consumers and businesses remain hesitant to spend because of so much lingering uncertainty about where the economy is headed.

For the past several years, the US government has made desperate attempts to stimulate the groggy economy and get the wheels turning again. Through a practice known as quantitative easing (QE), the Federal Reserve has injected massive amounts of liquidity into the US financial system in order to prop up flagging institutions and keep the economy growing. After several multibillion-dollar purchases of US Treasuries and Mortgage-Backed Securities had little positive impact, the Fed continued to take additional QE measures, most recently in September 2012, which could be likened to throwing more logs onto a smoldering fire, hoping it will ignite.

Here's the all-important question: Once a spark takes hold, will the government be able to control the potentially raging fire that results? Many economists believe that so much excess liquidity in the markets will backfire and lead to high inflation.

Similar predicaments exist in governments around the world that are still reeling from the global financial crisis that began in the United States. After issuing their own massive bailout measures to prevent system-wide collapse, they now face staggering national debts. Relatively minor players such as Greece and Portugal have led the headlines, but the crisis also impacts major European powers including the United Kingdom, Italy, France, and Germany. In the East, the Chinese economy has been weakening in part because of decreased demand for the products it exports, and Japan faces its own debt crisis.

In sum, the world's solutions to the financial debacle of 2008–2009 might have set the stage for the next crisis.

What Could Happen

Like the basketball team that waits to find out who its next opponent will be, many investors find themselves wringing their hands over the uncertainty of the global financial markets.

Unlike the conclusion of a basketball game, however, the world's economic problems will not suddenly end when a clock runs out. Also, the complex developments affecting investors will not be easily categorized as a win or a loss. More likely, a chain of related outcomes will unfold over time. Nevertheless, investors will have to take decisive action or watch their portfolios get tossed about by the winds of change.

In the sunniest scenario, the world will heal itself. Governments will collaborate to arrive at shrewd decisions about fiscal and monetary policy. The stimulus efforts already underway will finally break the ice that grips the world economy, and investors once again will enjoy a long period of steady, predictable growth. We can hope, right?

Unfortunately, many experts are not so optimistic. Some feel that the world's economic wounds are just too deep and too extensive to patch up. They believe all signs are pointing to another possible recession in America and beyond.

Another possibility is that the massive money-printing measures of struggling governments will finally explode and set off hyperinflation and skyrocketing interest rates.

WHAT YOU CAN DO ABOUT IT

You would have to be the world's greatest economist to have all the answers (because the PhDs at the Fed and on Wall Street are still scratching their heads). But there are a few things I can advise with confidence.

First, do not invest based on headlines. They change faster than you can speed-dial your broker. Recall that most of the advice in this book encourages you to build a well-diversified portfolio and trust in it, not to shuffle the deck willy-nilly every time there is a market scare. Strategic adjustments to deal with long-term trends can be appropriate. Just make sure you're making them for a good reason.

One such good reason would be to diversify into asset classes that tend to perform well in each of the potential economic environments. In other words, hedge your bets. For example, during periods when inflation is high and rising, real assets such as real estate, energy, and other commodities tend to outperform stocks. On the other hand, if inflation continues to be low and rises slowly, stocks and short-term bonds (less than five-year maturity) become more attractive. Like the basketball coach, it is wise to be prepared for each scenario rather than guess in one direction and hope you're right.

Finally, do not attempt to revamp your game plan alone. Seek the advice of experienced professionals who have access to the latest information and sophisticated planning tools. Remember, even the most seasoned investors can benefit from the specialized knowledge and objectivity of good advisors. Financial planners cannot see the future, but they likely will see things in the present that you cannot. And those insights will help prepare you for whichever steely-eyed opponent lurks just out of sight.

READINGS FOR HOOPS FANS

Auriemma, Geno, with Jackie MacMullan, *Geno: In Pursuit of Perfection*. New York: Grand Central Publishing, 2006, 2009.

Knight, Bob, with Bob Hammel, *The Power of Negative Thinking: An Unconventional Approach to Achieving Positive Results*. New York: New Harvest, 2013.

Krzyzewski, Mike, with Jamie K. Spatola, *Beyond Basketball: Coach K's Keywords for Success*. New York: Business Plus: Hachette Book Group, 2006.

Pitino, Rick, with Pat Forde, *Rebound Rules: The Art of Success 2.0*. New York: HarperCollins Publishers, 2008.

Smith, Dean, with John Kilgo and Sally Jenkins, *A Coach's Life*. New York: Random House, 1999.

Wooden, John, with Jack Tobin, *They Call Me Coach*. New York: McGraw-Hill, 2004.

About the Author

Chuck Thoele is a partner at the independent advisory firm of Robertson, Griege, and Thoele based in Dallas, TX, and Irvine, CA. He is a Certified Financial Planner (CFP)™, Chartered Financial Analyst (CFA), and Certified Public Accountant (CPA), with more than thirty years of broad experience in many aspects of financial planning and investing. Chuck is active in the Dallas community, having served on the boards of various non-profit organizations benefiting underprivileged children, the arts, and education.

Chuck grew up in Indiana, is an Indiana University graduate, and is a die-hard college basketball fan. This book connects two of his greatest loves—helping people manage their money and the annual spectacle of the NCAA Tournament.